# Replaceable You

# Replaceable You

## Engineering the Body in Postwar America

DAVID SERLIN

UNIVERSITY
OF
CHICAGO
PRESS

CHICAGO
AND
LONDON

David Serlin is a historian, writer, educator, and the coeditor of *Artificial Parts, Practical Lives: Modern Histories of Prosthetics* (2002). He lives in Brooklyn, New York.

The University of Chicago Press, Chicago 60637
The University of Chicago Press, Ltd., London
© 2004 by The University of Chicago
All rights reserved.  Published 2004
Printed in the United States of America

13 12 11 10 09 08 07 06 05 04        1 2 3 4 5

ISBN: 0–226–74883–9        (cloth)
ISBN: 0–226–74884–7        (paper)

Library of Congress Cataloging-in-Publication Data

Serlin, David.
    Replaceable you : engineering the body in postwar America /
David Serlin.
        p. cm.
    ISBN 0-226-74883-9 (cloth : alk. paper) — ISBN 0-226-
74884-7 (pbk. : alk. paper)
    1. Biomedical engineering—United States.
    2. Regeneration (Biology)—United States. 3. Prosthesis—
United States. 4. People with disabilities—Rehabilitation—
United States. I. Title.
    R856.S457 2004
    306.4'61'097309045–dc22

                                        2003022009

FOR BRIAN          **Famous Artist to Her Majesty the Queen**

A society cannot live with a consciousness of its deepest motivations, any more than you can speak a language while being conscious of all the rules of grammar to which you are subject.

HENRI-JACQUES STIKER, *A HISTORY OF DISABILITY*

—There used to be a me, but I had it surgically removed.
—Um, can we change the subject?

PETER SELLERS AND KERMIT THE FROG ON *THE MUPPET SHOW*

# CONTENTS

**Can Humans Be Rebuilt?**


*1952.* IN WASHINGTON, DC, a handsome male amputee, a veteran of World War II, holds a book of matches with his new prosthetic hand and lights a cigarette with the other while a photographer captures the image for posterity. In Hiroshima, Japan—a city
occupied by U.S. military forces—a group of physically disfigured
young women, survivors of the atomic bomb, sit in a church base-
ment and dream of how American plastic surgeons will fix their
bodies and their futures. Meanwhile, in New York City an intro-
verted young illustrator from Pittsburgh (soon to be famous for his
images of soup cans and Brillo pad boxes) wins an award for his
advertising designs and dreams of one day changing his nose
through cosmetic surgery. In Los Angeles a lesbian star famous during the Harlem Renaissance tells the world how estrogen treatments
not only have made her heterosexual but also may have revived her
ailing career. And in Copenhagen, Denmark, a reporter for an
American newspaper discovers that a shy male photographer from
the Bronx, a former GI, is recuperating in a hospital bed after having been transformed into a beautiful woman.

Besides their synchronicity, what do these stories have to tell us
about the meanings that ordinary individuals attached to medical
science in the years following World War II? In *Replaceable You* I
explore how, in the late 1940s and early 1950s, medical procedures
used to rehabilitate or alter the human body enabled a new alignment of civic goals and national imperatives, of material form and
ideology, of private possibility and public responsibility. In its

four chapters, the book describes how certain procedures and technologies—such as prosthetic devices, plastic surgery, hormone treatments, and sex reassignment—were appropriated by the rhetoric of Americanism, which was configured as a peculiar form of hypernationalism in the period immediately after the war. Each chapter charts how physical rehabilitation became an allegory of national rehabilitation and the capacity for medical procedures to make such rehabilitation not only visible but also literal on the human body.

The allegorical tales told in *Replaceable You* are intended to offer new interpretations of postwar American culture. They explore not only the meanings that ordinary Americans attached to medical science but the meanings they attached to bodies—sometimes their own, sometimes those of others—that they perceived to be different, abnormal, or in some way extraordinary.[1] Historians, biographers, and memoirists tell us that, in the 1950s, individuals who were routinely stigmatized for being physically or psychologically different were encouraged—and sometimes forced—to use medical procedures to conform to social standards. Those without access to such procedures were often required to conceal their differences and tolerate the effects of living complex and often dissatisfying lives. In Deirdre N. McCloskey's memoir *Crossing* (1999), the author characterizes the moral hypocrisy typically associated with the postwar era by describing some of the "secrets" that Americans were forced to maintain, usually at the expense of their own integrity:

In the 1950s a lot of people were keeping secrets, personal and state: the obedient wives, the hidden handicapped, the closeted homosexuals, the silenced socialists, the blacks under Jim Crow. After the liberation [of the 1960s] and the talk that followed they are no longer disgraceful Others or pathetic victims, or merely invisibles . . . but people whose stories are heard and talked about and might even be imagined as one's own. It's the difference between shame and life.[2]

McCloskey makes a fundamental historical distinction between the two decades. She differentiates between the preliberation "shame" of the 1950s, for those "others" whose identities encompassed physical, sexual, political, or racial difference, and the post-liberation "life" of the 1960s embraced by Americans who wanted to imagine a new way to exist in the world. While this familiar narrative of individual and collective progress—out of the closets and into the streets—was no doubt true for many Americans (McCloskey included), it was also true that in the late 1940s and early 1950s medical procedures enabled some Americans to experience their bodies, in material form, as both public expressions of national conscience and individual expressions of personal identity. Indeed, far from living passively under an ideological regime that forced them to keep "secrets, personal and state," many Americans aggressively pursued medical procedures to reconcile their secret selves with what they believed to be their public selves. Rather than merely containing physical or sexual differences, medical procedures served as tools of consensus building, and the fanfare they generated helped to promote medicine as the apotheosis of domestic engineering. Bodily transformation also obliged Americans to confront the social and moral opprobrium with which they typically greeted the idea of the unnatural. What, after all, did the so-called natural body mean if an engineered body approximated one's sense of self far more persuasively than the body one was born into?

The stories in *Replaceable You* are anchored by the emergence of what might be called medical consumerism, the broad promotion of which reflected Americans' shift from the wartime economy of the 1940s into the productive economy of the 1950s. The relation between medicine and consumerism was certainly not a new one; it was articulated early in the twentieth century as medical products came to be understood as amenities of a prosperous economy and a modern social self.[3] In the 1920s, for example, plastic surgery was associated not only with reconstructing veterans of World War I, but increasingly with offering the promise of a new appearance to celebrities, vain matrons, and even international criminals seeking asylum under foreign governments. But this well-documented rise in medical consumerism after World War II is not in itself enough to explain why Americans in the postwar period gravitated toward medicine as a tool of self-realization.[4] By the early 1950s, the mood of the United States had changed after two decades of Depression-era deprivation and wartime anxiety. The specific economic and cultural contours of postwar life—including, among other things, the prosperity enjoyed by more and more Americans—transformed procedures and treatments previously associated with emergency medicine or with elite society into panaceas for those looking to rehabilitate their identities along with their bodies. Popular newspapers, magazines, and journals of the postwar period championed "medical miracles" as outgrowths of military research. Such "miracles" included the unprecedented and widespread use of lifesaving and life-extending technological resources including blood plasma, sulfa drugs, substitute bladders, dialysis machines, respirators, plastics, and stainless steel as well as the establishment of banks for human skin, eyes, organs, and blood. "It will be possible to replace whole organs that are diseased," *Collier's* predicted in a 1950 article titled "Can Humans Be Rebuilt?" "It will be possible, even, for a person with two diseased kidneys to have them replaced with sound ones. Or do you wish a new leg, or lung, or a whole eye? All of these will be theoretically possible if [medical] researches succeed."[5] A 1953 article in *Ebony* asserted that "in much the manner as manufacturers have developed spare parts for automobiles, surgeons and researchers have gone to great lengths to make available to the ill and disabled dozens of replacements for worn-out or destroyed parts of the body."[6] For scientists and consumers alike, medical science had come to epitomize, as Paul Starr has written, "the postwar vision of progress without conflict. . . . Here was evidence that life was getting better."[7]

This vision of "progress without conflict," however, was intensified by the urgency of a growing Cold War mentality. The post–World War II period was very much like the period after World

War I in that it witnessed the rise of aggressive and reactionary
political values that defined American identity in opposition to
anything or anyone that challenged it. In the 1920s, appeals to
Americanism were often used to justify nativist or racist policies
at home or abroad. Similarly, after World War II, the appeals to
Americanism to justify imperialist policies abroad were often
manipulated to transform health care into a weapon in the global
fight against Communism. Writing in 1945, for instance, journalist Stanley Hiller recommended that in the fight against nondemo-
cratic governments that were hostile to the American way of life,
the United States should try "exporting our standard of living."
"Chinese peasants with an excess of income," Hiller predicted,
"would not hesitate . . . to employ the services of physicians and
dentists using the latest instruments or techniques, or to pay for
services that would bring them a greater degree of freedom from
pain and famine."[8] In an era of geopolitical insecurity, what could
represent a nation better than boasting about the normal, healthy
bodies of its citizens?

Such an attitude was equally strong among those who sought to
use American medicine to combat domestic insecurity. In 1950—the
same year Senator Joseph McCarthy first pointed his finger at
alleged Communist infiltrators and the Senate sponsored its first
extensive investigations into the lives of alleged homosexuals
employed by the federal government—master Cold War paranoiac
and alleged cross-dresser J. Edgar Hoover published a conspicuous "guest editorial" in the *Journal of the American Medical
Association* under the title "Let's Keep America Healthy":
"Communist germs, spawned in the swamps of iniquity and terror,
have blotted out . . . the sunshine of free thought, independent
research, and unfettered inquiry. They have 'sickened' many nations
and literally killed countless persons. These germs are infectious
and deadly, easily transmitted and often difficult to detect."[9] After
making specious parallels between Communism and infectious
disease, Hoover concluded that physicians were a vital link in protecting national security, and he encouraged them to report to the

FBI any information of a dangerous nature. "A healthy body," Hoover argued, "like a healthy nation, must receive the unstinting cooperation of all of its component parts. . . . Like you, as physicians, we want to know the unvarnished facts of the case." By linking the "unvarnished" objectivity of Hoover's agency to the objectivity of medical science, the editorial implied that organized medicine could be an effective force in combating the virulent influence of Communism in American society.

In another sense, however, Hoover's editorial may have implied that physicians could help in eliminating the Left-leaning and potentially Communist biases within organized medicine. Beginning in the late 1930s, progressive medical organizations with liberal to Left affiliations, such as the Physicians' Forum and the Committee for the Nation's Health, challenged the authority of the AMA. At the time, the AMA had come out as publicly opposed to a universal health insurance policy, declaring it antithetical to the American way of life.[10] In 1946 novelist and journalist Richard Wright opined that "it would be far easier to confiscate private property than to violate, under however laudable a pretext, the contemporary metaphysical canons of organized medicine in America."[11] In protest of the AMA's authority, the Physicians' Forum sent a telegram to President Harry Truman in 1949 and declared that its three thousand physician-members endorsed the passage of the Wagner-Murray-Dingell bill, which would have brought compulsory health insurance to every American citizen.[12] To counter these threats, which they readily identified with state-controlled socialized medicine, the AMA inaugurated a series of red-baiting campaigns to discredit the Wagner bill, which was subsequently defeated in Congress.[13] As a result, the AMA, which had been at best neutral in most national political debates, took a more aggressive and proactive position of leadership as a professional organized body. In addition to creating political lobbies to support conservative candidates like Dwight Eisenhower and Richard Nixon who openly opposed universal health care, the AMA endorsed the Doctor Draft Act and the use of the "loyalty oath" among practicing physicians well into the 1950s.[14] Thus the spectacular coincidence of Hoover's correlation of organized medicine with anti-Communist politics and the *Journal of the American Medical Association*'s decision to print Hoover's editorial came at a decisive moment for organized medicine at midcentury.

I do not intend to describe American medicine as only a set of diabolical professional interests that dominate the bodies of hapless and vulnerable citizens. Much has changed in the half century since Hoover's editorial was published: from the triumphant (the decoding of the human genome and the potential to eliminate genetic diseases) to the humbling (the emergence of a new class of infectious diseases that resist even the most sophisticated tools of high-tech biomedicine). Yet the language of health care continues to borrow freely and without shame from the lexicon of free market economics refined during the postwar era. A 2002 policy report by the RAND Corporation titled "Make World Health the New Marshall Plan," for example, indicates how far contemporary health campaigns have absorbed the language of Cold War economic liberalism.[15] Indeed, in the early twenty-first century, the rhetoric behind Hiller's "exporting our standard of living," which endorsed using medicine to combat Communism, has been retooled to combat a far more intractable enemy: those who resist for-profit health care. For managed care organizations looking to transform health from a social entitlement into a profit-making venture, or for the corporate strategists and marketers in the billion-dollar pharmaceutical industry, the world's poor and sick—including those in the United States—are a captive audience whose hearts and minds are waiting to be won.

One difference between our world and the world of the postwar era is that in the late 1940s the exploitation of medicine for profit did not seem inevitable. For scientists and clinical researchers at places like the National Institutes of Health, the concept of basic research, with no immediate expectations and no strings attached, was a cherished part of the culture. Should we become too despondent about the future of health care in our era, we need only be

mindful of the larger political environment in which some of the
initial strategies for public health during the Cold War era first
developed. The 1947 creation of the World Health Organization as
well as the drafting of the Universal Declaration of Human Rights
(approved in 1948) that followed the Nuremberg Trials after World
War II marked a fundamental shift in the ways that doctors, law-
makers, and political leaders conceived of the relation between
health status and citizenship. These legislative and institutional
actions were predicated on the moral and political convictions that
access to health care and the protection of the human body would
be matters of international policy for modern nation-states.
Attitudes toward global public health in the late 1940s and 1950s
arguably paved the way for movements in support of human rights
and postcolonial liberation in the second half of the twentieth
century.

     As more resources and decision making went into implementing
new health care strategies around the world, Americans in the age
of modern medicine, freed from the immediate dangers to public
health such as infectious disease and inadequate nutrition that
defined the 1930s and 1940s, could afford to focus on chronic illnesses such as cancer, diabetes, and heart disease that reflected an
affluent, postscarcity society. They were in the enviable position of
regarding medical treatments such as steroid hormones and cosmetic surgery as modern amenities to be privately consumed rather
than publicly distributed. This does not mean that public health was
not overtly addressed or explicitly politicized in the United States
during the postwar era. Indeed, the eradication of polio and the
growth of environmental health awareness in the 1950s, the imple-
mentation of Medicare and Medicaid legislation in the mid-1960s,
and the 1972 whistle-blowing that culminated in the end of the
forty-year-long Tuskegee syphilis experiment were milestones in the
history of public health that should not be underestimated. Equally
important, however, is the emergence, since World War II, of certain
conceptions of individual health care that have come to define the
contours of American identity: a certain self-consciousness about

what, exactly, it means to have a modern American body; what constitutes health for a First World nation; and, furthermore, what it means to export certain medical procedures and technologies of health care as envoys of American foreign policy. Throughout this book, I treat the history of postwar medical procedures and technologies as a lens through which to view the intertwined histories of nationalist politics and individual self-making so relevant to our contemporary world.

IN THE SECOND HALF of the twentieth century, the social boundaries of American identity that had formerly been associated with public sphere activities such as voting and consumption were increasingly shaped by what had formerly been associated with the private sphere. The contested nature of Supreme Court cases as diverse as *Engel v. Vitale* (constitutionality of prayer in schools, 1962), *Roe v. Wade* (constitutionality of abortion rights, 1973), and *Bowers v. Hardwick* (constitutionality of sodomy laws, 1986) confirm how formerly private activities were transformed into matters of public discourse and national concern. In 2003, the landmark decision in *Lawrence v. Texas,* which overturned *Bowers* and confirmed that consensual sex acts like sodomy are protected by the Constitution, shows explicitly how this shift in emphasis has profoundly redefined the concept of civil rights in the United States and, in turn, the concept of American identity. For citizens struggling to articulate and codify the dimensions of a national identity, the Court's decisions for better or worse serve as benchmarks of our national polity to be protected or challenged, affirmed or dismantled.

The often diametrically opposed experiences of private and public that many Americans have attempted to reconcile through law or medical procedures may well be perceived as an updated version of the attempt to reconcile the Cartesian split between mind and body. In 1903 this philosophical debate was given a peculiar new shape after the historian W. E. B. Du Bois, following on the work of Hegel, introduced his concept of "double consciousness." For Du Bois, double consciousness represented a divided state of mind in which identifying both as black and as American was in fact impossible and compromised social status and personal integrity.[16] Du Bois's concept of double consciousness articulated the cultural dissonance felt by many members of minority populations and, to a certain degree, was philosophically instrumental in propelling the modern civil rights movement in the United States, postcolonial liberation movements abroad, and the sexual liberation movements in the 1960s and 1970s.

Du Bois's concept of double consciousness, however, takes on more complex meanings if one interpolates the experience of the physical body. If for African Americans the burden of double consciousness could not be resolved without full civil rights legislation, those designated as physically or sexually nonnormative—those we might now identify by the imprecise social markers of queer or disabled—were thought to bear the burden of a double consciousness that could not be resolved without full medical intervention. For much of the twentieth century, moral pieties rather than compassion guided scientific ideas about how to ameliorate the tragic double consciousness of the physically or sexually nonnormative. After World War I, psychiatry and rehabilitation medicine—for just two examples—reorganized nonnormativity as a public health issue rather than a badge of personal shame that must be suffered in private. Individuals became case studies. Physical differences or sexual aberrations were perceived as social problems that could be not only solved but triumphed over. In almost all cases, this entailed teaching the physically or sexually nonnormative to adopt and follow some kind of easily recognizable cultural narrative: how to become whole, or how to become beautiful, or even how to become the right kind of person and achieve the right character.

The rise of a counterculture, or counterconsensus, in the 1950s and 1960s gave a certain license to individuals who sought ways to put their private bodies and public identities into alignment. Some began to create individual narratives that matched what they saw as the liberating potential of their new bodies. Consider the title of the famous early feminist volume *Our Bodies, Ourselves,* first published in 1969 by the Boston Women's Health Collective. The book was not an affirmation of a traditional narrative about the female body that women had been expected to follow for generations but instead was an alternative narrative that challenged the contemptuous attitudes toward female bodies held by physicians, by the medical industry, and often by women themselves. On the other hand, consider the difference between Christine Jorgensen, the first internationally known "sex change" recipient, who rose to fame in the early 1950s, and Renée Richards, the transsexual personality of the early 1970s. Unlike Jorgensen, who followed a more socially conservative narrative of 1950s glamour and femininity, Richards fulfilled her personal story as a tennis champion who sought to disentangle her physical self from the gender expectations of the era as well as the expectations about who she was supposed to be.[17]

This book follows those Americans who, like Jorgensen, regarded certain medical procedures as part of the amenities of a modern and seemingly meritocratic social order made possible by the benefits of modern science. They believed that the promise of medicine could enable them to make their unconventional bodies more conventional, which would allow them to express an American identity in a more palpable way. They were not alone in this commitment. For example, the development of cortisone in the late 1940s, and its use to treat arthritis and other inflammatory diseases, was heralded as one of the great medical innovations of the twentieth century. Similarly, Jonas Salk's vaccine for poliomyelitis, a disease associated with children as well as with President Franklin D. Roosevelt, achieved a similar cultural status when it was introduced in 1955. Along with Alexander Fleming's penicillin and Paul Ehrlich's salvarsan, Salk's vaccine promised to eradicate not only a disease but the memories of the disease, which festered in the collective American consciousness along with other Depression-era public health panics such as tuberculosis, diphtheria, and syphilis. Of course, the deployment of medicines and other technologies of health care as social interventions in the lives of ordinary citizens long predates the era of cortisone and the polio vaccine. The growth of federal policies for veterans of the Civil War and World War I, for instance, joined health benefits to the rights of those who had served their country.[18] After World War II, however, nationalist imperatives, guided by the triumphalist rhetoric of Americanism, had an enormous impact in leading Americans to perceive medical care as a social means to larger civic ends. A 1945 article in *Popular Science* proudly claimed that "injuries . . . [today] are erased entirely or mended so subtly that no one knows of them except the men themselves and their families. . . . War's rehabilitation engineering may well become the *social engineering of the future.*"[19]

Saturated by the discourse of physical rehabilitation, many Americans were increasingly persuaded that putting one's physical body and one's social identity into some kind of coherent alignment was a way to enter a new phase of modern society.[20] Such attitudes were sustained long after the immediate postwar period. In 1965, President Lyndon B. Johnson's vision of the "Great Society" democratized health care as a social entitlement for all citizens in the form of Medicare and Medicaid. Almost a decade later, in 1973, the Nixon administration boosted federal funding exponentially for what Nixon inaugurated as the "War on Cancer," a military concept that also referenced the familiar language of Johnson's mid-1960s progressive social commitment to the "War on Poverty." One could argue that Johnson's and Nixon's attitudes toward health care in the 1960s and 1970s were shaped by memories of the patriotic aplomb with which advocates endorsed the medical "miracles" that emerged after World War II. Ironically, however, the postwar era's focus on medical "miracles" and the benefits of rehabilitation also introduced the potential for social friction and persuaded some physicians and social scientists to reconsider the causal relation they had taken for granted for at least a century. Indeed, modern medical science might be interpreted as a beleaguered contest between scientific perceptions of what constitutes the natural body and social perceptions of the natural pecking order. Nineteenth-century European social scientists such as Alphonse Bertillon and Francis Galton believed that the body told the truth about one's identity no matter how much one tried to disguise it, and they developed systems of classification for criminals and immigrants that relied on this belief.[21]

In the United States during the late nineteenth century, scientific convictions about the truth held by the natural body encouraged nativist attitudes and policies that sought to protect Americans— and in particular white Americans—from incipient flooding of the American gene pool by ethnic bodies deemed inferior in what popular discourse termed the "immigrant menace."[22] Undergirded by Galton's new science of eugenics, American nativism established allegedly objective criteria for measuring normal bodies considered to represent the best of the nation and vilified any body that deviated from that norm.[23] Nativists claimed that the fate of civilization depended on giving precedence to those bodies that were inherently superior in the natural order of things.[24] The widespread celebration of infants at "beautiful baby" contests held at county fairs across the country continued to operate as a vernacular form of eugenics, and to this day these contests remain fixtures of American popular culture, although most mothers (and all babies) remain oblivious of their specious origins. In 1927 the majority decision in the Supreme Court case of *Buck v. Bell* advocated the medical sterilization of women designated "feebleminded" to prevent problem births. *Buck v. Bell* was significant in legislating which kinds of bodies actively promoted ideal forms of citizenship and respectable social roles, not to mention ideal gender roles and reproductive health.[25]

Intellectual leaders in the American eugenics movement, such as Charles B. Davenport, believed they could distinguish superior from inferior bodies and show a direct correlation between natural bodies and social status. In 1918 the U.S. War Department commissioned Davenport and Albert G. Love to mobilize data about racial and ethnic groups for future use. By measuring and comparing the physical characteristics of recent immigrants against those of old-stock Americans, they produced such notable manifestos of institutional surveillance as *Defects Found in Drafted Men* (1920) and *Army Anthropology* (1921).[26] In the 1930s, Harvard physiologist

William Sheldon developed the concept of the somatotype, an amalgam of eugenic science and physical anthropology that produced descriptive terms for bodies such as ectomorph (tall, thin, or wiry body types), endomorph (short, heavy, or stocky body types), and mesomorph (symmetrical, classically proportioned, naturally sculpted body types).[27] Using somatotyping as a way to confirm the biological basis of social organization, scientists and policymakers could declare with certainty that the physical body determined one's identity, a belief encapsulated in Sigmund Freud's famous observation that "anatomy is destiny."[28]

By the early 1950s, however, the conviction that one's external body did not necessarily represent who one was, and that its constituent parts could be altered to match one's innermost idea of who one wanted to be, could be realized on a much larger scale than anyone had ever anticipated. Medical procedures now enabled individuals to transform their own bodies to be compatible with a private identity that had been hidden from public view. Their increasingly widespread use meant that people could change their bodies to remove, or at least temper, the relation between what they looked like and the stories their bodies told about their identities. Indeed, medical procedures allowed people to disrupt that easy causal connection between body and identity by encouraging them to thwart social expectations and take control over what was assumed to be their anatomical destiny. This is how making one's body commensurate with what one believed to be one's true self became an established pillar of American identity. The widespread availability of new or refined medical procedures made it possible for Americans to uncover something dormant within them that they now wished to make visible. It also made possible, as we shall see throughout the stories in this book, a new kind of subjectivity. Those Americans who experienced their lives, and thus their identities, through the veil of the extraordinary body could use the tools of medical science to insert themselves into a national narrative in which rehabilitating one's physical body made one more tangibly and visibly American than ever before.

The process also resulted in the sustained promotion of medical science as one of the most potentially transformative forces in the world.

THE STORIES IN *Replaceable You* engage with a variety of historical sources and scholarly disciplines. They draw heavily on recent works that investigate the history of the body, especially Sander Gilman's *Making the Body Beautiful,* Rosemarie Garland Thomson's *Extraordinary Bodies,* Elizabeth Haiken's *Venus Envy,* Valerie Hartouni's *Cultural Conceptions,* and Donald Lowe's *The Body in Late Capitalist U.S.A.*[29] My thinking about the American body is also highly indebted to groundbreaking works of scholarship in gender and sexuality studies such as Gail Bederman's *Manliness and Civilization,* John Howard's *Men Like That,* Kathy Peiss's *Hope in a Jar,* Siobhan Somerville's *Queering the Color Line,* and Robyn Wiegman's *American Anatomies.*[30] All these works are themselves interdisciplinary, drawing on American studies, critical race theory, science and technology studies, and media studies as they also push the boundaries of these individual scholarly areas in new and provocative ways. *Replaceable You* locates itself at the intersection of histories of the body, gender and sexuality studies, and American cultural history but also encompasses the rich interpretive tools offered by Cold War culture studies as well as disability studies and queer studies. Rather than telling one single story in a monographic fashion, the four chapters show how the national and international politics of the immediate postwar era were made to ramify within the politics of everyday life, and how the meanings attributed to Americanism shaped the bodies of citizens in myriad ways that were both consonant with and distinct from more familiar arenas of social policy or political discourse. In this sense the book is primarily offered as direct response to and departure from historical studies of United States culture during the postwar era that have charted the ways we currently understand the period's central historiographical themes. These books include Paul Boyer's *By the Bomb's Early Light,* Mary Dudziak's *Cold War*

*Civil Rights,* Elaine Tyler May's *Homeward Bound,* Alan Nadel's *Containment Culture,* and Stephen Whitfield's *The Culture of the Cold War.*[31]

In chapter 1, "The Other Arms Race," I explore the significance of prosthetic devices designed and built during the late 1940s and early 1950s in the context of the emphasis that postwar United States society placed on certain normative models of masculinity. Throughout the war, and especially afterward, the federal government made extensive efforts to rehabilitate veterans and reintegrate them into civilian society. Responding to these perceived needs, through military-university collaboration researchers and engineers created new prosthetic devices, providing revolutionary options for paralyzed soldiers and amputees and creating some of the earliest precedents for bioengineering.

I examine how the development of prosthetic devices for veteran amputees coincided with popular distortions of normative male behavior that produced deep anxieties in the masculine psyche: from Alfred Kinsey's revelations about male sexuality to the evolution of widespread 1950s heterosexual male archetypes such as the "white-collar" executive and the swinging *Playboy* bachelor. Prostheses designed and built in the 1940s and 1950s, then, were not merely symbolic or abstracted metaphors for a body-machine interface; they were medical technologies whose design and development expressed postwar culture's need to reengineer the physical body to accommodate the social mandates of the era. In 1955 the noted industrial designer Henry Dreyfuss worked in conjunction with the Veterans Administration to create a model prosthetic hand. The successful design of Dreyfuss's stainless steel split hook device, still in use today, demonstrates how prosthetic technologies during the 1950s reflected emerging technology in materials science and industrial robotics as well as ideals of "human engineering" and industrial design. The hand's functionalist styling and modern use of materials represented the perfect armature with which veterans could challenge the emasculation often associated with their amputation.

palimpsest?

In chapter 2, "Reconstructing the Hiroshima Maidens," I recount the story of twenty-five young female survivors of the atomic bombing of Hiroshima who were brought to the United States in 1955 for plastic surgery. I show how, in many ways, the reconstructive surgery that American doctors performed on their patients was only the most visible part of the women's story. Historians, sociologists, and medical anthropologists who have analyzed plastic surgery have shown how it reflects a host of irreconcilable cultural concepts about beauty, normalcy, and disability that extend far beyond any discussion of the Hiroshima Maidens. For many contemporary feminist critics, plastic surgery exemplifies the worst excesses of modern medicine, and in particular Western culture's devaluing of the integrity and inviolability of the human body, especially the female body.[32] The efforts of the sponsors and surgeons in the Hiroshima Maidens project, however, were not only to reconstruct the women's hands, faces, and bodies but also to make them over as subjects of medical and social transformation.

The Maidens' physical scarring from the bombing impaired their ability to appear normal, but it also stigmatized them psychologically as young women whose faces and limbs were perceived as dangerous and even exaggerated distortions of the female body. Unlike the veteran amputees in chapter 1, whose disability carried contradictory messages of both emasculation and patriotism, the Maidens experienced their disability as personal shame and national embarrassment. While their sense of self-worth as women seemed irrevocably damaged, as Japanese women they also had to endure their time in the United States, an occupying power that already regarded Asians as physically different. Regardless of how they looked or what they said or how they moved, the story of the Hiroshima Maidens represents a palimpsest of assumptions about gender, ethnicity, nationality, and disability as inscribed literally on the bodies of a former wartime enemy. The history of the Maidens demonstrated how postwar medical science imagined plastic surgery in the process of repairing and erasing physical trauma and cultural memory.

In chapter 3, "Gladys Bentley and the Cadillac of Hormones," I describe how the desire to change or erase seemingly aberrant physical traits was also manifest in the science of endocrinology and in the properties of hormones—in particular, synthetic versions of the steroid hormones known by the familiar names estrogen and testosterone. The emergence of synthetic hormones during the 1940s meant that these treatments took on new cultural meanings for postwar consumers. They were used not simply to treat diseases or glandular disorders but also to regulate sexual behavior, ameliorate delinquency, improve personality, and transform physical characteristics to conform to contemporary social standards. To explore the political and cultural ramifications of these hormone treatments, this chapter focuses on the life story of Gladys Bentley (1907–60), an African American pianist and performer who openly identified herself as a lesbian during the Harlem Renaissance. Her successful career was followed by mild cult status, but Bentley made a brief comeback when, in a 1952 issue of *Ebony,* she claimed that estrogen therapy not only had transformed her body but had corrected her sexual orientation and made her a well-adjusted heterosexual woman.

Like other contemporary consumers of medical procedures, Bentley chose to undergo hormone treatments because she equated medical rehabilitation of her body with social rehabilitation of her identity. Hormone therapies, particularly estrogen, were regarded as appealing amenities for upwardly mobile women at the same time that physicians promoted their use as tools of racial and sexual regulation. Endocrinologists applied steroid hormone therapy to individuals such as Gladys Bentley in order to generate physical traits and characteristics that would be more compatible with postwar gender roles and cultural values. For Bentley, however, the allure attached to endocrinology was accelerated not only by the period's compulsive need to reinvent the self but also by the domestic, middle-class sensibilities of many African Americans. I argue that women like Bentley were seduced by the promises of a bourgeois black identity in the period just before the mainstream civil rights movement in the second half of the 1950s brought debates over the economic, legal, and social status of African Americans to national urgency.

Finally, in chapter 4, "Christine Jorgensen and the Cold War Closet," I examine the early history of Christine Jorgensen (1926–89), the first American citizen to become an international sensation as a male-to-female transsexual personality. In the fall of 1950, a twenty-four-year-old Bronx photographer named George Jorgensen traveled to Copenhagen to undergo extensive estrogen treatments in order to neutralize the already low levels of testosterone in his body. When in December 1952 newspapers announced her chemical and surgical transformation from George to Christine, Jorgensen was widely regarded as a "medical miracle," and she rode an unprecedented wave of popularity as "the most talked-about girl in the world." Six months later, however, in April 1953, Jorgensen's celebrity status was challenged when investigative journalists revealed that Danish surgeons and endocrinologists had not in fact made Jorgensen into a biological woman—that is, one capable of menstruating or reproducing—but had merely castrated George. American society saw her gender betrayal as unpatriotic, and her celebrity status was compromised by a common perception of her transformation as social deviance. In the hysterical political climate of the early 1950s, Jorgensen's "conversion" was met with the zeal of rabid anti-Communist paranoia, arousing the scrutiny of the public and its (un)officially designated commentators. Consequently, I try to understand Jorgensen's rise and fall as an allegory of national pride and domestic comfort, as reflected in the meanings that Americans projected onto Jorgensen in both male and female incarnations.

Following chapter 4 a short epilogue, "The Golden Slipper Show," brings Jorgensen's life story into the orbit of another American original, Andy Warhol. In late 1956 Warhol exhibited a set of portraits of famous celebrities done in his own inimitable style that included Jorgensen as a pair of glittery golden pumps. Jorgensen's appearance in Warhol's exhibition suggests an interesting intersection of themes that prove critical to understanding the trajectory of Warhol's own emerging aesthetic, which in the 1960s helped to spawn a subculture transfixed by the possibilities of a body, or an image, or an object that was anything but natural.

Scholars have often tended to regard American culture in the fifteen years between 1945 and 1960 with condescending superiority. It is treated either as a maudlin moment of crassly sweet nostalgia and embarrassing kitsch or as a painful moment of moral hypocrisy fueled by social intolerance and political violence. Depending on one's temperament, these versions of our recent past seem either seductive or distasteful to our early twenty-first-century sensibilities. Yet the fear and panic that geopolitical conflict or domestic chaos inspired in Americans have remained constant and are perhaps more salient than ever, particularly in light of recent transformations at home and abroad since the terrorist attacks of September 11, 2001. Rhetorical appeals to Americanism that were manipulated for ideological ends in the Cold War era are still regularly exploited more than a half-century later to wage wars, contain dissent, further political agendas, and keep us trapped in a perpetual state of anxiety. Meanwhile, American culture at the beginning of the twenty-first century, whether consumed at home or exported, seems to offer few if any solutions for the ills that afflicted the psyche five decades ago. Americans seem unfazed by the paradox of fearing biological weapons of mass destruction while pursuing injections of toxic microorganisms (in the form of Botox treatments) directly into their foreheads and armpits. Both seem to be our rightful inheritance, proving that we often get exactly what we wish for. Perhaps we underestimate the capacity of ideology to unravel and, under conditions of its own choosing, to reconstitute itself in complex ways that often exceed our abilities of explanation. This book turns a critical eye on the years immediately following World War II as one source, among many others, for tracking the ideological and cultural effects of Americanism that continue to haunt us, especially in those pockets of domestic life where we naively least expect them to occur.

## ONE

# The Other Arms Race

IN THE NOVEMBER 1946 issue of *Fortune*, famous photographer Walker Evans presented some views of perfectly ordinary men walking the streets of downtown Detroit in the late afternoon.[1] Evans, a master of social realism whose photographic work for the Farm Security Administration in the mid-1930s culminated in his masterpiece with James Agee, *Let Us Now Praise Famous Men* (1939), had moved into a new phase of his career, this time focused largely on representations of postwar labor.[2] Evans's pictures of American working men in a variety of guises—in broad-brimmed caps and overalls, or in work pants and white T-shirts—were familiar to the American businessmen who made up the vast majority of *Fortune*'s readers. Since the 1920s they had been accustomed to looking at images of men who marked physically the masculine exuberance and patriotic spirit embodied in icons of American commercial production.[3] Even into the 1950s, a disproportionate number of advertisements in *Fortune* that depicted men at work showed blue-collar workers.

For Evans, such icons of American labor were fundamental to the health of the postwar economy, since they promoted the strength and vitality of the American workingman. The text that accompanied the *Fortune* photo-essay (which may have been written by Evans himself) observed:

The American worker . . . is a decidedly various fellow. His blood flows from many sources. His features tend now toward the peasant and now toward the patrician. His hat is sometimes a hat and sometimes he has moulded it into a sort of defiant signature. It is this diversity, perhaps, which makes him, in the mass, the most resourceful and versatile body of labor in the world. If the war proved anything, it demonstrated that American labor can learn new operations with extraordinary rapidity and speedily carry them to the highest pitch of productive efficiency. Though it may often lack the craftsmanly traditions of the older worlds, American labor's wide spectrum of temperaments rises to meet almost any challenge: in labor as in investment portfolios, diversification pays off. There is another thing to be noted about these street portraits. Here are none of those worn, lusterless, desolated faces we have seen so frequently in recent photographs of the exhausted masses of Europe. Most of these men on these pages would seem to have a solid degree of self-possession. By the grace of providence and the efforts of millions including themselves, they are citizens of a victorious and powerful nation, and they appear to have preserved a sense of themselves as individuals. When editorialists lump them as "labor," these laborers can no doubt laugh that off.[4]

From its focus on the American worker's ability to be "resourceful" and "versatile" to its insistence that what characterizes American labor is individual pride—"a solid degree of self-possession"—and not union affiliation or a European (read socialist) working-class identity, Evans's text exemplified the compulsive need among many commentators in the postwar era to correlate the male American worker with the qualities of a certain brand of normative masculinity: independence, reliability, efficiency, resiliency. With the excitement of industrial production from a military economy still fresh, using one's body remained one of the primary ways that citizens (and, despite Evans's protestations, men who identified as organized members of the American working class) forged identities and affiliations with industrial economies. In the years immediately following World War II, vast pockets of the United States were still heavily industrial. Many older cities in the Northeast and Midwest relied almost exclusively on steel, coal, iron, lumber, and oil as well as the nexus of related industries including railroads, automobile and appliance manufacturing, production of chemicals and plastics, and shipping and storage technologies. In this industrial milieu, the image of the blue-collar man still carried substantial power as a dignified symbol for corporate strength. The prominent service-oriented FIRE industries (finance, insurance, and real estate) that we now associate with large American cities for the most part represented only one segment of their diversified financial output. The image of the city as a hive of gleaming office towers housing white-collar corporate capital was still only a dream of urban planners, economic theorists, and real estate moguls that would not be realized in cities like Detroit until the 1970s.[5]

Evans's 1946 photo spread for *Fortune* was characteristic of images of the workingman's body in action, found in abundance throughout mass culture. One could trace these icons of the masculine work ethic to images by Progressive Era photographers like Lewis Hine or, somewhat later, works by muralists and photographers who created public art for the Works Progress Administration during the 1930s. Film representations of ruggedly masculine American men like James Cagney and Clark Gable were enjoyed by Depression audiences who found admiring such handsome figures a convenient escape from the economic deprivation of the era. During the work shortages of the Depression, conservative critics had sounded a note of fear over the perceived erosion of masculinity among American men. Their worst fears were realized in the early 1940s when the mobilization of hundreds of thousands of women in the labor force, combined with the prolonged absence of men from traditional positions of family and community authority, began to give a new shape to civilian domestic culture. Many were displeased by new configurations of family and marriage, not to mention the new sexual divisions of labor on the home front. In the best-selling *Generation of Vipers* (1942), for example, Philip Wylie coined the term "Momism" to describe what he perceived to be the emasculating effects of aggressive mothers and wives on the behavior of passive sons and husbands as a consequence of the reconfiguration of traditional gender roles. One could argue that after the attack on Pearl Harbor in December 1941, and the war that followed it, the bodies of American men were marked simultaneously by their solidity and their fragility, the dual norms of American heterosexual masculinity. As Walker Evans's photographs demonstrate, the two constituent aspects of the male body—its relation to productive labor and its relation to heterosexual masculinity—took on increased significance.

Professional and public discussions of workingmen, as well as representations of them working, became more complex as a result of the return of veterans—many of them wounded, disfigured, or traumatized—to positions in civilian society. One of the foremost concerns of the era was what effect trauma and disability would have on veterans' self-worth, especially in a competitive economy defined by able-bodied men. Social workers, advice columnists, physical therapists, and policymakers during and after World War II turned their attention to the perceived crisis of the American veteran, much as they had done after the Great War some thirty years earlier. As Susan Hartmann has written, "By 1944, as public attention began to focus on the postwar period, large numbers of writers and speakers . . . awakened readers to the social problems of demobilization, described the specific adjustments facing ex-servicemen, and prescribed appropriate behavior and attitudes for civilians."[6] Recent studies of disabled veterans of the two world wars have emphasized that such men often carried collective and national anxieties about the transition from wartime to civilian labor and its relation to the precarious status of the male body. For many workingmen these anxieties seemed hardly visible. But many male veterans of World War II with visible (and not-so-visible) disabilities came back to a country where, among other changes they encountered, gender roles were far less comprehensible or predictable than they had once seemed. How did normative models of masculinity affect disabled veterans who had to compete against the reputation and image of the able-bodied American workingman?

This chapter examines the status of disabled veterans of World War II, looking closely not only at veteran amputees but also at the design and representation of prosthetic devices developed for amputees who wanted to return to the workplace. I read the stories of veterans and their prostheses as neglected components of the historical reconstruction of gender roles and heterosexual male archetypes in early Cold War culture. Like artificial body parts created for victims of war and industrial accidents after the Civil War and World War I, prosthetics developed during the 1940s and 1950s were linked explicitly to the fragile politics of labor, employment, and self-worth for disabled veterans.[7] Discussions of prosthetics also reflected concomitant social and sexual anxieties that attended the public specter of the damaged male body. As this chapter argues, the design and construction of prostheses help to distinguish the rehabilitation of veterans after World War II from earlier periods of adjustment.

Prosthetics research and development were catalyzed, to a great extent, by the mystique attached to "medical miracles" and scientific progress in the late 1940s and early 1950s. The advent of new materials science and new bioengineering principles during the war and the application of these materials and principles to new prosthetic devices helped transform prosthetics into its own biomedical subdiscipline. The convergence of these two areas of research—making prostheses as physical objects and designing prosthetics as products of engineering science—offers important insights into the political and cultural dimensions of the early postwar period, especially in light of what we know about the social and economic restructuring of postwar society with the onset of the Cold War. By the mid-1950s the development of new materials and technologies for prostheses had become the consummate marriage of industrial engineering and domestic engineering.

This chapter uses the term "prosthetics" in two distinct though clearly overlapping ways. While the word obviously refers to artificial additions, appendages, or extensions of the human body, after World War II it referred increasingly to a biomedical and engineering subdiscipline—what mathematician Norbert Wiener, beginning in the late 1950s, would call "biocybernetics" or "cybernetic medicine." Before World War II, prostheses were made of organic, often familiar materials—such as leather, wood, glass, and metal—or were changed to accommodate the synthetic products of late nineteenth-century industrial processes such as vulcanized rubber or early plastics. By the late 1940s and early 1950s, however, prosthetic devices were constructed from a variety of new materials such as acrylic, polyurethane, and stainless steel. Furthermore, by the late 1950s and early 1960s, new biomechanical principles and cybernetic control systems had begun to be applied to the operation of artificial arms and legs. Because of these myriad changes, prosthetics themselves were entirely reimagined by the designers and engineers who made them as well as by the veteran and civilian amputees who wore them. The distinction between prosthetics as objects and prosthetics as science also enables us to reclaim both the ideological foundation and the material foundation of postwar prosthetics—to look at prostheses and the prosthetic sciences not merely as metaphorical tropes or linguistic conceits but as forms of embodied technology that predate our affinity for talking about cyborgs and cyberculture.

Many books of the past decade use the extended metaphor of the prosthesis to analyze the artificial objects that mediate human relations as well as cyberculture's mandate of virtual reality.[8] In these works, a prosthesis can refer to any machine or technology that intervenes in human subjectivity, such as a telephone, a computer, or a sexual device. As a result, the prosthesis is regularly abstracted as a postmodern tool or artifact, a symbol that reductively dematerializes the human body. As Kathleen Woodward has written, "Technology serves fundamentally as a prosthesis of the human body, one that ultimately displaces the material body."[9] Despite ubiquitous representations of prostheses or cyborgs in late twentieth and early twenty-first century culture, they hardly begin to understand the complex historical and technological origins of the body-machine interface for amputees and other prosthesis wearers. They also fail to give agency to the people who use prosthetic technology every day without glamour or fanfare.

Far from transforming them into supermen or cyborgs, prostheses provided veteran amputees with the material means through which individuals on both sides of the therapeutic divide imagined and negotiated what it meant to look and behave like a so-called normal, able-bodied workingman. For engineers and prosthetists, artificial parts were biomedical tools that could be used to rehabilitate bodies and social identities. For doctors and patients, prosthetics were powerful anthropomorphic tools that reflected contemporary fantasies about ability and employment, heterosexual masculinity, and American citizenship.

## PATRIOTIC GORE

Long before World War II ended in August 1945—the month that Japan officially surrendered to the United States after the bombing of Hiroshima and Nagasaki—images in the mass media of wounded soldiers convalescing or undergoing physical therapy occupied a regular place in news reports and popular entertainment.[10] In John Cromwell's film *The Enchanted Cottage* (1945), a young soldier played by Robert Young hides from society and his family in a remote honeymoon cottage after wartime injuries damage his handsome face.[11] *The Enchanted Cottage* updated and Americanized the substance of Sir Arthur Wing Pinero's 1925 play of the same title. Pinero's drama focused on a British veteran of World War I who symbolized the plight of facially disfigured veterans (sometimes called *les gueules cassés* by their countrymen), who were often considered social outcasts by an insensitive public.[12] In the 1945 North American production, as in the original, the cottage protects the mutilated soldier and his homely, unglamorous fiancée from parents and family members who take pity on the couple for their abnormal physical differences.

Many amputees who returned from war to their homes, hometowns, and places of work—if they could find work—suffered from a similar lack of respect, despite the best efforts of federal agencies like the Veterans Administration to meet their needs. Physicians, therapists, psychologists, and ordinary citizens alike often regarded veterans as men whose recent amputations were physical proof of emasculation or general incompetence, or else a kind of monstrous defamiliarization of the normal male body. Social policy advocates recommended that families and therapists apply positive psychological approaches to rehabilitating amputees.[13] Too often, however, such approaches were geared toward making able-bodied people more comfortable with their innate biases so they could "deal" with the disabled. This seemed to be a more familiar strategy than empowering the disabled themselves.

In William Wyler's Academy Award-winning film *The Best Years of Our Lives* (1946), real-life war veteran Harold Russell played Homer, a sensitive double amputee who tries to challenge the stereotype of the ineffectual amputee while he and his loyal girlfriend cope valiantly with his new split-hook, above-elbow prosthetic arms. Given the mixed reception of disabled veterans in the public sphere—simultaneous waves of pride and awkwardness—scriptwriters made Homer exhibit tenacious courage and resilience of spirit rather than the vulnerability or rage that visited many veteran amputees. As David Gerber has written, "The culture and politics of the 1940s placed considerable pressure on men like Russell to find individual solutions, within a constricted range of emotions, to the problem of bearing a visible disability in a world of able-bodied people."[14] Recurring images of disabled soldiers readjusting to civilian life became positive propaganda that tried to persuade able-bodied Americans that the convalescence of veterans was not a problem.

Such propaganda was to be expected in the patriotic aftermath of World War II—especially given the War Department's decision during the early 1940s to expunge all painful images of wounded or dead soldiers from the popular media.[15] The American media regularly circulated stories about amputees and their triumphant use of their prostheses. The circulation of such unduly cheery narratives of tolerance in the face of adversity implied a direct relation between physical trauma—and the ability to survive such trauma—and patriotic duty.

In the summer of 1944, for example, United States audiences were captivated by the story of Jimmy Wilson, an army private who was the only survivor of a ten-person plane crash in the Pacific Ocean (fig. 1). When he was found forty-four hours later amid the plane's wreckage, army doctors were forced to amputate both of his arms and legs. After Wilson returned to his hometown of Starke, Florida, surgeons outfitted him with new prosthetic arms and legs, and he became a poster boy for the plight of thousands of amputees who faced physical and psychological readjustment on their return to civilian life. In early 1945, the *Philadelphia Inquirer* initiated a national campaign to raise money for Wilson. By the end of the war

FIGURE 1 Quadruple amputee Jimmy Wilson, right, with his wife, Dorothy Mortenson Wilson, using the celebrity status that the war veteran achieved in the mid-1940s to cheerfully promote public awareness for Wilson's fellow amputees still recuperating in service hospitals. Photograph taken in Philadelphia, November 1, 1951, © Bettmann/Corbis.

in August the *Inquirer* had raised over $50,000, collected from well-known philanthropists and ordinary citizens alike, such as a group of schoolchildren who raised $26 by selling scrap iron.[16] By the winter of 1945, Wilson's trust fund had grown to over $105,000, and he pledged to use the money to get married, buy a house, and study law under the newly signed GI Bill. Wilson's celebrity status as a quadruple amputee peaked when he posed with Bess Myerson, Miss America 1945, in a brand-new Valiant, a car (whose name itself championed Wilson's patriotic reception) that General Motors designed specifically for above-ankle amputees.[17] Wilson learned how to operate the car by manipulating manual gas and brake levers on the car's steering column. Demand for the Valiant was so great that in September 1946 Congress allocated funds that provided ten thousand of these automobiles to needy amputees.[18]

If men like Jimmy Wilson were regularly celebrated as heroic and noble, it was because tales of their perseverance and resilience grew with the fervor of a Cold War mentality. Instead of allowing them to speak for themselves, the media transformed amputees into powerful visual and rhetorical symbols through which war-related disability was unequivocally identified with heroism. In the fall of 1945, for example, the Washington, DC, edition of the *Goodwill*, Goodwill Industries' newsletter devoted to raising money and collecting supplies for the war effort, published a provocative image of a handsome young veteran on crutches. Dressed stylishly in pleated pants, a twilled cotton shirt, and the greased, well-coifed hair typical of young civilian men in the early 1940s, the relaxed veteran beams beneath a visual collage including the Capitol, the Washington Monument, and the Lincoln Memorial. The text on the front of the newsletter bears a striking proclamation of patriotic support:

WE ARE FIGHTING FOR HIM and others like him—Not only veterans of the war—but all who are handicapped. . . . In the general confusion of National Reconversion—we wish to eliminate as many difficulties for them as possible—NOW, more than ever, WE ARE IN NEED OF YOUR WHOLE-HEARTED SUPPORT! WE MUST NOT FAIL THEM![19]

Although the message is remarkable for its inclusion of all people with disabilities, the rhetorical power of words like "victory" and "support" clearly invokes the economic and social needs highlighted by veterans. The reference to "National Reconversion" addresses the expectations of a new economic organization—one that emphasizes the viability of disabled veterans as competent workers—in which public commitment to the social welfare of the disabled is one way of exercising one's patriotic duty. By making an implicit connection between the disabled veteran's individual transition to civilian society and the military's transition to a civilian economy, the newsletter amplifies the need to understand that such a transition is about both individual and collective sacrifice.

At approximately the same time, in late 1945, the Coast Guard press corps captured a different kind of amputee, in full military dress, that made explicit the needs of disabled veterans within the discourse of patriotism and military masculinity. In figure 2, the small body of Thomas Sortino of Chicago is framed deliberately against the Olympic-sized statue of Abraham Lincoln. The accompanying caption proclaims, "A fighting coastguardsman . . . poses for a Memorial Day tribute to the Great Emancipator at the Lincoln shrine here." Like the *Goodwill* cartoon, the photograph uses Sortino's familiar gesture to endorse the democratic ethos of sacrifice, as if his amputation had been nothing less, or more, than what the government demanded of all its citizens during wartime—"pitching in," buying war bonds, tending victory gardens, and rationing consumer goods. Under Lincoln's attentive glare, the visual and verbal cues here invoke a nostalgia for the Civil War, reinforcing the idea that those disabled during World War II fought and won the war to preserve democracy. Two newspaper articles published about the same time in the *Washington Evening Star* confirm this theme. One, about the Quebec-born amputee Fernand Le Clare, declares in a headline, "Canadian GI Proud to Be an American," while the other, about the Hawaiian-born disabled veteran Kenneth T. Otagaki, assures us that "This Jap Is Justly Proud That He Is an American."[20] The particular brand of normative domestic politics expressed by these images and

... So That 'Freedom Shall Not Perish From the Earth'

A fighting coastguardsman, who lost his right arm in battle, poses for a Memorial Day tribute to the Great Emancipator at the Lincoln shrine here. The guardsman, who took part in the invasion of North Africa, is Thomas Sortino, of Chicago.

FIGURE 2 Coast Guard amputee Thomas Sortino of Chicago expresses his patriotism at the Lincoln Memorial. Undated newspaper clipping, ca. 1944, from the Donald Canham Collection, Otis Historical Archives, Armed Forces Institute of Pathology, Walter Reed Army Medical Center, Washington, DC.

headlines is precisely what Tom Englehardt has described as the "victory culture" of the late 1940s and early 1950s.[21]

The media's use of images of male amputees (with and without their prostheses) was a deliberate strategy that reminded the public of the recent war, but it also served to memorialize the war-honored dead and disabled. It was, after all, yet another period all citizens would need to acclimate to, another period that mandated massive social reconstruction, policymaking, and productive transitions to civilian life for millions of people, both able-bodied and disabled, civilian and veteran. Moreover, amputee veterans were a significant part of the popular image of soldiering itself and of military culture in general. Their public presence blurred the techniques of physical rehabilitation with tacit forms of democratic participation and civic duty.[22] In 1951, for example, Senator Joseph McCarthy antagonized Secretary of State Dean Acheson (who McCarthy believed was a Communist) at a congressional hearing by invoking the name of Bob Smith, a recent veteran amputee of the Korean War, to contest some of Acheson's recent foreign policy proposals. Seamlessly combining anti-Communist hysteria with homophobic intolerance, McCarthy contrasted Smith's masculine resilience with Acheson's perceived effeminate and aristocratic stance. "I suggest that . . . when Bob Smith can walk," McCarthy asserted, "when he gets his artificial limbs, he first walk over to the State Department and call upon the Secretary if he is still there. . . . He should say to Acheson: 'You and your lace handkerchief crowd have never had to fight in the cold, so you cannot know its bitterness. . . . [Y]ou should not only resign from the State Department but you should remove yourself from this country and go to the nation for which you have been struggling and fighting so long.'"[23]

The ideological links forged between public exhibitions of disability, heterosexual masculinity, and patriotic commitment— usually exercised in a less spectacular fashion than McCarthy's exploitation of Smith—were not new. Since the 1860s, photographers had developed a sophisticated visual lexicon for depicting able-bodied and disabled soldiers and veterans. Alan Trachtenberg, among others, has discussed how images of wounded amputees sitting graciously for portrait photographs were rhetorical expressions of extreme patriotism (for both Northern and Southern veterans) distilled into visual form.[24] For many of these disabled veterans of the Civil War, the amputation stump, the artificial limb, and other physical markings that proved sustained injury were visual shorthand for military service. Disability, then, became their permanent uniform (fig. 3). Medical photographs of amputees in the nineteenth century, as Kathy Newman has argued, were sophisticated enough to capture the subjects' brutal amputations yet polished enough to preserve the genteel conventions of Victorian portrait photography.[25] This must explain why, in such photographs, the male body often appears as both disabled spectacle and eroticized object. For those reading the photographs today, these portrait sittings of handsome young men with deep wounds, radical amputations, or artificial limbs become

FIGURE 3 This studio portrait of Union volunteer soldiers from Maine, New York, Ohio, and Wisconsin demonstrates how visual representations of veteran amputees after the Civil War were textured with late nineteenth-century ideals of masculine resilience and postwar patriotism. Photograph ca. 1870s, © Bettmann/Corbis.

material reflections of the photographer's desire to recuperate the soldiers' putatively lost masculinity. Perhaps medical photographers believed that by using an "objective" science of surveillance, they could displace the potentially emasculating effects of the camera's penetration into the intimate spaces of the amputee's body.

Through the public circulation of these images of veteran amputees, we begin to see the formation of arbitrary (though no less hierarchical) categories for thinking about disability itself. How differently, for example, does a society view disability that results from war injury or industrial accident as opposed to disability that results from congenital deformity, acquired illness, or even self-mutilation? Part of this delineation relies on the perceived difference between disability induced by modern technology or warfare and hereditary disability, attitudes toward which were influenced by antiquated notions of a "monstrous birth" even as late as the 1950s.[26] In the former, disability is material proof of one's service to the military, to the modern state, to industrial capitalism: these help to preserve patriotic values and respectable citizenship. In the latter, disability is a material stigma that marks one's rejection from competent service to society. Among men, such stigmas may confirm the male body as weak, effeminate, and inimical to normative heterosexual versions of manly competence. In the aftermath of war and the rise of the hyperpatriotic culture of the late 1940s, veteran male amputees constituted a superior category on an unspoken continuum of disabled bodies, suggesting that hierarchies of value are constructed even *within*, and sometimes *by*, groups of differently abled individuals.

## MAKING MEN WHOLE AGAIN

The social and political climate of the late 1940s directly affected the ways in which images of veterans were disseminated in the public sphere. Images of amputees undergoing rehabilitation—learning to walk, eat, and perform other "normal" activities—were often used in tandem with materials to promote the agendas of postwar science and technology. This was especially true after the passage of NSC-68, the National Security Council's 1947 resolution to allocate enormous sums to the "containment" of Communism by any means necessary, which increased exponentially the military aggression and technological competition already mounting between the United States and the Soviet Union. At large, well-funded research institutions with other government contracts—such as Case Institute of Technology, Massachusetts Institute of Technology, Michigan State University, New York University, the University of California at Los Angeles, and Western Reserve University—the development of new prosthetic designs arose concomitantly with new technologies used to protect and defend national interests. Writing in 1954, Detlev Bronk, president of the National Academy of Sciences, made clear the responsibilities to nation and citizenry that were articulated through the relation between military research and rehabilitation medicine:

Those whom this committee first sought to aid were those who suffered loss of limb in battle where they were serving their fellows. In times of war scientists have fortified the courage of our defenders by applying science to the development of better weapons. They have done significantly more; during times when it was necessary to sacrifice human lives they marshaled the resources of science for the protection of health and life. . . . [The development of prostheses] is a vivid reminder that human values are a primary concern of the scientists of freedom-loving nations.[27]

This was not the first time new materials and techniques had been applied to the design and creation of new prosthetic parts for those wounded during war. Industrial processes in the nineteenth and twentieth centuries had enabled the production of materials, such as vulcanized rubber, synthetic resins, and plastics, for use in prosthetic devices developed for veterans of the Civil War and World War I. What made new prostheses different from earlier models is that they represented the marriage of prosthetic design to military-industrial production. Both materials science and information science—hallmarks of military research and federal funding—

figured prominently in experimental prosthetics developed in the late 1940s. According to Wilfred Lynch, "The development of dependable [prostheses] proceeded at a snail's pace until the emergence of 'exotic' new materials in answer to the needs of the military in World War Two. The subsequent aerospace program and the high volume of burgeoning new postwar industries made the commercial production of these unique materials practical."[28] Some of these represented the conversion of military needs for civilian ones in materials such as Plexiglas, Lucite, polyester, silicone, titanium, Duralumin, stainless steel, ceramics, and high-grade plastics that flooded the industrial and consumer markets. By the fall of 1947, funding from Congress had made artificial limbs constructed from lightweight plastics available to over five thousand veterans. Newly patented technologies used in later experimental prosthetic models, such as Velcro and Siemes servomotors, grew out of wartime research in materials science and miniaturization of solid-state electronics.[29] Furthermore, scientists attempted to apply new engineering techniques derived from military-industrial research to veterans' artificial limbs. In late August 1945, just two weeks after the war ended, Paul E. Klopsteg, chairman of the National Research Council's Committee on Prosthetic Devices, announced a research program devoted to creating "power-driven" artificial limbs that resembled the "real thing" by "introducing power, either hydraulic, pneumatic, or electric" to prosthetic limbs.[30]

The association between amputees and state-of-the-art prosthetics research may have been an intentional strategy to link disabled veterans with the cutting edge of new scientific discoveries. In 1943, for example, the War Department commissioned Milton Wirtz, a civilian dentist, to develop artificial eyes using the new wonder material, acrylic.[31] Wirtz's expertise with acrylic derived from using the new material in forging dental prostheses for patients. It made him the ideal candidate to supply the armed forces with hundreds of prototype acrylic eyes, which proved to be more durable, lighter, and even more realistic than glass eyes. Wirtz's kits provided low-skilled technicians at military hospitals with easy-to-follow charts for matching the patient's eye color, and they even contained red-brown threads for simulating blood vessels. In a similar fashion, the Naval Graduate Dental Center in Annapolis, Maryland, developed a full complement of acrylic facial parts, including eye, nose, cheek, and ear prostheses. Surgeons in the field adapted these parts temporarily to the patient's face before the soldier was transferred to a military hospital for reconstructive surgery. In 1944 the Naval Graduate Dental Center also built customized cases for holding these parts that looked like velvet-lined candy box samplers. They included, among other facial features, a "Negro" ear and a "Caucasian" cheek. Interestingly, these navy prosthetists used a single mold to cast each facial part they created. This process made fabrication of parts easy; at the same time, it may have had the effect of neutralizing, or even erasing, the perceived phenotypic differences between white and black facial characteristics. One could argue that, in some small way, such a technical feat of prosthetic science anticipated by several years President Harry S. Truman's desegregation of the U.S. military in 1948.

Prosthetists and engineers working to rehabilitate disabled veterans relied on technical expertise; but they were also directly influenced by the fiercely heterosexual culture of postwar psychology, especially its orthodox zeal to preserve a soldier's masculine status. A 1957 rehabilitation manual developed by physical therapists at the University of California at Los Angeles, for example, explicitly correlated physical disability with the perceived heterosexual anxieties of the male amputee: "Will he be acceptable to wife or sweetheart? Can he live a normal sex-life? Will his children inherit anything as a result of his acquired physical defect? Can he hope to rejoin his social group? Must he give up having fun?"[32] This professional concern was associated with increasing panic about homosexuality, which predated the war but was formalized in the public imagination after the 1948 publication of Dr. Alfred Kinsey's *Sexual Behavior in the Human Male*. Among military and university researchers, this emphasis on rehabilitating the amputee's masculinity along with his body was an artifact left over from the military's deep-seated and overt homophobia.[33] As Allan Bérubé has described it, the armed forces maintained statistics throughout World War II on soldiers excused from military service for perceived homosexual behavior or for having otherwise unmasculine psychological or physiological traits.[34] At New York University, rehabilitation therapists expected that prostheses not only would permit able-bodied activity but also would confer positive self-esteem on those who participated in an experimental, technologically innovative laboratory study: "[A] good prosthesis, provided in an atmosphere of understanding and interest by people who are looking to him as a *man*, a human being, and as an important cog in an experimental program fills two interwoven needs. He can feel a lessening of the threats against which he must continually arm himself and he can utilize the potentialities of the prosthesis to a much greater extent."[35]

Attitudes like this, which equated independent activity with the perquisites of heterosexual masculinity in order to resist the potentially feminizing interventions of family members, were hardly unique in postwar rehabilitation culture. Throughout the late 1940s and 1950s, physicians, psychologists, and engineers imagined amputees as potentially troubled and socially maladjusted. Most were not even expected to fulfill their routine daily chores, let alone discharge their civic duties as sons, husbands, and citizens. For example, the physical therapists Donald Kerr and Signe Brunnstrom writing in 1956 encouraged amputees to reclaim their masculinity by rejecting dependence on others and observing strict rules of self-reliance: "From the time of surgery until he has returned to a normal life in the community, the amputee is beset by many doubts and fears. . . . The amputee must recognize that these attitudes are based on lack of knowledge, and he must not permit them to influence his own thinking. . . . [T]he family [should learn] to ignore the amputation and to expect and even require the amputee to take care of himself, to share in household duties, and to participate in social activities."[36] In this institutional climate, prostheses were regarded not only as prescriptive tools for rehabilitating amputees but also as cultural weapons with which they might defend them-selves against the onslaught of social criticism or the scrutiny of their male peers.

Apparently the social emphasis put on productive labor and its relation to masculine independence made such weapons mandatory for many veterans. Even while they were manipulated as symbols of American patriotism and stalwart defenders of national values, veterans and amputees often suffered explicit discrimination from employers in both white- and blue-collar industries. According to a 1947 interview with Fred Hetzel, director of the U.S. Employment Service for Washington, DC, "during and immediately following World War I, employers were eager to help disabled men." The dif-ference between these two postwar periods, Hetzel argued, was that "now that the labor market has tightened up, [employers] hire the physically fit applicant almost every time. They seem to want a Superman or a Tarzan—even though wartime experience showed that disabled men often turned in better work than those not handicapped."[37]

Hetzel's comments about the privileges of the able-bodied and the biases of the "tightened" labor market echoed a storyline that was published in the comic strip *Gasoline Alley* in May and June 1946 (fig. 4). The comic ran at approximately the same moment when double amputee Harold Russell and quadruple amputee Jimmy Wilson had ascended to popular consciousness (fig. 2). *Gasoline Alley* tells the story of Bix, a veteran of World War II who "lost both legs in the war and has two artificial ones" and the responses of able-bodied men who are impressed and won over by the display of Bix's normalcy. In the brief narrative, Wilmer, the shop owner, protests foreman Skeezix's decision to hire Bix as a new employee on the warehouse floor. Wilmer tells Skeezix, "It's nice to help those fellows, but we've got work to turn out—lots of it!" When Wilmer hires a former sailor for the position, he is amazed to discover that he is the same double amputee Skeezix had hired the day before. The cartoon echoes the promotion of rehabilitation medicine as one of the perquisites of the postwar economy. Skeezix

declares, parroting the rhetoric of medical miracles that saturated the postwar media, "Modern medicine and surgery have been doing wonders for war casualties. . . . [Bix] tells me he was out dancing last night!" Apparently Bix was not alone on the dance floor. In a 1946 autobiography the writer Louise Baker observed that "[a] great wave of slick stories has pounced [on] the public recently in which disabled soldiers bounce out of their beds, strap on artificial legs, and promptly dance off with pretty nurses. . . . [One nurse] not only affected a miraculous cure of the poor boy's complexes, she practically put blood and bones in his [prosthetic] leg."[38] By the social standards of the mid-1940s, what evidence was more reasonable assurance of an American's normal status than Darwinian competition with other males on the dance floor?

Artifacts of popular culture like *Gasoline Alley* suggest that some sectors of the public were only too aware of the harsh standards amputees were judged by. These were standardized versions of normal, heterosexual masculinity that few men, able-bodied or otherwise, could deviate from without fear of reprisal. That Bix is able to "pass" as an able-bodied, virile veteran—and is not immediately identified as a delicate or effeminate war casualty—is the comic's principal message. While watching Bix carry an enormous carton across the shop, Wilmer declares, "You sure put one over on me. I didn't suspect [Bix] wasn't perfectly *normal*." Skeezix replies, "Practically he is. . . . He wants to show he's as good as anybody. That makes him better."

As the *Gasoline Alley* comic demonstrates, preconceptions about amputees as maladjusted, fragile, or even neurotic were widespread and powerful. Yet such preconceptions did not just disappear at the behest of cartoonists; they significantly influenced the way prosthetics research was conducted—and consequently represented—during the 1950s. Such representations, in other words, were hardly the purview of mass culture alone. The photograph on the cover of this book, for example, was taken at Walter Reed Army Hospital in March 1952. It was undoubtedly meant to capture a veteran amputee in a familiar able-bodied activity: enjoying a cigarette. As usual, what was at issue was not simply his vocational or domestic rehabilitation but the crucial preservation of his masculinity. The dramatic lighting and crisply graduated shapes of the amputee's body, however, seem like conventions of celebrity iconography directly descended from photographers such as Cecil Beaton or George Platt Lynes. The photograph also suggests that the prosthesis will help the veteran preserve his male competence and self-reliant citizenship. Like other objects that celebrated the scientific and technological progress of postwar culture, such photographs taken at a military hospital known for its advanced prosthetics research were self-conscious attempts to illuminate and maintain the essential gestures of masculinity.[39] These familiar icons were circulated and disseminated throughout the world—not unlike Hollywood films, modern art, swing dancing, or phonograph records in decidedly American genres—as evidence of both domestic rehabilitation policies and the enduring legacies of American male toughness and resiliency.

Similarly, a photograph of an older veteran reading the newspaper, taken at Walter Reed in 1949, challenges the notion that all amputees were young and virile embodiments of virtuous American character and identity (fig. 5). Difficult to discern in the photograph, but no less poignant, are the pinup girls painted on the amputee's legs—icons more characteristic of the noses of airplanes or the backs of bomber jackets. Customizing one's legs with images of calendar girls perpetuates the tradition of proudly decorating jeeps, tanks, airplanes, and other military transport.[40] Photographs like these did double duty: first, they served as promotional materials for large rehabilitation centers like Walter Reed, advertising their progress in prosthetics research.

Such consciously crafted publicity images also assured the general public that amputees suffered no loss of ability, mobility, personality, or—most important—manhood. Smoking, reading the sports section, and in Bix's case swing dancing, were glorified matter-of-factly as normal American expressions of heterosexual male behavior. In the case of this older man, perhaps the pinup girls

FIGURE 5 This double amputee challenged the popular reputation of veteran amputees as emasculated or socially maladjusted by painting tattoo-like images of calendar girls on his prosthetic legs. Photograph ca. 1949, from the collections of the Otis Historical Archives, Armed Forces Institute of Pathology, Walter Reed Army Medical Center, Washington, DC.

let him identify with blue-collar workers. Looking like rugged tattoos, they may have connoted a particular mechanical aptitude or technological competence beyond merely sitting at a desk all day. The seductive lure of blue-collar accoutrements like tattoos never disappeared but in fact expanded among white-collar workers after the United States shifted from industry to a service economy in the 1960s and 1970s. To a large degree, the singular image of the happy, efficient white-collar organization man in his corporate office may have been only a triumph of postwar marketing, the genius of Madison Avenue.[41]

## BUILDING A NEW WORKFORCE

The rapid development and diffusion of new prosthetic materials and technologies in the postwar period made it possible for thousands of veterans to return to their jobs or to pursue alternative careers. Engineering departments and rehabilitation centers still needed to exercise extreme care in selecting which amputees would make good candidates for receiving experimental prostheses. Clearly the United States had a surfeit of veterans eager to participate in new research programs at military and university hospitals—most notably those sponsored by the Veterans Administration and the National Research Council's Advanced Council on Artificial Limbs. But with the fate of large federally sponsored contracts on the line, doctors and administrators made a concerted effort to choose just the right applicants as research subjects. As we have already seen, many professional discussions of veterans' social and psychological stability focused on the male amputee and his work competence, an especially potent set of concerns during a period when Freudian psychoanalysis, lobotomies, and shock therapy all held enormous medical authority as solutions to the problem of the maladjusted individual. Psychologists in both military and civilian practice in the 1940s and 1950s emphasized social adjustment—what sociologist David Riesman described in his critique of the "outer-directed personality"—in endorsing manliness and self-reliance among veterans and amputees.[42] Prosthetic laboratories, it seems, were no different.

At New York University and the University of California at Los Angeles, for example, engineers routinely gave potential prosthesis wearers a battery of psychological tests, all of which assumed that amputees suffered from war-related neuroses. In 1957 amputees at the UCLA School of Medicine were given the California Test of Personality, "designed to identify and reveal the status of certain fundamental characteristics of human nature which are highly important in determining personal, social, or vocational relationships."[43] UCLA also asked potential prosthesis wearers to describe in their own words their personal concepts of "self reliance; sense of personal worth; sense of personal freedom; feeling of belonging; freedom from withdrawing tendencies; and freedom from nervous symptoms." These questions in the testing manual all fell under the ominous category "Personal Security." In 1953, clinical researchers at NYU's College of Engineering gave prospective prosthesis wearers the Ascendance-Submission Reaction Study, a psychological test developed in the late 1930s "to discover the disposition of an individual to dominate his fellows (or be dominated by them) in various face-to-face relationships of everyday life."[44] This study examined the amputee according to his "early development—home setting; conforming or non-conforming behavior; neurotic character traits; attitude to parents; siblings; friends; cheerful or gloomy childhood; position of leadership; [and] attitude toward crippling." Through these examinations, engineers who built experimental prostheses believed they could quickly estimate the amputees' psychological profiles and citizenship values, including what the UCLA examiners called the test subjects' "social standards; social skills; freedom from anti-social tendencies; family relations; occupational relations; [and] community relations."

The relationship between psychological health and ideas about citizenship in rehabilitation programs underscored the assumptions made by engineers and therapists that much more was at stake than

making the amputee a productive laborer. While the language in
these manuals seems at first glance to partake of the Cold War's
obsession with character and conformity, the use of the prewar
Ascendance-Submission Study to measure an amputee's "conforming or nonconforming behavior" or "neurotic character traits"
demonstrates that the concern with the amputee's social and
political orientation in relation to his rehabilitation was not entirely
new. The Cold War may have normalized the use of some of this
language, but the psychological dimensions of rehabilitation medicine for amputees belonged to a much older historical discourse
about the care of citizens and workers under government bureau-
cracies and industrial management. After World War I, for instance,
European social scientists like Jules Amar applied principles from
management to the rehabilitation of amputees and veterans in hospitals in Paris. Their concern was the treatment of the neurotic
individual in society, but in the economic depressions that followed
the Great War they were equally concerned about the impact of a
generation of neurotic young veterans and amputees on the financial and political vitality of their respective nations. In the United
States, where the Great War ushered in a period of unprecedented
economic prosperity, psychologists also helped to develop vocational
training programs for veterans to meet the needs of assembly-line
production and other forms of industrial labor.[45] For rehabilitation
doctors and efficiency experts between the wars, making the damaged male body productive was perhaps the greatest conceptual
challenge to modern industrial capitalism.

After World War II, the new possibilities offered by prosthetics
research meant that rehabilitation programs could use prostheses as
technological interventions to meet the social mandates of the era,
especially as they reflected a new set of economic and political attitudes about the future of work in American society. In the late 1940s
Norbert Wiener, the MIT mathematician and communication theo-
rist who coined the term "cybernetics" in 1947, was commissioned
to explore the social benefits of independent function by applying
advanced electronics to the problem of the inefficient prosthesis.

Wiener theorized rhapsodically about "electronic control techniques to amplify pulses provided by commands from the amputee's brain."[46] In 1949 Wiener argued that engineers had the capacity to control muscle power through electrical motors attached to self-adjusting electronic feedback chains in a classic cybernetic system: "There is very little new art in connecting an electric motor to the numerical output of the machine, using electrical amplifiers to step up the power. It is even possible to imitate the kinesthetic sense of the human body, which records the position and motion of our muscles and joints, and equip the effector organs of the machine with telltales, which report back their performance in a proper form to be used by the machine."[47] Wiener's theorizing about a cybernetic-controlled prosthesis was not unprecedented. Experiments with power-assisted prostheses had begun in earnest in Germany in the late 1940s and by the mid-1950s were taken up in Britain, the Soviet Union, and the United States. Some of these included myoelectric prostheses, which used internal batteries or external amplifiers to stimulate muscles that had survived amputation, and pneumatic limbs, which were powered by small pneumatic gas canisters attached to the body. By the end of the 1950s, cybernetic control systems were considered to be in the vanguard of artificial limb research, and prosthetists and engineers in the United States saw self-contained power sources as the future of prosthetic science. Wiener later helped to design one of the earliest myoelectric arms. Using a battery-operated amplifier, it magnified existing nerve impulses into a self-regulating feedback chain, which generated enough consistent power to lift and move the arm.[48] Variously called the "Boston arm" and the "Liberty Limb," the myoelectric arm was developed in the early 1960s by Wiener in conjunction with Harvard Medical School and sponsored by the Liberty Mutual Insurance Company of Boston.[49]

Wiener's design for a cybernetic prosthesis was humanitarian in its vision, intended to rebuild the human body rather than displace or destroy it. The "Liberty Limb" was a new biomechanical model that promised self-control and self-sufficiency for individual prosthesis wearers. Reflecting the period's emphasis on self-reliant citizenship, the myoelectric prosthesis theoretically could perform independent functions using an internal power supply. For Wiener, the internal mechanism of the cybernetic prosthesis—pulleys, cylinders, and the like—echoed the postwar society's emphatic belief that medical technology could rehumanize the physical body rather than dehumanize it. In creating a group of electronically controlled, self-sustaining artificial limbs that replaced conventional prostheses, Wiener imagined a futuristic body in which applied technical expertise and cybernetic sophistication brought mobility and independence to the nonproductive citizen, who was almost always imagined as male and predominantly working class.

In retrospect, however, Wiener's vision was diluted by the politics of international scientific competition at the height of the Cold War. At the 1958 World's Fair in Brussels the USSR's pavilion of new technological breakthroughs under Soviet science featured the world's first commercially available myoelectric artificial arm. A. Y. Kobrinski and his colleagues at the Institute of Machine Technology of the USSR's Academy of Sciences and the Central Prosthetics Research Institute perfected and built the arm in the mid-1950s.[50] Meanwhile, in the United States during the same period, Wiener's experiments with cybernetic arms had bypassed the rehabilitation center completely and ultimately found their way to a very different end-user: the industrial robot. The United States exhibited the remote-controlled robot without showing its application in a myoelectric arm, let alone any medical device utilizing cybernetic technology. The result of this discrepancy between Soviet and American approaches to prosthetic technology—the former serving rehabilitation medicine, the latter serving industry—is one of the crushing ironies of postwar labor in the United States. Wiener's good-faith efforts with the principles of cybernetics, which started with the initial intention of helping amputees achieve self-sufficiency and return to work, became principles of exploitation after they were appropriated and promoted by industry, as the United States pavilion at the Brussels World's Fair demonstrated. By 1963, when they arrived en masse, robotic arms had begun to displace manual laborers in almost every facet of manufacturing and commercial production in the United States.[51]

Anxieties over the rise of complex automated processes in the workplace were not new for American workers in the 1950s. Automation had been a point of contention between labor and management since the early part of the century, beginning with Ford's assembly lines and picking up steam with the popularity of machine-made industrial objects and technocratic management styles in the 1930s.[52] The appearance of industrial robots—which worked tirelessly and without complaint on both day and night shifts and for which coffee breaks, safe working conditions, and overtime pay were nonissues—seemed like the death knell for American laborers, who saw their bodies and their status as workers as potentially obsolete. Furthermore, this new generation of industrial robots perfectly matched the new generation of managerial theories propounded by white-collar economists and business executives in the 1950s, who spoke rapturously about the new opportunities for leisure and relaxation that would be afforded to the American worker. For older workers who had experienced these so-called leisure opportunities during the Depression, as well as for younger workers and returning veterans of the recent war, the rise of industrial robots represented yet another disruptive historical force that challenged the capacity of male workers to express their masculinity through their physical bodies.

In the scheme of postwar prostheses, Wiener's "Liberty Limb" was atypical: designed as an experimental model, it did not become available commercially in the United States until the late 1960s, and then its exorbitant cost was anathema to most patients and many insurance companies. More typical were prostheses that would help allay men's work anxieties. Updated designs meant to create work opportunities were far more common than new designs meant to produce unemployment. Designer Henry Dreyfuss, for example, whose work promoted the social benefits of ergonomics, engineered and built a prosthetic hand for the Veterans Administration in

1955, and the design is still in use today. One might say that Dreyfuss's work as an industrial designer for the federal government marked the perfect cohesion of prosthetics as a tool of social engineering and of Cold War science. As he declared in his 1955 manifesto *Designing for People,* "The goal in [military projects] is a contribution to morale, the intangible force that impels soldiers to have confidence and pride in their weapons and therefore in themselves and that, in the long pull, wins battles and wars."[53] Dreyfuss had many experiences adapting his design sensibility to serve military-industrial science and technology.[54] In 1942, for example, Dreyfuss contracted with the Coordinator of Information and the Office of Strategic Services to plan strategy rooms and conference rooms for the armed forces. Dreyfuss also designed Howitzer rifles and carriages for 105-millimeter guns for the army and ship habitats for the navy. Well into the 1950s his services were retained, and he designed missile launchers as well as the ergonomic interiors of the M46 and M95 tanks. Completing the collaborative symbiosis between government and industry that so marks the Cold War period, Dreyfuss served as a consultant for Chrysler's confidential missile branch from 1954 to 1956. Following the war, however, from 1948 to 1950, Dreyfuss served as a consultant to the National Research Council's Advanced Council on Artificial Limbs.

A photograph of Dreyfuss Associates' prosthetic hand created for the Veterans Administration's Human Engineering Division was published in *Designing for People* (fig. 6). Appearing alongside images of familiar industrial objects, such as the round Honeywell thermostat and the black Bell telephone, the photograph would have been a noticeable departure from advertisements for artificial arms—let alone legs, hands, or facial parts—typically produced by nineteenth- and twentieth-century prosthesis manufacturers. As Stephen Mihm has argued, late nineteenth-century catalogs by esteemed limb makers such as A. A. Marks routinely included images of workingmen using their artificial arms and legs to operate threshers and other heavy farm machines. Such images demonstrated that an artificial arm in no way compromised either the worker's

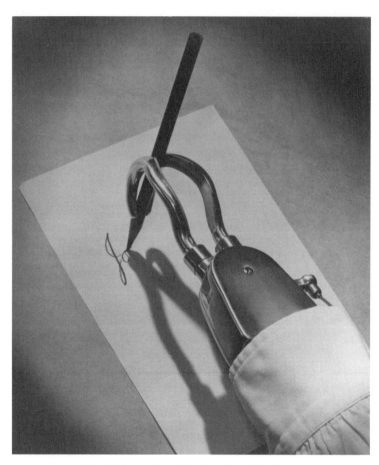

FIGURE 6 Henry Dreyfuss's prosthetic hand, produced for the National Research Council in 1948–50, was designed as a new kind of hand for a new kind of labor. Reprinted with permission from the Henry Dreyfuss Collection, Cooper-Hewitt National Design Museum, Smithsonian Institution.

masculinity or his ability to earn a living.[55] As one A. A. Marks catalog declared in 1908, "The wholesome effect an [artificial] arm has on the stump, that of keeping it in a healthy and vigorous condition, protecting it from injuries, forcing it into healthful activity, together with its ornamental aspect, are sufficient reasons for wearing one, even if utility is totally ignored."[56] By contrast, the Dreyfuss hand would have been a self-conscious alternative to these photographic images and manufacturers' endorsements. It provided a "civilized" alternative to the otherwise painful and traumatic representations of amputees and prosthesis wearers that were displayed in public, especially those doing blue-collar work, such as Bix from *Gasoline Alley*. As one can see in the photograph, Dreyfuss's hands for above-elbow amputees were shiny, rounded stainless steel hooks that imitated the curve of fingers. Beginning a signature in beautiful longhand, with its mechanics hidden tastefully by a crisp Oxford-cloth shirtsleeve, the gleaming steel hand twinkles within a well-lit and expertly framed composition. Clearly, Dreyfuss was concerned with aspects of the hand that would not have provoked much interest, or comment, among prosthesis makers or amputees fifty years earlier.

Similarly, Dreyfuss commented in *Designing for People,* "If 'feel' is of importance to the housewife at her ironing board, imagine how infinitely more important it is in the artificial limbs of an amputee. We learned a great deal about this in our work for the Veterans Administration. To understand the plight of the amputee, members of our staff had artificial limbs strapped to them."[57] Dreyfuss's interest in "feel" was, again, not a conceptual category of design that was useful or even recognizable to many early manufacturers of prostheses. Even in the 1950s, the typical goal for prosthetists was to make the worker as productive and efficient as possible, while not discounting necessary comfort and daily utility. The search for some ergonomic standard of "feel" would have stimulated the interest only of an industrial designer, especially one concerned with the appearance and feel of commercial products and home and business environments. The Dreyfuss hand may have harked back to the image of a managed worker's body from the early twentieth century, but its aesthetic details were undeniably *moderne,* a product of the design-conscious mid-1950s. The Dreyfuss hand followed the objectives of an industrial designer whose goal was to package all consumer objects according to the aesthetic criteria of beauty, harmony, and use-value. After all, Dreyfuss not only designed telephones and thermostats, but also designed window displays for Marshall Field's in Chicago and Macy's in New York as well as theatrical spaces at the 1939–40 New York World's Fair. For someone of such catholic tastes, designing and representing a prosthetic hand held similar aesthetic and ergonomic challenges. Mechanical hardware must be hidden either by the stainless steel casing or by the long-sleeved shirt in order to obey Dreyfuss's own strict design injunctions: no visible screws, a single housing, no exposed seams or joints, and no distracting colors or patterns. As this photograph shows, Dreyfuss's prosthetic hand was a model of solidity and sophistication.

To whom, then, were these new Dreyfuss hands pitched? As we have seen from representations of amputees engaged in what appear to be ordinary tasks, images of men performing as men in familiar and recognizably masculine endeavors, both individually and collectively, were an extremely important part of rehabilitation. In the Dreyfuss photograph, however, we see historical evidence of industrial designers and commercial photographers grappling not with the needs of factory workers or GI amputees but with the postwar period's growing desire for a new model of American masculinity. Such an image, ideally, would accommodate a growing army of corporate white-collar workers, not to mention those blue-collar workers encouraged—or forced—to make the professional transition to a service economy.[58] For this reason, the functionalist imperative in the Dreyfuss hand might be understood as one way of normalizing and marketing able-bodied function for amputees whose professional aspirations did not include assembly-line work. This, then, was "the other arms race" of the postwar period: not the

technological cum political competition with the Soviet Union
but the competition between white-collar masculinity (as symbolized by the Dreyfuss arm) and that of the blue-collar worker who
formerly had proved his worthiness and aptitude through the labor
he accomplished after completing rehabilitation. By the 1960s, both
able-bodied and disabled men who had been trained for certain
types of physical labor were seen as increasingly obsolete as more
and more jobs shifted from the industrial and manufacturing sector
to service contexts. The uneasy relationship between the workingman and his body remained the premier site where American masculinity continued to be refashioned throughout the postwar era.
This is why Dreyfuss's arm is historically so important: it was an
image that offered corporate bureaucrats a vision of a white-collar
hand for the newly emerging white-collar world that would come to
dominate the workscape of American cities. Indeed, the hand form-
ing a signature—"John"—vindicated the consumerist ethos that
dominated the 1950s by demonstrating that even amputees could
sign their lives away through credit debt. The Dreyfuss hand may
have promised to restore anatomical function and neutralize emasculation, but perhaps it could also confer self-esteem and cultural
capital. This may be why the white-collar sophistication that
Dreyfuss's design team attempted to impart through both product
and marketing reflected not the contents of contemporary rehabilitation manuals but those of period magazines like *Playboy* and
*Esquire*, whose advertisements regularly featured high-tech appli-
ances or multifunctional Herman Miller furniture.[59]

The arms race in prosthetics demonstrated, in material form, the
shift in ideas about labor for men as well as the status of the prosthesis as a form of social engineering. It offered a proud new
consumer item that reflected a profound new sense of prosperity,
as predicted by the era's foremost economic theorists and carried
out by service economy workers. At the end of the war, an ampu-
tated arm or leg may have provoked associations between anatomical dysfunction and a lack of reliability, sturdiness, fortitude, or

commitment. But by the mid-1950s, the utterly functionalist, aesthetically integrated, and mass-produced Dreyfuss hand offered a new kind of social prestige as well as a new model of masculine labor. Many must have believed that the Dreyfuss hand would be the wave of the future. It was a whole new hand for a whole new kind of labor.

## TWO

**Reconstructing the Hiroshima Maidens**

IN 1950 THE FAMOUS Japanese American sculptor Isamu
Noguchi made a historic pilgrimage to Japan, where he lived and
worked intermittently for the rest of his life.[1] Throughout the early
1950s, Noguchi pursued a successful series of projects in Japan,
including a sculpture garden at the Reader's Digest building in
Tokyo, an exhibition of his works at the Mitsukoshi department
store, and a memorial for his father at Keio University. Noguchi
also designed stone railings for two bridges in Hiroshima. The
Great Bridge for Peace (called *tsu kuru,* translated as "to build" or
"life") and the Great Western Bridge for Peace (called *yuku,* translated as "to depart" or "die") were meant as symbolic thorough-
fares by which travelers could visit Hiroshima's newly constructed
Peace Memorial Park (fig. 7).[2] The park, the brainchild of the
Committee for the Reconstruction of Hiroshima, was first conceived in 1947 to honor the citizens and city ravaged by the 1945
atomic bombing, although it did not achieve conceptual maturity
until 1955.[3] Before working on the bridges in Hiroshima, Noguchi
also proposed a design for a "Memorial to the Dead," an exquisite
six-foot black granite cenotaph that would function as the official
monument for Hiroshima's war dead. As Noguchi himself described
the sculpture, "[The cenotaph] was to be the place of solace to the
bereaved—suggestive still further of the womb of generations still
unborn who would in time replace the dead."[4] Despite the proposal's
poignant simplicity, Noguchi's elegant cenotaph design was rejected.
The Committee on the Construction of the Peace Memorial City

FIGURE 7 Hiroshima survivors Sakae Okubi, left, and Mariko Matsumoto pose beside Isamu Noguchi's Peace Bridge on the ninth anniversary of the atomic bombing. The two women were among the thousands of female *hibakusha* who did not come to the United States for the Hiroshima Maidens project. The sartorial contrast between Okubi's Western outfit and Matsumoto's traditional kimono suggests some of the underlying tensions that occurred during the reconstruction and modernization of Hiroshima in the 1950s. Photograph taken August 13, 1954, © Bettmann/Corbis.

felt it was inappropriate for an American citizen, regardless of ethnic heritage, to design a memorial that commemorated the destruction of Hiroshima.[5] Even though "the atomic bomb ceno-taph is a symbol of recognition and retrospection for everyone," wrote Noguchi in 1953, "the Japanese said they did not need a foreigner's help."[6]

At approximately the same historical moment, and not far from the Hiroshima Peace Memorial Park, the Reverend Kiyoshi Tanimoto was seeking foreign help for an altogether different kind of project. Tanimoto, a Methodist minister who had trained at Emory University in the 1930s but returned to serve in his Japanese hometown, wanted to bring a group of young Hiroshima women who had been badly burned and disfigured by the atomic bomb to the United States for plastic surgery.[7] For most of their adult lives, the young women had been kept out of sight by their embarrassed families, who understood their disfigurements as subjective reflections on their families' status rather than as the objective effects of atomic warfare. As a result, the young women bore deep physical and psychological wounds. Around the city, they were known informally as Tanimoto's "Keloid Girls," an awkward term of endearment that referred to the hard scar tissue that formed from their radiation burns. In 1951 Tanimoto was introduced to Norman Cousins, the influential editor of the *Saturday Review of Literature*. Cousins had commenced a series of well-publicized tours to increase public awareness for the plight of Japanese orphans and war victims both in the United States and abroad. Tanimoto implored Cousins to help him arrange for a cross section of the Keloid Girls to travel to the United States and undergo reconstructive plastic surgery. Over the course of four years, Cousins was finally able to grant Tanimoto's wish. Although British and German doctors had imported Western medicine to Japan in the mid-nineteenth century, Japanese surgeons did not develop plastic surgery as a medical specialty before the 1960s.[8] By contrast, advanced reconstructive techniques had put British, French, German, and American surgeons at the forefront of modern surgery. Beginning in late spring 1955, a team of plastic surgeons at Mount Sinai Hospital in New York City performed over 140 necessary operations on twenty-five of Tanimoto's Keloid Girls. Soon known in the United States and abroad as the "Hiroshima Maidens," they recuperated in the metropolitan New York area in the homes of Quaker families who had agreed to sponsor them. For eighteen months, from May 1955 until

November 1956, the travails and triumphs of the Hiroshima Maidens achieved international recognition. By the end of 1956, when the last operations were complete, the Maidens returned to Hiroshima where they were expected to begin new lives.

In what ways are these two seemingly unrelated stories about postwar Hiroshima connected? One might argue that Noguchi's cenotaph and Tanimoto's Maidens illustrate two different strategies that were devised by citizens of Japan and the United States to memorialize, and ultimately repair, the physical and psychic damage done to Hiroshima and its citizens by the atomic bomb. As Lisa Yoneyama has proposed, the city of Hiroshima itself is a powerful locus for understanding the political exigencies of memory: not only for the *hibakusha,* the survivors of the original 1945 atomic bombing, but also as a constantly shifting metaphorical site within contemporary Japanese cultural politics.[9] For Noguchi, the proposed cenotaph registered the horrors of war by proudly memorializing the dead. For Tanimoto, Cousins, and the Maidens themselves, plastic surgery registered the horrors of war by successfully repairing the living. This emphasis on surgery as a tool of reconstruction should not be surprising. After World War I, when the techniques used in modern plastic surgery first emerged from exclusively wartime use to civilian use in Europe and the United States, practitioners and patients regularly referred to plastic surgery as "sculpture in the living," and in the 1930s it had acquired a reputation as something of an art form.[10] These were applications of medical technology aimed at a consumer audience that transcended the destruction and disfigurement caused by war.

Noguchi's memorial cenotaph and the Maidens' plastic surgery were technological projects that expressed entirely different, and even contradictory, concepts of national identity for a postwar Japanese culture seeking meaning in the aftermath of trauma. Noguchi assumed that the Committee on the Construction of the Peace Memorial City denied his proposed contribution solely because of his American citizenship. But the Committee's expression of nationalistic integrity was hardly that simple.[11] Since Japan opened its doors to Western cultural influences in the 1850s, Japanese leaders in both the public and private sectors had adopted numerous Western policies and practices, especially the promotion of Western industry, education, and technological development. Before it was transformed into an important military center for war production during World War II, Hiroshima was an unremarkable though picturesque city of approximately 280,000 citizens whose livelihoods were sustained by a bustling fishing economy and a small commercial sector concentrated in its downtown business district. After 1946, however, when it began the slow process of rebuilding itself, Hiroshima envisioned its future as a new "modern" city of wide boulevards and bridges, memorial parks and green public spaces, and Western-style architecture. Through this rebuilt landscape, individuals and civic groups realized the cultural and material benefits promised by applying Western ideas and technologies to the native environment. This attitude was partly derived during the Occupation of Japan (1945–52), during which time General Douglas MacArthur headed the Supreme Command of the Allied Powers. As Carl Mosk has noted, "Western ideas and goods started streaming into Japan as isolationism collapsed under American pressure in the early 1950s." After the war, according to Mosk, "the Japanese government exhibited a strong 'supply side' technological bias in its health/population quality maintenance and enhancement programs, eschewing social engineering . . . in favor of importing Western medical and public health methods and knowledge."[12]

The stories about Noguchi and the Maidens both embody the political and philosophical contradictions that lay at the heart of what Masao Watanabe has identified as "Japanese ethics, European science."[13] In this dialectic, both Noguchi's critics and the Hiroshima Maidens' sponsors sought a cosmopolitan postwar Japanese identity while also laboring to disavow the provincial values associated with prewar Japanese nationalism. According to this logic, plastic surgery's exotic status carried with it the elusive mark of modernity, providing tangible evidence of Western technical proficiency. Tanimoto and Cousins, guided by a similar and deliberate

*inimical*
*atavism*

privileging of Western cultural and technological forms, sought out American surgeons precisely because they used Western medical procedures that were heretofore unavailable in Japan. In such a mindset, Noguchi's traditional cenotaph would have been regarded as a sculptural form that was inimical to postwar enthusiasm for Western design, such as modern architecture, and thus something of a nostalgic atavism.[14] As Sachio Otani has observed, "Most Japanese perceived traditional culture to be tainted with nationalism, and consequently it was almost automatically rejected, a sort of expiation of war guilt."[15] The decision to send the Maidens abroad for medical care paralleled the rejection of Noguchi's sculpture in the sense that both actions symbolized, as James R. Bartholomew has written, the "deeply engrained Japanese belief that what had been 'proven' abroad" was preferable to anything domestic.[16]

Scholars and journalists have tended to offer complex interpretations of the story of the Hiroshima Maidens, more often than not seeing it as a shining expression of medical humanitarianism that attempted to repair some of the physical and political scars left by World War II.[17] Others have been more critical of the project: in 1961, for example, literary critic Edmund Wilson observed, "We have tried to make up for our atomic bombs by treating and petting the Japanese women whom we disfigured or incapacitated. We like to read about this in the papers."[18] This chapter examines the reception and promotion that surrounded the Maidens' surgeries in the United States from May 1955 through November 1956, using both public records and heretofore unexamined private documents. As we shall see, the Maidens project should be understood as a medical narrative of normalization that was galvanized by the futuristic tenor of plastic reconstructive surgery (especially cosmetic surgery) in the postwar years. Their surgical rehabilitation crystallized around popular fantasies—both international and domestic—about the possibilities of upward mobility and self-improvement that were embodied in plastic and cosmetic surgery. This chapter also examines the *non*surgical techniques that the Maidens' American sponsors used to rehabilitate the physical bodies and social identities of these young women. The cultural fantasies attributed to plastic surgery's material effects may help us understand why and how the Hiroshima Maidens project was pursued at the very same time that Noguchi's memorial cenotaph was rejected on what were essentially the same grounds.

## BUILDING THE "NEW" JAPAN

In the late 1940s, the Reverend Kiyoshi Tanimoto organized a weekly support group for about forty young women from downtown Hiroshima who were so badly burned and disfigured by exposure to the heat and radiation of the atomic blast that their families hid them from public view.[19] In 1951 the young Japanese minister approached Norman Cousins on one of his tours of Japan. Tanimoto believed that, with Cousins's help, he could raise enough money and support for the young women to undergo plastic reconstructive surgery, permitting them to hold jobs and lead "normal" lives. Japanese surgeons who had tried to repair the Maidens' damaged bodies had done a bad job, so much so that in some cases they made the scars worse and left them in a nearly inoperable state. The heavy, inexpensive makeup the young women often wore sometimes led to rashes or skin infections. Their disfigurement was also exacerbated by the genotypical reaction to atomic radiation that many Asians experienced. The outermost layers of their skin either had been burned off completely or had formed keloids, fibrous pieces of scar tissue that cemented elbow or leg joints at right angles and made movement difficult or nearly impossible.

Tanimoto persuaded Cousins that the best possible medical care for the Maidens was in the United States and that he should move heaven and earth to help them as quickly as possible.[20] Cousins was moved by the plight of these young women, whom he affectionately dubbed the "Hiroshima Maidens," an awkward English translation of the Japanese name with which they had christened themselves—the "Unmarried Young Ladies of Hiroshima."[21] In 1953 Cousins approached Dr. William Hitzig, his personal physician at Mount

Sinai Hospital in New York City, and asked him to assemble a team of plastic surgeons who could perform the necessary major and minor operations. Hitzig and his colleagues flew to Hiroshima and selected twenty-five young women they believed could benefit most from the reconstructive surgery. In late April 1955, just days before the Maidens began their weeklong trip from Hiroshima to New York City, a group of American photojournalists traveled to Japan to capture their preparations for their historic journey. Such journalistic interventions were intended to inure the young women, all of whom had lived in involuntary privacy since 1945, to the routine elements of celebrity journalism. In the candid spirit of paparazzi photography—which used, among other things, the rhetorical pretension of "before" and "after" portraits—the journalists sought to familiarize the American public with recognizable images of the women that they expected would circulate in the media over the next few months.[22]

In one photograph, two of the Maidens, Atsue Yamamoto and Suzue Oshima, stand before the burned-out and exposed rotunda of the Industrial Promotion Hall, the Gothic tower built in 1908 as the leading commercial structure of Hiroshima Prefecture's business district (fig. 8).[23] Indeed, the Industrial Promotion Hall was one of the few buildings left standing after the atomic bomb was dropped, and for many in the city it became a triumphant metaphor of the enduring spirit of the "old" Hiroshima. It is known today as the "A-Bomb Dome." After 1947, when Hiroshima Prefecture passed a bill that declared a section of the city a Peace Memorial Park, the Hall became the organizing symbol around which the city's team of urban planners proposed their renewal project for the entire city. When the first group of Maidens returned to Hiroshima in July 1956, photographers for *Collier's* even posed them in front of the famous building again, only this time standing on a grassy knoll that looked down on the Industrial Promotion Hall as well as the whole of the Peace Memorial Park.[24]

To a large degree, the dual focus on both the Industrial Promotion Hall and Yamamoto and Oshima in their best clothes perfectly

FIGURE 8 "Unmarried Ladies of Hiroshima" Atsue Yamamoto, left, and Suzue Oshima pose before the Industrial Promotion Hall, one of the icons of the "old" Hiroshima now known informally as the A-Bomb Dome. Photograph taken late April 1955, author's collection.

expressed the momentum behind Tanimoto's vision. More than merely serving as visual propaganda, this poignant though obviously posed image of the Hiroshima Maidens standing symbolically before the Hall served as a key to the hopes and dreams with which both Japanese and American sponsors endowed the Maidens project.[25] Though Yamamoto and Oshima are posed in the foreground and lighted from below, the building is intentionally shown out of focus, a remote and hazy reminder of the past. The smiling Maidens, dressed in their best suits, gloves, and handbags and surrounded by barbed wire, make a stark contrast with the haunted building, whose missing windows are infused with gray, sunless light. Photographs like this one were undoubtedly the result of general policies during the Occupation regarding representations of the atomic bombings of Hiroshima and Nagasaki. Throughout the late 1940s and early 1950s, topographic photographs or reports of Hiroshima emphasized the architectural devastation of the city and later its rejuvenation. These images became symbols around which public discourse formed in the absence of photographs of *hibakusha* or those who were killed outright. Photographs of people killed or maimed were not published in American newspapers or magazines until late in 1952, the final year of the Occupation.[26] The absence of human beings in pictures of Hiroshima gave enormous power to the buildings themselves, so that the complete erasure of ordinary people from this historical record slyly avoided the human scale of destruction by which the bomb consumed Hiroshima's and Nagasaki's populations. In lieu of photographs of survivors, which were immediately censored by the State Department, images of the bleak, destroyed landscape—and the remains of public buildings like the Industrial Promotion Hall—became deliberate and extremely palpable substitutes for the people who could not be shown.

In May 1955, just weeks after this promotional photograph of Yamamoto and Oshima was taken, the State Department issued a classified internal memo that sought to downplay the atomic angle of the Hiroshima Maidens project. The State Department took great pains to identify the young women publicly as war victims. According to the memo, it wished to maintain the belief that "the death and mutilation inflicted by the atomic bombs are no different than those caused by conventional weapons."[27] This strategy, used throughout the 1950s to maintain funding for nuclear energy research, was also used, in effect, to displace American culpability for the Maidens' disfigurement as well as to make them seem like ordinary wartime refugees. Consequently, posing Yamamoto and Oshima in front of the Industrial Promotion Hall had the rhetorical effect of linking them visually to famous postwar photographs of recuperating civilians, especially women and children, in Cologne, Dresden, London, Warsaw, and other European cities devastated during World War II. Like those forlorn children posed before crumbling buildings or on the broken cobblestone streets of Paris, as in the famous humanist photography of Robert Doisneau or Willy Ronis, the Maidens in their Western-style suits and smiles suggest that they are merely victims of war stepping out momentarily from the daily demands of their busy lives, not living survivors of the only atomic bombing in world history.[28]

After 1945, the architectural reconstruction of Hiroshima became a kind of shorthand for the ones in whose name the media dared not speak. The photographic emphasis on the city's physical environment allowed the media to refer openly to Hiroshima's destruction without also having to choose whether to defend the nuclear arsenal (or for that matter the military-industrial complex) in order to appease the State Department. Associated Press articles about Hiroshima, for example, which appeared in hundreds of small and large newspapers across the world, affirmed the architectural focus on Hiroshima's modernity on the tenth and twentieth anniversaries of the atomic bombing: "Ten years after, Hiroshima has shaken off the scars of war and rebuilt a better city with sturdier homes and more industry" (1955); "Though the Fukuya Department Store, Hiroshima's largest, was destroyed in the blast, it's now back in business with modern interior design and display counters" (1955); "Slowly but surely Hiroshima is rebuilding from

FIGURE 9 View of the destroyed Hiroshima from the top of a Red Cross hospital emphasizing rubble and debris over images of *hibakusha*. Photograph taken August 1945, © Bettmann/Corbis.

the shattered ruins left by the atom bombing ten years ago" (1955); "From a sleepy city with narrow winding streets, Hiroshima has become a well-laid-out metropolis" (1965).[29] Norman Cousins asserted in 1955, in one of his progress reports about the Maidens to readers of the *Saturday Review,* that "Hiroshima is on the way to becoming one of the most exciting cities, architecturally, in Japan. Already, the general outlines are becoming clear. The new park areas have been laid out, the new boulevards are well past the half-way mark, the new and modern civic buildings are being built." (See figs. 9 and 10).[30]

The reconstruction of Hiroshima as a Peace Park also belonged to a greater national anxiety over the fate of Japanese cultural identity following the war. During the seven years that the Occupation government dominated domestic policies in the rebuilding of the

FIGURE 10 Aerial view of the rebuilt Hiroshima emphasizing modern office buildings, stores, and public transportation over images of *hibakusha*. The original caption, betraying a lack of subtlety, claimed "one has to look closely to find any scars of that terrible day when a city died." Photograph taken August 1, 1955, © Bettmann/Corbis.

country, Japan's attraction to Western science, technology, and culture accelerated as proof of the people's capacity to enter the brave postwar world of modernity, efficiency, and technological prowess.[31] As Sheldon Garon has written, "So powerful was the Japanese belief in modernization, progress, and science that neither the contradictions of the wartime campaigns nor the nation's disastrous defeat in 1945 rent the alliance for daily life improvement in the postwar era."[32] The push to democratize Japan came from powerful economic incentives provided by the United States government, which pumped over $2.2 billion into the Japanese economy between 1947 and 1952, $1.7 billion of it in grants that did not require repayment.[33] In addition to new economic programs, on May 3, 1947, the Supreme Command of the Allied Powers (SCAP), under the direction of General Douglas MacArthur, approved a new constitution for Japan. It demanded that the nation break up concentrated wealth among the Japanese aristocracy and within large corporations, dismantle the state's military power, and disband all nationalist groups and associations, especially those that had germinated during wartime. According to Garon, the SCAP also forced all textbooks harboring "ultranationalist propaganda" to be replaced by what was perceived to be nonideological, democratic language approved by American supervisors.

Elizabeth Gray Vining, a Philadelphia Quaker commissioned in 1946 by the emperor of Japan to tutor his son the Crown Prince Akihito, experienced firsthand the postwar shift in Japanese culture from its feudal political organization toward democratic principles imposed during the Occupation. "Many of the Americans were indeed the 'crusaders' that General MacArthur has called them," Vining wrote in her memoir, *Windows for the Crown Prince* (1952), which championed the democratic values of American culture after the war.[34] "In their effort to produce a perfect model of democracy they sometimes instituted measures that would be advanced experiments in many of our own states and which were bewildering to the Japanese, who were only learning their democratic ABCs. 'But why,' they would say, 'shouldn't they avoid the mistakes we made?'" Like its academic counterpart *The Chrysanthemum and the Sword* (1946), Ruth Benedict's classic anthropological study of Japanese value systems in the modern era, Vining's book tried respectfully to comprehend a foreign nation (and former enemy) undergoing enormous social change under direct American influence.[35] In 1947 socialist prime minister Katayama Tetsu launched the "People's Campaign to Build a New Japan," which espoused values that would come to embody the "new" Japan, including thrift, morality, hard work, love of homeland, and intolerance of crime and delinquency. Also instituted under the new campaign was what was termed "social education," which included everything from home economics to personal and public hygiene. This crusade to reform and regulate social behavior had fairly unambiguous political implications when, in 1959, the government sponsored its newest social program, the "Campaign to Beautify Japan."[36]

The legislative and cultural mandates that sought to forge a new and integrated Japanese identity were mirrored in debates over the architectural and spatial reconstruction of Japanese cities. Since the 1920s, several prominent Japanese architects had maintained an aesthetic dialogue with European and avant-garde movements in modernist architecture, most notably the German Bauhaus and visionaries like France's Le Corbusier. By the late 1940s and early 1950s, new visions for recreating Japanese cities were futuristic fixations that must have seemed extremely forward-looking to postwar Japanese culture.[37] In 1951, for example, Kenzo Tange, the architect who was awarded the contract to design the cenotaph to the war dead for the Hiroshima Peace Memorial Park, revealed his *Plan for Tokyo, 1960*. Describing his ideas for the Japanese capital, Tange wrote, "We are not trying to reject the Tokyo that exists and build an entirely new city. We wish instead to provide the city with a revised structure which will lead to its rejuvenation. We are talking not merely of 'redevelopment,' but of determining a direction along which redevelopment should proceed."[38] Tange's plan for a "revised" Tokyo consisted of a vast series of concentric rings of small residential units linked by bridges and water transport that emanated from a central commercial and industrial hub. Tange's vision captures the essence of contemporary architectural and technological fantasies of the "new Japan." This is because the idea of social progress during the Occupation often privileged urban planning projects that replaced Japanese tradition with European and European-derived American modernism. Such projects were often directly inspired by American architectural visionaries like Buckminster Fuller and Raymond Hood. For Tange and his contemporaries, the "new" Tokyo could symbolize the ideal organic marriage of the structural demands of the modern city with the technical demands of modern architecture. It could serve its inhabitants not merely as a functioning city but as a symbol of Tokyo's ascent to the status of world-class international capitol. This impulse toward internationalism and modernity would fulfill what architectural critic Arthur Drexler first saw bubbling underneath new Japanese building styles; as he wrote in 1955, "Modern architecture in Japan must first be international—that is to say, visually and structurally related to twentieth century technology—before it can become specifically Japanese."[39]

In smaller cities such as Hiroshima, reinventing the landscape for the purposes of urban planning and reinvigorating economic growth held a particular appeal, especially since it linked them to a progressive, modern renovation. Plans for redevelopment in Hiroshima were formally set in motion in August 1949, when a law was promulgated mandating the reconstruction of Hiroshima as a "City of Peace." The charter for this law decreed, "The purpose of reconstructing the city of Hiroshima as a peace memorial is to create a symbol of our desire for lasting peace. . . . Besides the usual city planning, plans will be made to construct memorial spots for peace and cultural facilities which are suitable for a 'Peace City.'"[40] By 1965, on the twentieth anniversary of the atomic bombing, American newspapers celebrated Hiroshima through its topographical features, describing it as "a lively city of broad boulevards, green parks, modern buildings, a half a million people."[41] By 1985 John Hersey called Hiroshima "a gaudy phoenix . . . risen from the ruinous desert of 1945 . . . with tall modern buildings on broad, tree-lined avenues crowded with Japanese cars, all of which had English lettering on them and appeared to be brand-new."[42]

Was the commercial transformation of Hiroshima inevitable? The Hiroshima Peace Memorial Park was clearly built to commemorate trauma, death, and destruction, but apparently it also enabled planners to conceive urban renewal projects for the entire city. This careful execution paralleled similar renewal projects under the Marshall Plan that transformed the physical landscape of war-ravaged cities throughout Europe—as well as economically depressed inner-city areas in the United States—during the late 1940s and throughout the 1950s and 1960s. The prominent urban renewal paradigm of the 1950s—applied with remarkable overlap in cities as diverse as Hiroshima, Cologne, London, Los Angeles, and New York City—meant that municipal governments would be shaped and funded by commercial interests, economic boosterism, and tourism. Many inner-city areas became singularly committed to tearing down obsolete buildings and replacing city streets with pedestrian shopping malls to create fountains, gardens, plazas, and other public spaces that would obviate the perceived "urban dangers" of the inner city. Critics of urban planning have routinely asked for whose benefit such renewal projects are ultimately undertaken, and with good reason. Urban renewal, as Norman Klein has noted in his focus on postwar Los Angeles, often erases local history, privileging political and economic alliances between local government and corporate interests over the civic rights of its inhabitants.[43] For architectural historians like Christine Boyer and Elizabeth Wilson, these strategies of renewal call to mind the controlling machinations of the City Beautiful movement, which was zealously pursued by civic-minded Progressive Era reformers in the United States during the early decades of the twentieth century.[44]

As early as 1947, citizens who attended public hearings about the reconstruction of Hiroshima expressed complete indifference to the green parks and flowerbeds promised to them. They demanded adequate housing, transportation, and food. Instead, in 1951

Hiroshima Prefecture gave eviction notices to the landlords of 320 buildings occupying space on the grounds of the Peace Memorial Park. In 1955 the editors of *Japan Letter,* a monthly newsletter published in San Francisco on behalf of Hiroshima orphans and refugees, commented that "the progress made in the rebuilding of the city of Hiroshima shows the courage of its people. Yet, between the new buildings there still remain many ruins and poorly built shacks. Ten years later, when the memories of war have begun to fade, the victims of the atomic bomb find it no easier to maintain themselves mentally, physically, and economically."[45] For many Japanese activists, the economic emphasis on urban renewal obscured the greater symbolic significance of the Hiroshima Peace Memorial Park, which they envisioned as the obvious geopolitical locus for a growing international antinuclear movement. This was precisely what the State Department feared. On May 6, 1955, the day after the Maidens left Tokyo for the United States, the State Department sent an anxious telegram to the American Embassy in Japan expressing "concern . . . that [the] Hiroshima girls['] medical treatment in U.S. can generate publicity harmful not only [to] our relations with Japan but particularly [to] our worldwide efforts [to] avoid playing up [the] destructive effects [of] nuclear weapons."[46] Had the Maidens decided to delay their trip by one more day, it is not clear whether the Air Force plane commissioned to carry them to the United States would have been given permission to take off. The State Department feared that antinuclear propaganda, like Communist ideology, would spread and infect other grassroots movements and organizations. Three years earlier, for example, in August 1952, concerned Japanese citizens organized the Hiroshima Symposium for Peace, a rally "in conjunction with labor organizations and some thirty other peace and democratic groups," which protested the war in Korea and sought to "promote friendship and trade among Asians . . . [and] people throughout the world united in a struggle for peace." In mid-August 1955, just three months after the Maidens had arrived in America and on the ten-year anniversary of the bombing, antinuclear groups of various political stripes mobilized in Hiroshima to sponsor the World Conference to Ban the Atomic and Hydrogen Bombs. The State Department regarded such potentially subversive events with great suspicion, seeking ways to disarm them whenever possible.

By the end of the 1950s, many viewed the creation of the Hiroshima Peace Memorial Park as an unnecessary and even hostile economic program motivated more by real estate opportunism than by a desire to memorialize the city's war dead. Despite these criticisms, in 1958 the city continued the steady march of progress, forcibly removing 105 buildings—many of which were still functional and occupied by families and businesses—in order to complete the 122,000 square meters of the Peace Memorial Park. By 1970 the Italian labor leader Daniel Dolci (described by the Japanese press as a "leader of an Italian civic movement") remarked critically on the Park's excesses: "Sprawling lawns, carps in the pond. . . . The ruins of Hiroshima should have been preserved as they were."[47]

Debates over the political meaning of Hiroshima's urban renewal projects took shape in universities, government buildings, and urban planning committees. Meanwhile, Japanese foreign policy initiatives were responsible for exporting a decidedly more provincial version of Japanese architectural identity for Western viewers to see. For example, in 1953 the Museum of Modern Art (MoMA) in New York City installed in its interior garden the Exhibition House, a model of a traditional Japanese home constructed in Nagoya, to highlight the relation between Japanese architecture and modern Western architecture. This was a period when, as Serge Guibault has argued, MoMA was the institutional epicenter of modernism in the United States.[48] The Exhibition House was part of a larger effort by MoMA and the Japanese Embassy to introduce to discriminating American audiences Japanese arts that included, among other things, the public premiere of the Japanese No plays in the United States.[49] For mid-1950s MoMA patrons, the traditional Exhibition House with its simple frame construction, sliding screens that blurred indoor and outdoor areas, elegant demarcations of public and private interior spaces, and paucity of furniture or other visible emblems of domesticity must have been a truly exotic spectacle.[50] This emphasis on the Exhibition House and other traditional elements of Japanese culture enabled institutions like MoMA, for all their diplomatic and aesthetic efforts, to tame the strategies of modernization that were concurrently taking place in Japan. Exhibitions like MoMA's, like so much of postwar politics, relied on an active preference for safe, nostalgic images that effectively displaced wartime memories and downplayed national atrocities. Like the photographic emphasis during the Occupation on buildings without people, the Exhibition House offered the odd juxtaposition of architecture with the complete physical absence of living denizens: a Japanese house without any Japanese. In disseminating the elements of traditional Japanese culture, institutions like MoMA perpetuated the idea of the Japanese as irredeemably alien, successfully reclaiming the benign Oriental fantasy of Japan familiar to Americans before World War II.

In contrast to these retrograde illusions about Japanese architecture—or perhaps because of them—the Hiroshima Maidens project reflected the themes of renewal and progress associated with the rebuilding of Hiroshima, especially when ideas of architectural modernity were blurred with their surgical rehabilitation. The Maidens were portrayed as enthusiastic supporters of modern architecture, repeatedly commenting that they had never seen American skyscrapers and eagerly anticipated their first trip to the Empire State Building. When the Maidens arrived in early May 1955, the New York *Daily News* reported that they "were most astounded by the tall buildings of Manhattan. (In Hiroshima a six-story building is a tall one.) They said they want to climb to the top of the Empire State."[51] The New York *Herald Tribune* observed that "the thing that impressed [the Maidens] most on the trip, according to the guides, was the size of New York's buildings. In their own city, there are no buildings higher than seven stories."[52] Meanwhile Toyoko Minowa, one of the Maidens whom the group had selected to be their spokesperson to the press, "said the girls' first wish in New York was 'to climb up a big building to the top.'[53] Even in their alienation from routine social interactions with other Hiroshima citizens, the Maidens had learned enough to be thoroughly absorbed by the cultural sophistication associated with major architectural landmarks in cosmopolitan cities. The tall skyscrapers of the New York City skyline, like the surgical reconstruction the Maidens were about to undergo, became stand-ins for social progress and the embrace of the benefits of Western architectural modernism.

If the Marshall Plan served as a paradigm of foreign policy during the early years of the Cold War, the same could also be said of the Hiroshima Maidens before their arrival in the United States.[54] The orchestrated efforts by the Maidens' sponsors to reconstruct the young women's faces and bodies reflected the same desire for transformation that affected their native city. Since their physical revisions remained a familiar frame of reference for a postwar culture that equated progress through building with renewal through architecture, the Industrial Promotion Hall where they posed and smiled became not only a symbol of the "old" Hiroshima but an older model of living against which all future (and modern) architectural forms would be measured. Perhaps this contrast explains why Tomin Harada, a Japanese physician invited to learn plastic surgery techniques at Mount Sinai Hospital during the Maidens' tenure, selected the Industrial Promotion Hall for the cover of his 1983 memoir *Hiroshima Surgeon*.[55] The image of the Industrial Promotion Hall, visual evidence of the remains of a life before the evaporation of the city, provided a powerful contrast with more familiar high-rise buildings—like the iconic Empire State Building—which symbolized the economic prosperity and technological progress the Maidens project would seek to embrace. Because the Hiroshima Maidens project was invested with the collective desire to erase a difficult chapter of recent history and replace the scar tissue of the past with modern amenities and conspicuous comforts, the Maidens literally made visible the expectations of those who had witnessed the architectural reinvention of Hiroshima take physical shape on the city's body politic. By the time they arrived in the United States, the Maidens project embodied many of the complex goals of foreign policy used by the United States in Japan. These goals would now be configured in the tools of Western medical technology with which the Maidens' sponsors would begin to reinvent the young women's lives.

## COMING TO AMERICA

The Air Force plane carrying the Hiroshima Maidens left Iwakuni Airbase in Tokyo on May 5, 1955, at 10:00 in the morning. Along with the twenty-five Maidens, the aircraft carried Cousins, Tanimoto, surgeon William Hitzig and his daughter Candis, Helen Yokoyama, who served as the Maidens' translator and "den mother," and an entourage comprising Japanese surgeons, medical technicians, interpreters, and a representative from the *Nippon Times*. After a brief layover in Honolulu, where they were feted by former citizens of Hiroshima who had relocated to Hawaii after the war, the plane arrived at Travis Airfield, just outside San Francisco, at 7:00 in the evening on May 7.[56] Before the plane landed, civic groups from California, including the California Japanese Benevolent Society, had gathered to greet the Maidens with flowers. Four local women, representing the Northern California Peace Council, used the event to deliver a speech of protest against the hydrogen bomb. A newspaper reporter commented that this assertive act lent an unfortunate "sour note" to the otherwise benign proceedings, during which all overtly political acts were apparently sanitized from the public sphere.[57]

The four female protesters, their identities unknown, provided an interesting counterpoint to the Hiroshima Maidens themselves, whose voices were conspicuously silent until their arrival in New York City two days later. While the "sour" women of the Northern California Peace Council were ultimately prevented from attending the incoming ceremonies, they did represent a small but growing minority of domestic antinuclear activists in the United States during the mid-1950s. The newly created hydrogen bomb, an atomic weapon infinitely more destructive and infinitely more terrifying than the bombs dropped on Hiroshima and Nagasaki, had captured international attention approximately one year earlier in March 1954 after American scientists detonated one in the Pacific. The nuclear testing inadvertently killed twenty-three Japanese fisherman aboard the unfortunately named *Lucky Dragon*. The incident provoked the Japanese government to issue a protest on behalf of the dead fishermen by publicly memorializing the tens of thousands of *hibakusha* still untreated from the 1945 bombings. Activists like those in San Francisco demanded an end to the production and use of the hydrogen bomb, which was all the more subversive because it conflicted with the military's plans to associate the development of the H-bomb with the national security state. The patriotic rhetoric used against antidemocratic governments during World War II and the Korean War was regularly exploited to win support for the funding and maintenance of a forbidding nuclear arsenal, paralleling in interesting ways the exploitation of images of veteran amputees to promote prosthetics research that we saw in chapter 1.

One tangible result of this antinuclear activism was that the public became fixated on the Maidens' physical presence. While the photographs of buildings in Hiroshima had been used to display architectural progress and avoid engaging with American culpability for the bomb, photographs of the Maidens out in public—as well as the prospect of their imminent surgeries—brought the specter of culpability to the forefront. The visible presence of the Maidens opened the door to debate about the United States military's atomic weapons program. The State Department, however, believed that the love and altruism shown toward the Maidens could have a strategic purpose: to contain both foreign and domestic dissent about nuclear weapons testing. On June 2, 1955, less than a month after the Maidens arrived in the United States, Cousins requested a meeting with members of the State Department to clarify the goals of the project and to dispel rumors that he was using the Maidens for his own antinuclear agenda. Government officials who watched the project unfold were sensitive that the Maidens' arrival in the United States roughly coincided with the ten-year anniversary of the bombing of Hiroshima and Nagasaki. This was an anticelebration through which, it was feared, the rise of domestic and international antinuclear protests might expose cracks in the smooth rhetoric of nuclear deterrence theory then propounded by the American government. At the meeting Walter C. Robertson, assistant secretary to the Far East for the State Department, "commented that Orientals always inquire about the reasons why Westerners want to do certain things and that to satisfy those questions is very difficult." Norman Cousins asserted that "the Japanese have a strong sense of obligation in definite situations, but they are largely lacking in a feeling of altruism." In response to Cousins's observation, Robertson reasoned that "it would be a real triumph [for the United States] if the Japanese could appreciate the feeling of altruism underlying the project."[58]

The emphasis placed on steering the Japanese in the right direction is exactly what Cousins and Robertson seemed to imply in their desire to inculcate altruism in the Maidens and Japanese civic culture in general. During the first few weeks of the Maidens' trip to the United States, strategic images of ordinary Americans receiving them in New York circulated widely in the media, even though Cousins and Tanimoto had declared a general ban on photographs. There was also an immediate economic benefit to "altruism," no matter how much it was touted as a social or moral philosophy. After World War II, the push to export the American standard of living (usually characterized as "the American way of life") created opportunities for distributing American consumer goods and cultural products to a worldwide (and in many cases captive) audience. The Rockefeller Foundation, for example, forged social liaisons in Japan during the mid-1950s and laid the groundwork for international cultural institutions such as the Asia Society in order to expand the Rockefeller family's financial interests in China, in

Japan, and throughout Asia. The Rockefeller Foundation's Asian projects emerged from the same ideological moment that shaped Max Milliken and Walt W. Rostow's *A Proposal: Key to an Effective Foreign Policy* (1957), a set of economic initiatives developed from a conference sponsored by Massachusetts Institute of Technology in the early 1950s. The proposal recommended that the United States must strive to make developing countries compatible with the perquisites of American consumerism and national values. "Although our techniques must be adapted to local conditions abroad if they are to be effective there," Milliken and Rostow argued, "they represent an enormous potential for steering the world's newly aroused human energies in constructive rather than destructive directions."[59] During such a moment of massive political restructuring and cultural upheaval, diplomatic overtures toward altruistic foreign policy initiatives promised to develop leadership skills, stimulate the tools of liberal consensus, and instill confidence in the political process among people who had never known true Western democracy.[60] A May 1955 article about the Maidens in the *Newark Evening News,* for example, described how "Kiyoshi Tanimoto . . . helped the injured girls find work and regain courage to face strangers . . . with their disfigured faces."[61] With an emphasis on triumphing over the stigma of public appearance through being productive and selfless, the Maidens' sponsors envisioned them as the beneficiaries of a democratic culture who could become role models for the "new" Japan. Programs designed to instill altruistic principles in non-Western countries—especially those that might be lured by the "global drift" of Communism—exhibit a similar patriotic rhetoric to the type found in the rehabilitation programs that we examined in chapter 1.

Some Japanese, however, had a hard time demarcating the boundaries between selfless community service and self-serving ambition. According to journalist Rodney Barker, in the early 1950s Tanimoto publicly declared it his professional and personal quest to "slow down the surging Left wing movement in Japan that was attempting to make the H-bomb the symbolic rallying point against the 'American militarization' of Japan." Tanimoto insisted that the Japanese people should follow the American example and promote a "common humanity."[62] Yet John Hersey has famously described how Tanimoto used a large portion of the initial funds given on behalf of the Maidens to buy himself embarrassingly expensive presents. In one instance Tanimoto treated himself to a Cadillac convertible, imported from the United States, that had to be refitted with a coal-burning engine, since it was almost impossible to obtain gasoline in Hiroshima. Understanding this complex dialectical relation between altruism and luxury may help to explain, and make visible, the way American foreign policy during the Cold War often blurred together economic liberalism and political self-interest under the guise of social progress.

After the Maidens arrived in New York City on May 9, the State Department's worst fears immediately materialized (fig. 11). The visual and symbolic evidence of the women's damaged bodies, now in full public view, forged unavoidable links between their physical scarring and the devastation wrought by the atomic bomb, much to the State Department's chagrin. In large and small newspapers across the country, the young women were described variously as "bomb-scarred," "A-scarred," "Hiroshima-scarred," "A-burned," "Atomic-bomb-scarred," or simply as "A-girls" or "A-victims." These epithets exposed the incontrovertible fact that, regardless of state-sponsored propaganda or political intervention, not only would the Maidens retain an atomic resonance during their residency, but their relation to the bomb—and not, as the State Department had hoped, to the generic war tropes of World War II— would be forever sustained by the American public. The federal government did not make light of these associations. One week after the Maidens arrived in the United States, the Hiroshima Teacher's Union's graphic and controversial 1953 documentary film *Hiroshima* opened in New York City.[63] The State Department nervously issued an internal memo critiquing the "leftist" Union, fearing that the simultaneous release of the film and the Maidens'

FIGURE 11 Shigeko Niimoto, left, and the Rev. Kiyoshi Tanimoto drinking coffee at Mitchel Air Field on Hempstead, Long Island, before heading to New York City. Images like this promoted the humanitarian dimension of the project and thus assuaged the State Department's fears that Cousins and Tanimoto were using the Maidens as antinuclear propaganda. Photograph taken May 9, 1955, © Bettmann/Corbis.

arrival would generate negative publicity.[64] Walter C. Robertson maintained that "helping victims of misfortune is a very worthwhile endeavor but every effort should be made to keep the project involving the Hiroshima girls from stirring up propaganda against nuclear weapons."[65] Norman Cousins, feeling himself begin to buckle, confessed that the film's producers had attempted "to obtain [his] sponsorship or endorsement in exchange for one-half the box-office proceeds of the first week of the film's showing as a benefit for the Maidens." Cousins, however, had "refused the offer and informed the producers that the film had been made under Communist auspices and hoped they would not proceed without first ascertaining everything that ought to be known about it. . . . [T]he Maidens have had and will have no connections with the film."[66]

The Maidens did not need an affiliation with a documentary film. Cinematic narratives about their lives began to surface within days of their arrival in the United States. Almost immediately, apocryphal tales about the Maidens' disfigurement began circulating among the general public. Unlike survivors of conventional wartime damage, the Maidens elicited an unprecedented and, for many, unfathomable outpouring of medical anxieties and fears concerning the treatment of the body (and especially the female body) as disabled by the effects of radiation and nuclear fallout. In retrospect, this emotive outpouring ultimately illuminated more about American anxieties about radiation than about the Maidens' own physical scars. Bernard Simon, one of the Mount Sinai Hospital surgeons, recounted the popular but inaccurate story about Mitsuko Kuramoto, the Maiden who wore an eye patch to protect her damaged conjunctiva, the flap of skin just below her right eyeball (fig. 12).[67] Early reports about Kuramoto misunderstood the precise nature of her condition and claimed that her entire eyelid had disintegrated in the heat and light of the atomic blast. Many speculated that her eye wept tears uncontrollably as a result of her missing eyelid. As Simon explained, a person without an eyelid could expect to burn her cornea and probably become blind within a few days. Regardless of this quotidian fact, Americans held on to the story and perceived the eye patch as an object lesson. It was just as easily a potent metonym for the Maidens themselves. The story of her eye presented a sober reminder of what a nuclear future might look like.

The surgical treatment of Kuramoto's damaged eye—as well as the body parts of the other young women—was also a way to gauge publicly the success or failure of plastic surgery and rehabilitation medicine in general. During and after the war, Americans had come to expect miracles. Plastic surgery was promoted as an

FIGURE 12  Mikiko Kashiwabara, a Japanese American nurse, offers a bouquet of flowers to Shigeko Niimoto upon the arrival of the Hiroshima Maidens and their prominently displayed Pan-American Airways flight bags at Mount Sinai Hospital in New York City. Mitsuko Kuramoto, whose eye patch marked her as the "weeping Maiden," is seventh in line. Photograph taken May 9, 1955, © Bettmann/Corbis.

art developed as a medical specialty under the duress of wartime, bearing the distinct heritage of military efficiency and expertise. In 1946, for example, *Life* displayed shockingly graphic (but always handsomely rendered) photographs of various surgical treatments in order to reassure viewers that "refinements in plastic surgery and the new methods of bone grafting and nerve repair will restore many victims of the violences of peacetime."[68] Modern surgical techniques would constitute the first line of defense against the physically disabling effects of war or ordinary civilian accidents. For many, however, the presence of the Maidens both transcended and confounded the question of how to treat and care for their bodies. Their scars seemed unlike anything Americans had ever seen before, appearing inscrutable, elastic, and beyond control.

Popular media tried to craft an alternative narrative for describing the Maidens' disfigurements as wartime injuries that could be healed by modern medicine. One reporter's comment that the Mount Sinai team hoped "to finish the task of restoring [to] these girls what war took away" seemed to neutralize their physical difference by invoking the patriotic image of the American GI about to undergo reconstructive surgery in the theater of battle.[69] But such narratives, while largely benign, brought to the surface many of the unresolved legacies of anti-Japanese and, more broadly, anti-Asian sentiment in the United States, now configured through the indignities that the Japanese experienced as the members of a defeated nation. Treating *hibakusha* as "guinea pigs," for example, had been a well-established protocol for a little less than a decade for scientists working for the Atomic Bomb Casualty Commission (ABCC) in Hiroshima. The ABCC's decision to examine and study radiation victims while maintaining a strict no-treatment policy reflected what M. Susan Lindee has identified as the practice of "colonial medicine."[70] Despite the humanitarian ethos that surrounded the project, the potential for racism remained vexing for the Maidens as well as for the entire postwar generation of American citizens of Japanese descent for whom legal discrimination and government-sponsored internment camps were well within recent historical memory.[71] Making parallels between atomic bomb survivors and American veterans was a naive commingling of patriotism and nostalgia that served the State Department's desire to keep antinuclear propaganda out of the Maidens' visit. But it did not serve anyone trying to determine how to be Japanese in America, let alone how to be Japanese in postwar Japan.

The anxiety surrounding Kuramoto's status as the "weeping Maiden" made her a tragic figure of technological modernity. The emphasis put on her passivity and vulnerability, which could be rectified only through modern surgical techniques, also made her a poignant distillation of many popular stereotypes and Orientalist fantasies about Japanese girls and women. For many, such images not only were distortions but were in direct conflict with the traditions and expectations of Japanese society. In mid-May 1955, for example, an unidentified U.S. Army officer stationed in Kobe reported that "the Japanese are very disturbed by the circumstances that no men were included in the [Hiroshima] group. . . . [A]nyone who knows anything at all about the Japanese people and their culture knows that women have a secondary position and that the men are the more important element in their social structure." Cecil R. King, a member of Congress from California who supplied the officer's comments to the State Department, encouraged it to go out of its way to turn this negative publicity in a more positive direction.[72] To some degree, the project depended on collective gendered fantasies of the Maidens as docile Oriental caricatures to accomplish its altruistic goals. That only young Japanese women—and not young Japanese men or, for that matter, any Japanese veterans—were selected for reconstructive plastic surgery rationalized what Sheila Johnson has called the "feminization" of Japan within American popular culture. According to Johnson, the American fascination in the 1950s with Japanese architecture, paper and printmaking, flower arranging, Noguchi's kidney-shaped coffee tables, kimonos, calligraphy, Kabuki theater, and the existentialist-Eastern dialectic embraced by writers like Alan Watts and Jack Kerouac all stemmed from a cultural desire to replace the crafty, militaristic, kamikaze images of Japan with "soft" images in order to "repress wartime memories."[73] Such gendered strategies were used to promote acceptance of the women as well as greater acceptance of the project's vision of global cooperation and humanitarianism.[74]

On May 11, just three days after the Maidens arrived in New York City, a cross section of the project's entourage flew back to the West Coast to NBC television studios in downtown Los Angeles to create another soft image of Japanese culture for American audiences. In order to raise money for the group's surgeries at Mount Sinai, two of the Maidens, Toyoko Minowa and Tadako Emori, had agreed to accompany Tanimoto for his appearance on Ralph

Edwards's popular live television program *This Is Your Life*,[75] arguably one of the first reality TV shows to air in the United States. True to the perfunctory rules of the program's format, Edwards brought on a number of people who represented "voices" from Tanimoto's past. This was not as difficult an assignment as one might expect: although many of his acquaintances had perished in the bombing of Hiroshima, Tanimoto had spent some time in the late 1930s as an exchange student at Emory University's Candler School of Theology. Edwards delighted the audience when he brought out Tanimoto's wife, Chyssa, and their two children, whom Edwards had flown in from Hiroshima specifically for the event. Toward the middle of the program, however, Edwards surprised Tanimoto with another "voice" from his past, although it was one he had never actually heard before. Edwards brought out from behind a sliding translucent screen the nervous figure of Lieutenant Robert Lewis, copilot (along with Paul Tibbetts) of the *Enola Gay*, the plane that dropped the bomb on Hiroshima.

Lewis reportedly had spent the afternoon drinking himself into a stupor at a downtown bar in preparation for the encounter.[76] To the dismay of everyone on the program, and under the patronizing gaze of Edwards and the breathless amazement of the studio audience, Lewis walked forward and took his place to the left of Tanimoto, whose entire body recoiled in what seemed like agonizing revulsion. Responding to Edwards's query, "Would you tell us, sir, of your experience on August 6, 1945?" Lewis looked on the verge of collapse as a low wave of electric organ chords began, soap opera style, to make their chromatic descent. He wiped perspiration from his face and, in a soft New Jersey accent, recited unsteadily the words he had prepared for this moment of public reckoning:

Well, Mr. Edwards, uh, just before 8:15 a.m. Tokyo time, Tom Ferrebee—a very able bombardier—carefully aimed at his target, which was the Second Imperial Japanese Army headquarters. At 8:15 promptly, the bomb was dropped. We turned fast to get out of the way of the deadly radiation and bomb effects. First was the big flash that we got, and then the two concussion waves hit the ship. Shortly after, we turned back to see what had happened. And there, in front of our eyes, the city of Hiroshima disappeared. I wrote down later, "My God, what have we done?"[77]

One wonders whether Lewis's description of his target as the Second Imperial Japanese Army headquarters was a way of avoiding a reckoning with the devastation of the civilian population, perhaps underscoring the emphasis on buildings rather than humans that seemed to haunt postbomb discourse in the American popular media. Later in the program, Edwards asked Lewis and Tanimoto to shake hands, which they did as if both of them were under heavy sedation. Still sweating profusely, the embarrassed Lewis presented Tanimoto and the Maidens with a check for fifty dollars for the surgical treatment he had helped to make necessary. After the broadcast, Lewis returned to his regular life as personnel manager at Henry Heide Incorporated, a candy manufacturer in New York City. According to Koko Tanimoto Kando, Tanimoto's daughter, Lewis was later institutionalized for severe depression in a mental hospital in upstate New York. He died of a heart attack in 1983. In his remaining years, however, Lewis was said to have built a sculpture as an art therapy project: an enormous three-dimensional mushroom cloud with a single tear sliding down one side. The sculpture, which seemed to invoke the tears that Mitsuko Kuramoto putatively wept from her injured eye, also suggested that Lewis was like many in the postwar era, such as Isamu Noguchi, for whom a physical, sculptural form was the ideal therapeutic tool for memorializing the Hiroshima dead.[78]

The lurid voyeurism and brutal insensitivity of Lewis's appearance notwithstanding—a moment unprecedented on television in the United States—what truly disturbed *This Is Your Life*'s production staff was not the potential awkwardness of the on-camera meeting between Lewis and Tanimoto. It was the presence of Minowa and Emori on a live national broadcast. They had been deemed too hideous to be shown to American television audiences. Producers feared that their appearance would clash ignominiously with the program's regular sponsor, Hazel Bishop cosmetics. Edwards told the audience, "To avoid causing them any embarrassment, we will not show you their faces," and he pointed instead to docile silhouettes of the women hidden behind translucent screens. Edwards may have thought he had the Maidens' best interests in mind when he showed them in shadowy profile. On camera it was a disturbing exhibition-ist form that, ironically, made Minowa's and Emori's silhouettes reminiscent of undisclosed criminals, anonymous homosexuals, or finger puppets animated by the light of a nineteenth-century lantern slide. The production staff had also requested that Chyssa Tanimoto wear a kimono and wooden slippers during her appearance on the program, even though she normally wore modern Western apparel. It must have seemed necessary to extinguish the actual details of Chyssa's modern experience for the sake of transforming her and the Maidens into Oriental spectacles with which to elicit compassion from American viewers who might otherwise harbor residual resent-ment. In the last few minutes of the broadcast, Edwards presented Chyssa with a lovely gold charm bracelet. It was intended, as Rodney Barker argues, "to commemorate the happy moments in her life."[79] Was this appearance intended to rank among them? Clearly, by offering the public benign feminine images, *This Is Your Life* resembled foreign policy choices by the State Department and curatorial choices by institutions like MoMA. All three enforced nostalgic images of Japanese culture for the sake of political expe-dience, economic development, and to make certain that the pres-ence of the vulnerable, unprotected female body would soften the formerly aggressive image of wartime Japan.

## FROM UNMARRIED MAIDENS TO AMERICAN GIRLS

After Minowa, Emori, the Tanimotos, and the rest of the Maidens' entourage finished their time in Los Angeles, they returned to the East Coast, where they were reunited with the other members of the project. They were all invited to recuperate from travel exhaustion and media attention at Pendle Hill, a Quaker retreat in Overbrook, Pennsylvania, a sleepy enclave on the patrician Main Line just outside Philadelphia. As early as 1953 Norman Cousins had appealed to the Quakers—one of the most recognizable and vocal religious groups to protest war and the atomic bomb—and asked for volunteers who would serve as host families for the Maidens before and after their individual surgeries. The American Friends eagerly complied and formed the social and spiritual scaffolding on which the Maidens project took shape over the next few years.

On their way to Pendle Hill, the entourage stopped at Philadelphia's Reading Terminal Market, an enclosed farmers' market. The market, with a rich local history, specializes in foods from across southeastern Pennsylvania and is one of the few local outlets for Amish goods from nearby Lancaster County. In one publicity photograph, three of the Maidens pose with two Friends in front of a butcher's kiosk (see fig. 13). Standing below a sign at the butcher shop that asserts "Double Thick Steak and Chops," each woman holds a box filled with frozen cuts of meat. The photographer's decision to pose the Maidens with steaks seems to offer the same promise of American abundance and comfort that the featured Quaker hosts do themselves. In Hiroshima, steak was a luxury in the postbomb period when, according to Sachio Otani, curried rice cost a week's salary and people regularly worked and bartered just to buy grain.[80] Two of the Maidens smile obligingly. The others look resentful, contemptuous, or even humiliated because the photograph was taken.

Looking at the awkward commingling of painful facial expressions, it is interesting to consider this photograph in light of how the Maidens had been thinking about their own faces only days before their arrival in Philadelphia. During the various stages of their trip to the United States, a number of Maidens had composed what they called their "Hiroshima Maidens' Song" to pass the exhausting hours spent in cramped airplane cabins, airport lounges, and press conference rooms. The song, which they all sang together, was later

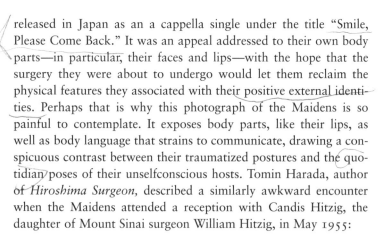

FIGURE 13 Five Hiroshima Maidens carrying gift boxes of "double thick steak and chops" pose uncomfortably with two of their hosts at Reading Terminal Market in Philadelphia before going to a Quaker retreat in Overbrook, Pennsylvania. Photograph taken ca. May 1955, author's collection.

released in Japan as an a cappella single under the title "Smile, Please Come Back." It was an appeal addressed to their own body parts—in particular, their faces and lips—with the hope that the surgery they were about to undergo would let them reclaim the physical features they associated with their positive external identities. Perhaps that is why this photograph of the Maidens is so painful to contemplate. It exposes body parts, like their lips, as well as body language that strains to communicate, drawing a conspicuous contrast between their traumatized postures and the quotidian poses of their unselfconscious hosts. Tomin Harada, author of *Hiroshima Surgeon*, described a similarly awkward encounter when the Maidens attended a reception with Candis Hitzig, the daughter of Mount Sinai surgeon William Hitzig, in May 1955:

The Queen of the reception was clearly Candis, the eldest daughter of the Hitzigs, rather than the Maidens from Hiroshima. Candis was just eighteen and had recently made her debut in New York society. It was announced at the reception that she personally had gone all the way to Hiroshima to invite the girls to come for treatment. She received many approving looks. Her beauty and elegant white gown made her look as if she were queen of the ball, and contrasted sharply with the scarred faces and simple clothing of the Maidens. The differences seemed to symbolize the contrast between America, the global power, and Japan, the vanquished nation. While many watched Candis, others, especially the Quakers, embraced the Hiroshima Maidens, and I felt at this reception I had seen a cross-section of American society.[81]

Like the contrast between the Maidens and Candis Hitzig, the photograph showing the male Quaker's handsome lumberjack's coat and the woman's sensible bobby socks—both of which can be read as symbols of all-American, white Pennsylvania friendliness—contrast with the disfigured faces and unfashionable clothing of the Maidens peeking out from behind them. It is a photographic dramatization that seems to capture the heart of the matter. The Maidens look at the camera. The housewife looks at the farmer. The farmer looks out into space. Smile, please come back.

In late May 1955, shortly after the Reading Terminal Market photograph was taken, the Maidens began working directly with the Society of Friends in New York City. The Friends helped organize what would become the Maidens' routine over the next eighteen months—surgery at Mount Sinai, followed by recuperation with Quaker host families living in wealthy enclaves in the New York metropolitan region such as Scarsdale, New York, Darien, Connecticut, and Upper Montclair, New Jersey. Ida Day, one of the members of the Society of Friends responsible for welcoming the Maidens, compiled lists to identify the characteristics of each of the young women. Day worked closely with Cousins and Tanimoto to collect enough information to place each one with a family that suited her individual needs. Day's intent was to provide the organizers of the Maidens project with descriptive assessments of each woman's personality traits, family background, and favorite foods, and what each wanted most from her experience in the United States. In retrospect, the following sample entries from Day's original detailed lists also reveal contemporary understandings of what was meant by the reconstruction of the Hiroshima Maidens. Betraying their surface appearance of common sense or compassionate hospitality—the putative reason for making such lists in the first place—these verbal snapshots convey much about the ways gender roles and class status were conceived by the middle-class imaginations of Americans living during the period:

Happy, not sensitive. Tries hard. Wants to do everything. . . . Is married (unlawfully). Not too intelligent. Low status—laborer father. Outgoing, easy. Put her with anyone with low intelligence.

Wonderful and gets along with anyone. Thinks for herself. Fair, unbiased. Dressmaking. Eyes affected by rays. . . . Reserved. More intelligent. Likes gardening. Not social. Small eater—don't worry. Studied dress-making 3 years. Not marriageable. Professional dress, or millinery.

Wants Western life and [to] learn Western ways. . . . Youngest child in family, spoiled, emotional, naive, hard adjustment. . . . [C]all Helen [Yokoyama, translator and "den mother"] if any difficulty.

Reliable, intelligent, good girl. Had millinery shop. Quiet, reserved, eager to learn. Studies hard. Very conscious of scars.

Lovable, not very intelligent, very appreciative. Naive, loves babies and little girls. Needs 9 or 10 hours of sleep each night.

Jr. College graduate. Likes parties. Wants to learn English, sewing, reading. Not lovable. Superiority air, objectionable to others.

Not disfigured. Would like to go to school and learn English.

Difficult, cynical, needs help, others afraid of her. Poor family, no father. Fatherly man wanted for host. Suicide in teens. Left church. Resents kindness. Touchable. Craves friend. No English, nor desire to learn.

Very good, sweet, better family. Willing to help. 8 years of ceremonial tea, also flower arrangements. Likes vegetables.[82]

What do such observations mean, outside of their historical value as indexes of the boundaries of social acceptability, respectability, or what made (or unmade) a person's reputation in the mid-1950s? One would have expected that the Society of Friends would have tried to protect the Maidens from (mis)apprehension by the superficial observations of detractors or hostile outsiders. Yet the Quakers, like their American contemporaries, constructed normative categories that imputed positive and negative social characteristics to the Japanese women. These lists seemed to denote explicitly, rather than connote implicitly, which ones among the Maidens were "lovable" and which were not, or what made a particular woman "marriageable," who was "intelligent," and even which young women were "difficult."[83] Standards were often applied to the Maidens in terms of their potential not only for surgical success, but also for upward mobility ("Wants Western life and [to] learn Western ways," and the enigmatic "Not disfigured"). Such potential was imagined to be either limited or catalyzed by the Maiden's class background ("Low status—laborer father," "better family"). Moreover, as we saw in the attitudes of prosthetists toward amputees in chapter 1, the authoritative power of personality played a large part in how the Society of Friends understood and consequently discussed the relation between the Maidens' bodies and their social identities. This clearly followed from the influence of contemporary sociologists like David Riesman and C. Wright Mills, who argued in the early 1950s that an "outer-directed personality" was the cultural capital that governed social relations. Apparently the Quakers were caught up in the same ideological nets that compelled them to seek out, and even perhaps to give preferential treatment to, those who exhibited the greatest potential for extroverted, even-tempered sociability. Smile, please come back.

Yet the prospect of social rehabilitation was integral to—if not the defining feature of—the Maidens' physical rehabilitation. Such concerns about rehabilitation, as we have seen in the case of veteran amputees, were not new but were typical of the era. After World War II, for example, Frances Cooke Macgregor became the first American sociologist to write extensively on the social and psychological repercussions of plastic surgery.[84] *In Facial Deformities and Plastic Surgery: A Psychosocial Approach* (1953), Macgregor showed photographs of patients with craniofacial disfigurements to a random sampling of interview subjects. Their published responses demonstrate that even the most cursory exposure to facial disfigurement incited pity, moral indignation, and even class bias among her interviewees:

"Was this a war casualty?"
"Probably a gangster."
"I don't think anyone would hire him."
"This guy looks like the real criminal type."
"Laborer."
"Probably does some kind of work by himself. Probably digs ditches or is a writer. He must have a tremendous interest in life. Seems to me he would want to destroy himself."[85]

Macgregor concluded that "facial features . . . serv[e] as false clues [that] . . . impute to these patients personality traits considered socially unacceptable but assign them roles and status on an inferior social level."[86] At the same time, she argued that plastic surgery constituted a humane, compassionate corrective for those who suffered from severe physical disability or social handicap owing to their impairments. Like many practicing plastic surgeons at the time, Macgregor maintained an important distinction between plastic surgery involving craniofacial disorders, cleft palate cases, and skin diseases and cosmetic surgery involving facelifts, blepharoplasty (eyelid surgery), and rhinoplasty (nose jobs). She regarded the rise in cosmetic surgery, however, as evidence that an obsession once only for the elite was now more widely available.[87]

The emphasis on the psychological, as well as physical, disabilities the Maidens experienced would have made perfect sense to the organizers of the project, who sought out a program that was holistic in its scope. This was not an uncommon attitude for those about to undergo plastic surgery.[88] As Sander Gilman has astutely observed, long before the mid-twentieth century, cosmetic surgery was shaped in equal part by medical ideals and by cultural expectations—both professionally sanctioned and personally internalized—about promoting socialization as well as smoothing out ethnic features to meet particular (usually white) standards of beauty.[89] As Elizabeth Gail Haiken and Joan Jacobs Brumberg have argued, elite American women in the 1910s and 1920s were deeply attracted to reconstructive—and, increasingly, cosmetic—plastic surgery as a tool of social status. Plastic surgery during the 1950s, according to Haiken, maintained its influence over the public, especially since it helped thousands of middle-class Americans anticipate the social and economic benefits of medical technology. Plastic surgery, like prosthetic devices, became one of the perquisites of postwar liberalism's redefinition of democratic public culture.[90]

Because of the equation of plastic surgery with consumerism, when the Hiroshima Maidens arrived in the United States for reconstructive surgery on their scars and burns, the distinctions between emergency plastic surgery used to ameliorate suffering and elective cosmetic surgery used to create beauty became blurry. The *Newark Star-Ledger,* for example, announced the Maidens' arrival in the United States with the headline "Disfigured Jap Girls to Get Facelifting," while the *New York World-Telegram* explained that "25 A-Burned Girls . . . Hope to Regain Beauty."[91] The social consequences produced by this conflation of surgical genres caused enormous criticism of the Maidens project. Some members of the Japanese press accused Cousins and Tanimoto of luring the

Maidens away for experimentation despite the seemingly objective language of medical humanitarianism espoused by American plastic surgeons. A May 1955 article in the Communist *Daily Worker* referred explicitly to the Maidens as guinea pigs of Western imperialism: "It is the supreme duty of the American workers to rescue mankind by taking the power from this ruling class whose disfigured face, pitted by the disease of degeneration of capitalism, can never be repaired by plastic surgery."[92]

In order to resist any possible associations between surgical treatment and imperialistic practices that haunted medical projects like the Atomic Bomb Casualty Commission, Bernard Simon and the other Mount Sinai surgeons made sure to distinguish cosmetic surgery (as reflected in headlines like "Disfigured Jap Girls to Get Facelifting") from what occurred in the operating theater. To make these distinctions material, between May 1955 and September 1956 the Mount Sinai team kept a precise log that recorded the names of each patient and the date and specific details of the surgical operations performed on her.[93] On June 16, 1955, for instance, lead plastic surgeon Arthur Barsky made a "formation of [an] abdominal tubed pedicle" for Toyoko Minowa, one of the Maidens who appeared on *This Is Your Life*. A pedicle is a small, tubular-shaped piece of healthy tissue that surgeons lift from an uninjured part of the body and then surgically graft to the site that needs reconstruction. Once the pedicle's tissue and blood vessels become independent, it can be cut and refashioned into whatever the patient requires. Grafting tubed pedicles was not "cutting edge" plastic surgery; it was a common technique among battlefield surgeons during World War II and remained a regular practice well through the 1950s. Simon later referred to such operations as "ballpark surgery," which, despite the phrase's reference to baseball, suggested a vernacular approach that removed it from plastic surgery's allegedly lofty orbit and put it back down on the ground with other emergency procedures. Similarly, on July 15, 1955, Simon performed an "excision and plastic repair of vertical scar of right cheek and right lower eyelid" for Mitsuko Kuramoto, the "weeping Maiden" who famously wore an eye patch. Apparently the rest of Kuramoto's physical body either was unharmed or did not warrant surgery, since she did not undergo any other procedures until the following April, when Barsky attended to the "scar of [her] right upper eyelid." Although such attention paid to "scars" might be interpreted out of context as cosmetic, Simon believed that such reparative surgery was not an issue of vanity. This was true of the work done by junior surgeon Samuel Kahn on May 15, 1956, when he crafted "bilateral naso-labial flaps to defects created by excision of scars of upper lip" on Atsuko Yamamoto, one of the two women who posed in front of the Industrial Promotional Hall publicity photograph. The use of the word "defects" in the description is not a critical judgment of the patient's nose but a reference to the scars created by inexperienced Japanese surgeons who had tried unsuccessfully to provide Yamamoto with relief for her damaged nostrils.

Surgeons strategically emphasized the professional distinction between reconstructive and cosmetic surgery to ensure that the Maidens project would receive the appropriate support from the public, who might resent Japanese girls' getting facelifts. According to Simon, in the 1950s those who performed nose jobs, facelifts, breast augmentations, and the like without board certification or the pedigree of a prestigious university or military training were routinely chastised in professional circles as "whores of the medical industry."[94] One could interpret Cousins's comment as elitist pride. But it also seemed to stem from a professional concern that the Maidens might be exploited in ways that would undermine the project. In 1952, for example, long before the women even arrived in the United States, a group of doctors from the Soviet Union approached them and said they would perform reconstructive surgery for free on condition that the Maidens speak out publicly against American imperialism and nuclear weapons testing.[95] Barsky, Kahn, and Simon were assigned the job of countering this propaganda and were identified in the media as heroic individuals, board-certified plastic surgeons who had distinguished service records during World War II. In order to promote the Maidens

project as not only humanitarian but also patriotic, it was imperative to establish American plastic surgeons as experts, free-thinking
promoters of American scientific superiority and humanitarian aid.[96]

Despite their actual work, the conflation of plastic surgery and
upward mobility persisted. The Maidens story often competed with
other stories published in popular magazines of the late 1940s and
early 1950s about young women whose scars, large noses, or misshapen chins compromised their careers. Typical were sensationalist
descriptions that played on the great pleasure postwar culture
derived from self-improvement narratives. In 1947, news magazines
ran feature articles on celebrity plastic surgeons such as Dr. John
Pick, who made "bad men better" by "correcting" the faces of ex-
convicts to make them more socially presentable and economically
viable after they left prison. As Pick explained, when selecting candidates for plastic surgery, "the reform school is the place to begin.
We could hope then to stop a criminal career right at the start."[97] By
contrast, what made a woman a career "criminal," apparently, was
her failure to attain even a minimally appropriate feminine appearance. As one *Saturday Evening Post* article put it in 1950, with the
drama of a radio play, "She was an attractive girl—except for one
shocking disfiguration. How could she earn a living with such a
tragic handicap?"[98] Postwar philanthropic groups, often composed
of prominent plastic surgeons, had begun to establish clinics to help
those with congenital facial deformities—and later to correct the
features of those lured by the transformative possibilities of cosmetic surgery.[99] A 1958 article in *American Mercury* titled "A New
Face for Christmas" described the charitable activities of Stanley
Slotkin, a Los Angeles businessman who established a foundation so
men and women could undergo plastic surgery in order to succeed
in their vocations. The article described Slotkin's secretary, Betty:
"On the wonderful morning when [Betty's] bandages were removed, she saw her beautiful face. A new chin brought with her a
look of strength and determination—and a promotion a few months
later. She's been moving upward in the agency ever since."[100]

The popular discourse surrounding cosmetic surgery shaped the public's understanding of the Maidens project, even if none of the Maidens' surgeries were explicitly cosmetic. None of the women, for example, received new noses or chins that marked them as "Western." Yet whatever initial otherness the Maidens brought with them on the airplane was neutralized by reconstructing them in the image of American women—if not physically, then certainly socially. Bernard Simon observed that when the Maidens got off the airplane in New York they not only were exhausted and airsick but were dressed in "ill-fitting" blue polyester "travel suits." They had teased their straight black hair into tangled knots that became, in Simon's words, "all frizzed out," since they assumed that all American women had their hair permed. The Quaker families immediately endeavored to change the Maidens' appearance and behavior. They gave them gifts befitting comfortable young American girls of a certain socioeconomic bracket and taste niche. According to Simon, many families bought the young women expensive tweed skirts, cashmere sweaters, and saddle shoes for daily wear, evening dresses and shawls for formal functions, and beauty products designed to restore their hair to its natural sheen. In addition, between surgeries, the Quaker families encouraged the Maidens to pursue professional and recreational interests at local community colleges, art schools, and vocational schools. Many took classes in painting, nursing, cosmetology, and secretarial skills, even if they anticipated that all the glamour would dissipate when they returned to the family fishing business.[101]

In the hands of their Quaker sponsors and American doctors, the Maidens became poster children for a new kind of postwar identity. They exemplified a generation of future citizens whose bodily damage, inflicted by the chaos of modern physics, could be healed through the miracles of modern medicine. Indeed, these miracles made it possible for them, as future citizens, to receive more than mere cultural opportunities or material gifts; it offered them an entrée into the triumphant global culture promised by Cold War economic liberalism. New York journalist Arnold Brophy claimed optimistically that "plastic surgeons hope to erase the scars [the Maidens] suffered in the bombing of Hiroshima," but he also mourned that "[the] bombing robbed them of their beauty—and of their status as normal human beings."[102] These responses reflected the implicit goals of the Hiroshima Maidens project: not only to normalize the women's physical features, but to normalize the terms on which modern science could absorb its capacity for recklessness and turn trauma into opportunity. Cousins claimed repeatedly during the Maidens' stay in the United States that the "girls [were] free of many of the misconceptions about plastic surgery that apparently exist in relation to this project in both the United States and Japan. They realize that it is beyond the reach of modern surgery to restore their faces perfectly."[103] Yet the Maidens themselves told reporters a different version of their inner world: a fantasy life enriched by the idea that plastic surgery would miraculously restore or, in many cases, dramatically transform them. In an article sensationally titled "Atom Blast Ruined Beauty, Sighs A-Victim," Toyoko Minowa was alleged to have claimed, with dramatic use of ellipsis, "I used to be considered beautiful, that is until . . ." while Michiko Sako explained that the Maidens "[were] hoping to recover the beauty that nature gave us."[104] Others told stories of how they sat "in the merciful dark of movie theatres, watching American movies, adoring James Stewart and Gary Cooper and wondering what it would be like to be as perfect and desirable as Elizabeth Taylor."[105] This fantasy, which sounds suspiciously like the desires of any number of insecure American teenage girls, helped to normalize the Maidens as female consumers who believed in a meritocracy based on beauty. Indeed, to further enhance their claim to a thoroughly modern identity, references to the Maidens described them in language redolent of American psychologists and advice columnists of the early 1950s: "For ten years these young girls have passed *their most sensitive years* aware of the ugly keloids on their faces."[106]

For the Americans that watched their transformation, the Maidens proved that plastic surgery, aimed at emergency cases as

well as at beauty's common denominator could serve as a democratizing force for these *hibakusha,* or for survivors of war, or for
those with ungainly appearances, or even for those with problem
personalities. In this sense the Maidens became literally the public
face of those foreign nationals to whom the magic and mystery
emanating from American goods and services flowed, giving the
aggressive foreign policy initiatives and equally aggressive conspicuous consumption of the Eisenhower years a visible manifes-
tation that one could not look away from. The term "Hiroshima
Maidens"—the awkward translation of their Japanese appellation—suggested that their homely identity as shut-ins would be the
first component of their personalities to go in their transition from
naive girlhood to modern womanhood. They may have been poor
female Japanese victims of radiation burns in real life, but this did
not prevent Americans from imagining the Maidens partly as
pioneers of innovative medical technology and partly as upwardly
mobile career girls. As the *New York World-Telegram* reported,
"For years [the Maidens] have avoided society's gazes and stares,
helpless in their common sorrow. But now there is hope. . . .
Twenty-five Japanese girls are seeing what America is really
like."[107]

## IMAGINARY TRANSLATIONS

Like an unresolved mystery or unconfirmed myth, the story of the
Hiroshima Maidens continues to invite reexamination and interpretation.[108] In 1994, for example, Daniel James Sundahl published
a short chapbook of poems titled *Hiroshima Maidens: Imaginary
Translations from the Japanese.* In modern free verse, the poems
recount—one might say project—the psychic impact that the bombing may have had on the young girls in Hiroshima. Sundahl's
stanzas are mostly written in the collective voice of the Maidens
who, in the book, are not distinguished as autonomous bodies but
are fused together, not unlike the features of their own bodies, as
one univocal entity. In an early section, for instance, in which the

Maidens remember their lives before the bomb was dropped, Sundahl writes:

what was past is not past
is not was but is / part
of our great longing.

we try to find some place
to go back to.

we remember:
long hair in braids,
feet gliding in satin slippers,
hands clasping paper roses,
lips singing morning prayers.[109]

At their best, Sundahl's "imaginary translations" are perhaps best described as poetic translations of a distorted American imagination, one that constructed a singular ideal of who these young Japanese women were and what they ultimately represented. Sundahl's description of the prebomb consciousness of the Maidens, while seemingly compassionate and eloquent, is refracted through several layers of misinformation about the class background imparted to their collective memory. Since the vast majority of them were born into poor working families of fishermen and seamstresses, none would have remembered the leisurely feel of "feet gliding in satin slippers," nor would many have spent their mornings "clasping paper roses." These were the daily activities of a kind of idealized, all-purpose Japanese handmaiden. Furthermore, the phrase "we try to find a place to go back to" belies the historical truth of their tribulations, since they had complex associations to their home country after Cousins and Tanimoto whisked them away to the United States in 1955. After the last of their surgeries were completed in September 1956, the Maidens remained for a final month and a half of recuperation and relaxation. Having left Hiroshima as poor disfigured girls, they packed their new luggage with memories of kindness and compassion and returned to Hiroshima with repaired faces, working hands and arms, and new confidence imparted through surgical success and material transformation. In November 1956, when they returned home to Hiroshima, they encountered a wide range of responses from Japanese citizens as well as from other surviving *hibakusha*. Much to their chagrin and through no fault of their own, they were not universally loved. Some saw the Maidens as victims of Cold War propaganda, who walked down the runway bearing the visible evidence of attempts by American surgeons to hide the pressing issue of nuclear weapons testing. Others saw them as victims of cultural assimilation, who walked down the runway under a veil of cosmetic improvements and shining new accessories, unaware that their time in the United States had put them in an exclusive bubble. Still others sympathized with them, regarding them as a bridge between former enemies, beneficiaries of a new world order in which medical procedures could be used as tools of modernization and foreign policy. Forty years later, Sundahl's poetry unconsciously captured the essence of that postwar moment when the Hiroshima Maidens became a screen onto which many citizens around the world projected their own cultural fantasies about these young Japanese women: who they were, how they looked, what they had become, and what it meant for them to come here in the first place (fig. 14).

In 1960, less than four years after the last of the Maidens returned to Japan, Rod Serling's controversial but popular television show *The Twilight Zone* broadcast its most famous and critically acclaimed episode, "Eye of the Beholder." In the episode, originally shown on November 11, the modern hospital becomes an Orwellian nightmare when Janet Tyler, a young woman with a horribly disfigured face, undergoes her eleventh surgical procedure to become physically acceptable. The doctors and nurses, whose faces we see only in shadow, are not unsympathetic to the young woman's plight but know that the surgery, certain to have no effect on her condition, will force her to be relocated to a segregated community of people

FIGURE 14 Filled with, as the original caption stated, "feelings of sadness and gladness," the first group of Hiroshima Maidens wave from the runway at La Guardia Airport in New York City and begin their long journey home. Sadam Takahashi, a Japanese surgeon, holds a box containing the ashes of Tomako Nakabayashi, the Maiden who died of heart failure in May during her third operation to correct her disfigured arm. Nakabayashi's death was underplayed in the American media but wildly overplayed by some Japanese newspapers, which maintained that the Maidens were guinea pigs of American medical experimentation. Photograph taken June 12, 1956 © Bettmann/Corbis.

who also suffer from her physical disorder. Although viewers never see Tyler's face while it is wrapped in tight, distorting bandages, they hear the character's plaintive voice as recorded by actress Maxine Stuart. In the final few moments of the episode, when the bandages come off, the woman is revealed as a stunning, physically normal blonde played by actress Donna Douglas, who later achieved fame as Elly May on *The Beverly Hillbillies*. The doctors and nurses, whose faces are finally brought out of shadow, have the grotesque misshapen noses, eyelids, and mouths of German Expressionist puppets.

Serling well understood television's role as a multivalent medium that conceptualized celebrity and beauty for different audiences and constituencies. Douglas Heyes, the director of this *Twilight Zone* episode, also knew that only a film noir approach to the mise-en-scène, punctuated by composer Bernard Hermann's dramatic score, would produce the desired effect. Heyes played with shadow and light so as not to reveal the program's characteristic ending twist. A promotional trailer shown in early November 1960 to drum up viewer interest recreated uncannily the Hiroshima Maidens' appearance on *This Is Your Life*. In it, Serling emerges from a shadowy silhouette to present the dark theme of the program. For the producers of *This Is Your Life*, the choice to show the Maidens in silhouette was a nod toward modesty and protection; for Serling, the silhouette heightened the program's intent to give the topic of plastic surgery an air of quasi-scientific menace. While many applauded the story, however heavy-handed, as an allegory of fascism and the dangers of mass conformity, organizations like the National Association for the Advancement of Colored People (NAACP) understood the program's social and political exploration of plastic surgery, appearance, and citizenship in racial terms. In honor of the poignant episode, the NAACP presented Serling with its 1961 Unity Award for Outstanding Contributions for Better Race Relations.

Unlike the surgical patient in the *Twilight Zone* episode, the Maidens were compassionately healed in a modern American hospital, free from the exploitation and manipulation that anchor

Serling's fictional story. But the utopian mystique imposed on plastic surgery in the 1950s placed them in a larger cultural narrative of social improvement through medical engineering that seemed to be the premise for Serling's allusions to plastic surgery as a tool used to promote political ideology. Furthermore, like Serling's episode, the American and Japanese supporters of the Hiroshima Maidens project conceptualized the women within Western paradigms of beauty and femininity. The sophistication imputed to their surgery allowed the Hiroshima Maidens to eschew traditional Japanese culture and embrace an American female identity increasingly defined by the medical appurtenances of scientific modernism. Their transformation—from Keloid Girls to Hiroshima Maidens—unfolded as a public drama through which ordinary citizens could engage with medical science and witness its visions of both technological enthusiasm and abject horror as projected onto the female body. In this sense, the women functioned both domestically and internationally as a medicalized version of the Marshall Plan. Like the lists that Ida Day compiled, rehabilitating them meant measuring them against the demands of a range of normative categories: physical and psychological; economic and political; gendered and able-bodied; and specific to the needs of Japanese-American relations in the era of reconstruction.

The public drama of the Hiroshima Maidens continues to unfold, in ways that have been essentially absorbed within the parameters of globalization. Toward the end of 1955, after doctors completed the Maidens' first round of surgery, Cousins acknowledged that because the surgeons at Mount Sinai had donated their services, and because the hospital had provided beds for the Maidens at little or no charge, a portion of the $55,000 collected on the women's behalf from philanthropic groups and public solicitations on the *This Is Your Life* broadcast had not been spent. Arthur Barsky, chief of plastic surgery at Mount Sinai and head surgeon for the Maidens project, suggested that the money be used for training Japanese surgeons in the reconstructive techniques that Barsky and his colleagues had performed on the Maidens. Barsky arranged for three young Japanese dermatologists—Kitaro Ohmori, Takua Onizuka, and Namba Katsuya—to come to Mount Sinai and train with doctors in the hospital's plastic surgery program. In 1958, Onizuka and Katsuya created the Japanese Society for Plastic and Reconstructive Surgery, which became the organization responsible for certifying practicing plastic surgeons in Japan. After 1958, dozens of plastic surgeons trained in Japan and learned Barsky's techniques, developing their own medical specialties of cosmetic surgery. By the early 1960s, surgeons in Japan, China, and Hawaii were recommending cosmetic surgery for men and women who wanted to Westernize their features.[110] By the late 1970s, blepharoplasty and augmentation rhinoplasty had become conspicuous consumer options among many Asian patients. Writing in 1980, Yoshio Hiraga, a prominent Japanese plastic surgeon, asserted, "Slit eyes are considered by some to make one look sad or ill-natured. Those with slit eyes are sometimes misunderstood and lose friends or even their work."[111]

One could argue that internationalizing plastic surgery techniques as modern social amenities suggests the breakdown of Western/non-Western binaries in terms of standards of beauty or access to particular medical technologies. The desire and willingness to undergo the knife in the name of physical improvement, one might argue, can no longer be regarded as a purely Western ideal foisted on unsuspecting populations. In a global marketplace dominated by goods and services that blur the cultural origins of an "authentic" national or ethnic heritage, identifying physical features as "Western" or "Eastern" may be an outmoded way of thinking. Yet the cautionary tale provided by the Hiroshima Maidens is that surgical options, no matter where they originate, retain their status precisely because people around the world have internalized medically normative ideas of what it means to have an appropriate or desirable body. In the late 1980s, cosmetic surgery became a widely publicized and hugely successful consumer product in so-called developing countries, where it is physical evidence of a particular standard of living. Some normative ideas of the body, however, speak more directly to medicine's Cold War legacies of cultural imperialism. In post-Communist Russia and Eastern Europe, as well as in many Asian and Pacific Rim cultures such as Korea, China, and the Philippines, cosmetic surgery continues to symbolize prestige, modernity, and access to lavish goods and services.[112] In 1993 the *Wall Street Journal* reported the story of a Korean cosmetic surgeon who encourages prospective patients, especially young urban professionals, to undergo cosmetic surgery by a sign outside his office that proclaims "Go Anglo!" As one of the surgeon's female clients explained, "[Cosmetic surgery] is different from buying luxury items. It deals with self-esteem. I admit we're looking Anglicized, but we're social animals, and we have to adapt to society."[113]

## THREE

**Gladys Bentley and the Cadillac of Hormones**

IN THE AUGUST 1952 issue of *Ebony* magazine, Gladys Bentley, an openly lesbian African American nightclub performer and cult figure in Harlem during the 1920s and 1930s, published her memoirs as an article titled "I Am a Woman Again."[1] In a rambling narrative, complete with photographs of herself at different stages of her life and career, Bentley described how she had banished her former lesbian past through successive treatments with the steroid hormone estrogen. She claimed that a program of hormone therapy, recommended by her gynecologist, had not only transformed the condition of her sex organs and enabled her to assume the physical status of an anatomically respectable woman but also enabled her to become completely heterosexual. These changes, Bentley argued, made her a true woman and not a shadowy creature compromised by an inferior natural body. "Today I am a woman again," she rhapsodized, "through the miracle which took place not only in my mind and heart . . . but also in my body—when the magic of modern medicine made it possible for me to have treatment which helped change my life completely."

Readers who remembered Bentley from her Harlem Renaissance heyday would have been confused and even shocked by her revelations, especially since her sexuality had hardly been a secret in her youth. Anyone who had been part of Harlem's ambisexual nightclub culture during the Jazz Age knew intimately that images of a big black piano-playing bulldagger presented in Carl Van Vechten's celebration of Harlem's after-hours crowd, *Parties* (1930), or Blair

FIGURE 15 Cabaret performer Gladys Bentley strikes a butch pose in her distinctive white tuxedo and top hat ensemble at a photo session in New York City, ca. 1928. Published in Bentley, "I Am a Woman Again," *Ebony* 7 (August 1952): 92–98.

Niles's *Strange Brother* (1931), were clearly based on Bentley.[2] Bentley also did not try to conceal from the public record the details of her wedding ceremony, held in Atlantic City in 1928, when she "married" her white girlfriend.[3] Bentley's performances were famous for her on-stage antics and unapologetic butch persona, whose defiant accoutrements included a custom-made white tuxedo, top hat, and jeweled cane that she used to entertain clientele as diverse as J. P. Morgan and the Prince of Wales.

After the onset of the Depression, however, Harlem's appeal as a taboo racial and sexual "interzone" for white bohemians could no longer sustain the nightclub culture that had once thrived there—owing in no small part to the repeal of Prohibition in 1933, which made liquor widely available.[4] The loss of Harlem's prominence as a tourist destination motivated many entertainers like Bentley to consider a change of venue. In 1937 Bentley went in search of a new commercial identity and moved with her mother to California, where she established herself as a cabaret performer. Recasting her act for more upscale West Coast supper clubs and bars, she remained a strong draw for black audiences and gay audiences alike, performing regularly at clubs in Hollywood like the Rose Room. An advertisement for Mona's Club 440 in the December 1942 issue of *San Francisco Life* billed Bentley as "America's Greatest Sepia Piano Artist" and the "Brown Bomber of Sophisticated Songs."[5] Capitalizing on her new popularity, she recorded some of her own material during this period, such as the revealing blues number "Gladys Isn't Gratis Any More." In her remaining years, Bentley made a few television appearances, but she turned heads again when she abandoned her cabaret act and joined the choir in the Los Angeles-based ministry Temple of Love in Christ, Inc.

The California phase of Gladys Bentley's career during the 1940s and 1950s suggests several ways we can interpret her personal history. Bentley's transformation of her body through hormones was in many ways a paradigm of the popular appeal of medical procedures in the United States after World War II. The discovery and synthesis of cheap and potent versions of steroid hormones during the 1930s made treatments for many physiological conditions and chronic illnesses—from menopause and rheumatoid arthritis to Addison's disease—widely available early in the next decade. Steroid hormones as well as other pharmaceuticals like sulfa drugs and penicillin were produced for a mass market as part of an arsenal of medical miracles that promised to cure the physical woes of civil society. They were so popular that, in 1948 one female physician wrote that she had found many of her patients were "endocrine conscious . . . [for] preparations which promise a kind of body Utopia."[6] While Bentley may have regarded her hormone treatments as miraculous, her understanding of them was also shaped by the scientific belief that products made from glands could regulate social behavior. In the late nineteenth and early twentieth centuries, during the discipline's infancy, physicians and scientists working in the field of endocrinology had postulated powerful connections between glands and individual identity. After World War II, the belief in the regulatory power of steroid hormones was still in wide circulation, but it was also reinvigorated by the fears and fantasies of the Cold War era. One longtime advocate of hormone therapy wrote in 1948 that "we may rehabilitate most gland-distorted persons (and many hardened criminals as well) by this new, humane use of modern endocrine wisdom. . . . [W]e cannot afford criminality in this deadly atomic age!"[7] Such sentiments were reminiscent of the reactions of many plastic surgeons to the facial features of perceived career criminals that we explored in chapter 2.

The lure of endocrinology's ability to transform bodies and regulate behavior was clearly a powerful incentive for consumers like Gladys Bentley. As she made clear in her declaration in *Ebony,* Bentley chose to undergo hormone treatments precisely because she equated medical rehabilitation of her body with social rehabilitation of her identity. Understanding the social and political—as well as scientific—contexts of hormone therapy is the key to historicizing Gladys Bentley's understanding of her body as an African American woman and, significantly, as a (formerly) self-identified lesbian who claimed that hormone treatments had set her straight. This chapter interprets Bentley's story to show how it illuminates, and is illuminated by, the various social meanings that American society imputed to steroid hormones such as estrogen in the immediate postwar era. To begin, however, it examines the racial implications of endocrinology as a medical subdiscipline in order to better situate the relation between Bentley's use of hormone therapy and twentieth-century cultural politics.

During the same period when endocrinology emerged as its own area of scientific study, the concept of "race" in popular and professional discourses encompassed a wide range of competing and often contradictory scientific and social meanings. In the late nineteenth and early twentieth centuries, the concept shifted as waves of domestic and international migrations and subsequent federal and judicial rulings—such as the Chinese Exclusion Act (1883), the Supreme Court's defense of "separate but equal" in the case of *Plessy v. Ferguson* (1896), and the National Origins Act (1924)—circumscribed access to the full rights and privileges of American citizenship by relying on race-bound definitions of national and ethnic identity.[8] Race was used with absolute scientific certainty to distinguish "superior" national or ethnic groups from inferior ones, especially as newly arrived immigrants from Italy, Ireland, and Eastern Europe rushed to join the ranks of "white" ethnic stock. As Matthew Frye Jacobson has argued, "a pattern of racially based, Anglo-Saxonist exclusivity dominated the years from 1840 to the 1920s, whereas a pattern of Caucasian unity [for "white" immigrants] gradually took its place in the 1920s and after."[9]

Twentieth-century developments in endocrinology, to a large degree, reaffirmed these legal and social understandings of race. But they also reflected the taxonomic systems that eighteenth-century scientists had developed to differentiate people into races.[10] Identifying endocrine glands as the biological source of an individual's physical traits—size, weight, color, physiognomy, and so forth—enabled physicians to associate glandular effects with the phenotypic characteristics of certain racial groups. By the 1920s, American physicians and reformers regarded endocrinology as yet another objective scientific tool with serious social and political implications.[11] In 1926, for example, physician Charles Evans Morris argued, "There is no proof to-day that the particular endocrine combination we are supplied with is so basic that it cannot be so altered in the course of time that the family characteristic or even racial tendencies cannot be obliterated."[12] Morris's pragmatism notwithstanding, one wonders exactly what "endocrine combination" he hoped to "obliterate," and to whom such an inferior-grade "endocrine combination" might belong. In the mid-1920s, at the height of nativist policies magnified by religious fundamentalism, Ku Klux Klan activity, and Palmer raids, obliterating or even containing physical differences through scientific means was idealized by some social conservatives as one possible method of enforcing assimilation. The intellectual potency of the eugenics movement and the influence of Supreme Court cases such as *Buck v. Bell* (1927), which legalized the sterilization of the "feebleminded," conferred a prescient authority to science in matters of public policy.

The desire to contain racial characteristics through the science of endocrinology was not merely the dream of xenophobic physicians, racist eugenicists, or mad Progressives, however. It was also a recurring motif of African American culture, especially among many middle-class blacks in the first decades of the twentieth century. Class-conscious organizations like the National Association for the Advancement of Colored People (NAACP), founded in 1909, attempted to fill a void by appealing to a new black bourgeoisie. The NAACP often concealed or downplayed familiar and visible phenotypic characteristics and promoted a safe, middle-class vision of the modern "New Negro." Cosmetic techniques such as skin lightening and hair straightening became some of the cultural tools used by an idealized, assimilated modern African American citizen. Even Charles Morris's description of endocrine therapy seemed to imply that concentrating too narrowly on race, rather than admitting to its inherent malleability, was an obstacle to the egalitarian spirit of modern society. Still, no matter how prosperous or adamant such proponents of racial assimilation were, the issue of what constituted "authentic" blackness remained under scrutiny by African Americans who did not subscribe to the idea of a neutralized and potentially deracinated black citizen. "A newly assertive political leadership" of African Americans, as Kathy Peiss has written, "pointed to the use of [hair] straighteners and [skin] bleaches as ipso facto evidence of self-loathing and the desire to appear and be white."[13] Instead, leaders like W. E. B. Du Bois and Marcus Garvey believed that one could be true to one's blackness—both physically and ideologically—as a tool of cultural citizenship rather than an obstacle. One could argue that the entire milieu of the Harlem Renaissance—the very movement in which Gladys Bentley flourished—was a contested terrain between forces promoting racial authenticity and forces promoting racial denial. In the cultural métier to which Bentley belonged, during the same year (1929) Wallace Thurman created the self-affirming race novel *The Blacker the Berry* . . . while Nella Larsen wrote *Passing,* the self-effacing and often painful novella of mulatto ambiguity. George Schuyler's aggressive 1931 science-fiction novel *Black No More* (taken from the name of a commercial skin-lightening agent) satirized the bourgeois affectations of many "high-yellow" African Americans who sought out ways to cosmetically erase their more pronounced Negro characteristics and turn themselves white.[14]

Clearly, Gladys Bentley's experience with hormones in the late 1940s and early 1950s encouraged her to assume, among other things, a heterosexual identity marked by excessive claims to authentic femininity and domesticity. But her desire as a black woman to reform her body and her identity was not an incidental component of this experience. For many women in the postwar era, hormone therapy defined the contours of a particular race consciousness. Seeking to distance themselves from women with what they perceived to be the attributes of a racially or ethnically inferior body type, they held up as endocrinology's glandular ideal a feminine norm implicitly coded as white. In this sense, Bentley may have located herself somewhere between the modern "New Negro" of the 1920s and politically conservative, middle-class African Americans in the period immediately preceding the mainstream civil rights activism of the mid-1950s. As Ruth Feldstein has argued, in the 1940s African American political figures as well as white supporters of the modern liberal state promoted the ideal of the refined and mature black woman. By focusing on middle-class and domestic images of black women rather than the more familiar and pernicious stereotypes, supporters of rights for African Americans could challenge the caricature of the "bad" or domineering African American wife and mother.[15] In this chapter, I show that Bentley's sexual and social "reform" through estrogen treatments reflected this pressure to define and realize an authentic African American social identity in the early 1950s while leaving many gender and racial stereotypes firmly intact. As we shall see, Bentley's 1952 explanation in the pages of *Ebony* for her use of hormone therapy was an artifact of an era when assimilation was the preferred option for many middle class African Americans who wanted to define themselves through consensus culture rather than struggle against it.

## A BRIEF HISTORY OF ENDOCRINOLOGY AND RACE BEFORE WWII

Although the word "hormone" itself was coined by British physiologists William Bayliss and Ernest Starling in 1905, the understanding of what hormones were and what they did was not exclusively a twentieth-century concept. At the dawn of scientific medicine in the late eighteenth century, many physicians and anatomists still subscribed to the ancient Greek concept of bodily humors, which hypothesized that humans produced small quantities of a number of mysterious chemical substances that were responsible for maintaining physical and emotional equilibrium. In the nineteenth century, chemists realized that certain hormonal substances originated with particular glands. In the late 1880s, for example, French physician Charles-Eduoard Brown-Séquard conducted famous experiments in which he injected castrated roosters with fluids extracted from their testes and watched as the treatment revitalized their withered combs.[16] By the early twentieth century, physiologists had thoroughly identified each of the major glands in the body: the pituitary, thalamus, thyroid, adrenals, ovaries, and testes. Each gland, they claimed, performed a discrete function that chemically controlled particular activities necessary for metabolism, digestion, and reproduction. In addition, physiologists linked glandular function, or dysfunction, to the etiologies of certain physical conditions and diseases such as dwarfism (pituitary hypofunction, or deficit of growth hormone), hirsutism in women (adrenal hyperfunction, or surfeit of adrenal hormone linked to androgen, the male hormone), or Addison's disease (adrenal dysfunction traced to a deficit of ACTH, the adrenocortical hormone that regulates adrenal activity).

Recent scholarship on the history of endocrinology has focused on reproductive endocrinology, showing how it has been used to manipulate social ideas about women's bodies. As Diana Long Hall and Nelly Oudshoorn have described it, over much of the past century reproductive endocrinology naturalized "normal" hormone production as the provenance of gendered "health."[17] Scientists exploited estrogen levels as objective gauges of feminine characteristics. It was assumed, for example, that ovarian hypofunction, or the low production of estrogenic hormones, indicated a female's inadequacy. Conversely, the excess of body hair called hirsutism (sometimes known as virilism in the medical literature), probably linked to a surfeit of testosterone, also indicated a woman's biological failure to achieve true femininity. By exposing these naive though powerful formulations, historians have shown how endocrinology has reflected sexist (and heterosexist) assumptions that have defined women's bodies through the gaze of scientists and gynecologists who were predominantly white, elite, and male.

Other historians have tried to denaturalize this biological imperative to an "authentic" female body and instead have shown how endocrinology has been used to manipulate social ideas about sexual identity and sexual orientation. Chandak Sengoopta and Stephanie H. Kenen, for example, have focused on how early twentieth-century European and American scientists sought out etiologies of homosexuality by analyzing hormone production among "effeminate" men and "virile" women. Similarly, Bernice L. Hausman has looked at the mystique surrounding hormones in the creation of modern transsexual identity beginning in the 1950s.[18] As a whole, such histories focusing on endocrinology, gender, and sexuality—both procreative and "deviant"—reflect the attitude espoused by group of medical historians at the Wellcome Institute of the History of Medicine, who organized a conference in 1997 on endocrinology as the "the glandular vision of life."[19]

Some feminist historians of science and medicine such as Donna Haraway and Jennifer Terry have attended more closely to the larger racialized implications of reproductive endocrinology by demonstrating how white male American and European scientists determined the direction and meaning of hormone research.[20] Such scholarship offers a potent political critique of endocrinology's endemic heterosexism in order to expose how bodies with putatively dysfunctional or "primitive" reproductive glands not only defied the concept of "normal" gender but also proved that the physiological and morphological features of such bodies were considered racially uncivilized compared to the rest of modern (white) society. During the late nineteenth century, when the nascent subdisciplines of evolutionary anthropology, sexology, and endocrinology emerged at precisely the same historical moment, anthropological theories of evolutionary development and scientific theories of sexual development supported one another.[21] Physically "primitive" or socially atavistic bodies were often regulated by scientific means and through legal channels. As Siobhan Somerville has shown, the entwined explanatory power of anthropology and sexology enabled scientists to understand the relation between "superior" classifications of humans that were defined by physical and physiological criteria.[22] The links between these emergent disciplines helped early anthropologists and sexologists to construct both homosexuals and African Americans as primitives who shared physiological and morphological characteristics. As Terry has argued, "The phantasmatic homosexual body, like savage bodies, became a text of telltale signs by which to measure moral character and the effects of civilization."[23]

Anglo-European models of physical development dominated these scientific disciplines and shaped racialized understandings of endocrinology and, in particular, reproductive endocrinology. Yet racial attitudes also thrived in the study of nonreproductive endocrine glands, namely, the pituitary, adrenals, and thyroid. By disaggregating the reproductive glands from the whole endocrine system, we lack a historical appreciation for the ways early physicians and scientists imagined the endocrine system as a *network* of glands working together as an integrated whole. While the specialized physiological functions attributed to the ovaries and testicles made them natural spectacles of popular curiosity, scientists and practitioners measured the activity of all the glands together as an endocrine network whose precise balance kept individuals healthy and productive. It is important, then, to establish that assumptions about the connection between hormones and race, which were exploited to privilege those with normal and productive bodies, did not reside solely in the reproductive organs. Assumptions about race were assigned to glands individually and the endocrine network collectively. Scientific justifications for racial ideology were clearly a part of the early history of reproductive endocrinology, but they ought to be included in studies of endocrinology more broadly as a professional and cultural practice.

From the 1890s through the 1930s, nonreproductive hormones were regularly administered through "organotherapy" and "pluriglandular" therapy, common terms for the application of animal gland extracts to human bodies. These were thought to be the next revolutionary phase of scientific medicine. Injecting juice squeezed from a sheep's thalamus, for instance, was thought to benefit those whose own thalamus was identified as the root cause of their physical ailments. Writing in 1916, physician Frank R. Starkey announced that pluriglandular therapy had brought about "brilliant results" "in children who are backward in either mental or physical development."[24] Like the activities of many Progressive Era physicians interested in social hygiene through therapeutic intervention, Starkey's description of "the utterly hopeless, abject picture of a pot-bellied, goggle-eyed dribbling idiot brought to normal by the administration of the derivatives of these glands" did not betray its eugenic roots.

Arguments made on behalf of the "natural order" of glandular values gave tremendous power to the pronouncements of these early manufacturers of pluriglandular products. Because endocrinologists and organotherapists used their professional knowledge to make distinctions between those with normal and abnormal glands, they constantly highlighted how hormonal science maintained dialectical concepts of normalcy and deviance. This may explain how the scientific authority imputed to understanding and controlling the endocrine glands reflected many of the social and political programs of the early twentieth century. Since proper glandular function was viewed as the biochemical definition of the normal and healthy and glandular dysfunction defined abnormal and unhealthy behavior, the seemingly lucid, though naive, causal links between endocrinology, physical maturity, and social productivity had the seal of common sense in the nativist milieu of American culture during the Progressive Era. In the same way that the failure to regulate and control the endocrine glands marked the failure of the human body to attain a mature plateau of natural progress, society's failure to regulate and control misfits (such as criminals, prostitutes, paupers, gamblers, homosexuals, and the feebleminded) marked its failure to attain a mature plateau of social progress. In 1938 a team of British endocrinologists claimed that the "failure of the endocrine factor leads to a regressive state, a state of development through which the [normal] adult has passed. . . . Since in some quarters insanity is regarded as the ultimate regression, it might be expected that some of these [hormonally imbalanced] cases would show some evidence of psychosis. This, in fact, was confirmed."[25]

Between 1910 and 1945, numerous discussions of the salutary influence of hormonal function and the deleterious effect of hormonal dysfunction circulated widely in professional and popular culture. For example, Chicago physician Theodore H. Larson's 1929 lay review of hormones, *Why We Are What We Are,* found in them the essential organic ingredients for perfecting the race, finding marriageable mates, and identifying appropriate physical types to perform appropriate social functions. As Larson argued, "It is . . . in the power of anyone to change the endocrine relativity by exercising and stimulating the endocrine glands, thus changing the endocrine exchange, which will ultimately change the endocrine relativity."[26] Inspired by the anti-immigrant and eugenic propaganda of the mid-1920s, Larson believed well-bred individuals could have a more lasting effect on society and ensure the future of "fitter families" in the United States. Unfit families were the result not only of breeding between so-called genetic defectives but also of the evils of miscegenation, a social problem that arguably had been made visible (to those watching) by Gladys Bentley's nonreproductive but no less controversial marriage to her white girlfriend one year earlier in 1928.

Larson used two allegorical portraits designed to illustrate the social value of attaining proper hormonal metabolism (see fig. 16). The nattily dressed, well-coifed young white man—clearly meant to represent a junior executive—is what Larson calls a "Master-Mind," a phrase that perhaps carried allusions to good "native American" stock (and what would come to be called, in an entirely different context, a master race). As proof of his superior mental capacities, the force of his actively engaged and thoroughly exercised pituitary radiates in every direction as the brain of a budding financier or young company manager might have been imagined during the rise of the middle-class professional of the 1920s.[27] In stark contrast, the sloppily dressed, disheveled young white man represents the eugenic ideal of an uneducated country bumpkin. Victimized by the "very small pituitary" that he "inherited," the young man's caricature embodies the phenotypic essentialism so crucial to the eugenics movement. As proof of his static mental capacities, his thumb is turned inward toward himself as he stares

THE EFFECT OF AN ACTIVE PITUITARY
*Keen Comprehension of the Entire World*

THIS young man was taught how to think logically and constructively while young. This he continued, until now we have before us a Master-Mind; which was produced by the proper stimulation of the pituitary, increasing it materially in size, which in turn stimulated the brain-cells to a much greater height of intellect.

This man has a most powerful mental control; is profoundly logical and sound.

FIGURE 16 Portraits of the "Master-Mind" and his opposite, the country bumpkin, conveyed some of the racial logic of early endocrinology in the 1920s. From Theodore H. Larson, *Why We Are What We Are: The Science and Art of Endocrine Physiology and Endocrine Therapy* (Chicago: American Endocrine Bureau/W. B. Conkey, 1929).

RESULTS OF AN INACTIVE PITUITARY
*Mental Sphere Very Limited*

THIS young man inherited a very small pituitary and has never been taught or trained to exercise it. The results are that this is not secreting more than one-third as much as it should; for this reason there is but very little stimulation to the brain-cells, with a correspondingly low mentality.

With proper attention this could have been greatly improved upon, if not wholly corrected.

blankly at his fellow local yokels sitting on boxes in front of a rural grocery store. The artist presumes that the grocery is the only social conduit through which the young man is destined ever to experience life or worldly conversation. In the years following World War I, when nativism reached fever pitch, such an atavistic image of the glandular-deficient genetic inferior supported the eugenic view that through overly generous immigration quotas or poor breeding stock the nation was producing too many bumpkins and too few Master-Minds.

Larson saw glands as proof of intellectual acuity, social skills, professional potential, and civic utility. Hormones were reliable quantitative (and, more important, *quantifiable*) evidence of whether an individual possessed adequate resources to succeed in a competitive society. Endocrinology, like eugenics, depended on a rigid hierarchy of racialized norms where healthy interventions made to the pituitaries could reform even the most pitiable poor white trash. In 1929, Boston citizen-reformer and philanthropist George Alexander self-published the provocatively titled pamphlet *You: The Story of Your Ductless Glands*. The pamphlet explicitly cataloged a host of glandular "anomalies" as perceived by a prime specimen of Boston Brahmin thinking:

> This Book Shows You What Causes
> The Giant—Dwarf—Bearded Lady
> Lion Faced Boy
> Youthful Mental Marvels
> Perverts and Murderers of the
> Hickman, Leopold, Loeb Type
> What makes the black man—Black
> What causes THE TERRIBLE CRETIN.[28]

The associations, whether casual or implied, that Alexander saw between psychopathic killers, circus performers, and African Americans seem not to be coincidental. If the genealogical connections between primitivism, perversion, and psychosis are too condensed in his logic to be properly disentangled, his scheme does offer an easily visualized continuum of physiologically distinguished types ranging from the abject ("lion-faced boy," "terrible cretin") to the superlative ("youthful mental marvels") who implicitly mirror a racialized scale of social evolution. Glandular dysfunction is correlated for Alexander with a host of social conditions ranging from the extra melanin in black skin (or, viewed another way, deficient melanin in white skin) to the infamous activities of wealthy Jewish sociopaths Richard Loeb and Nathan Leopold, whose 1927 murder of Bobby Franks in Chicago caused a national scandal. Although in the 1920s the phrase "mental marvel" was often attributed to the awkward savant-performers who were exhibited in circuses and sideshows along with the bearded lady and the lion-faced boy, here the marvel seems more like a cousin to Larson's upwardly mobile Master-Mind rather than a freak show curiosity. For Alexander, identifying such glandular types was part of his civic duty, embodying the concerns of many reformers and institutions in medical, psychological, or managerial fields that worked diligently to treat and improve the lots of individuals who were—in modern parlance—glandularly challenged.

## SYNTHETIC HORMONES AND THE DREAM OF DEMOCRACY

In the 1930s and 1940s, the discourse around endocrinology and race became more complex. As organotherapy gave way to what we now think of as hormone therapy, physicians and patients imagined hormones as consumer amenities for those who could afford them. In the early decades of the twentieth century, chemists working for pharmaceutical companies distilled androgenic, estrogenic, or adrenocortical materials from, literally, tons of ground bulls' testicles, sows' ovaries, or bovine adrenal glands. Steroid hormones, isolated in their most purified form, not only were hard to come by but were prohibitively expensive for all but the wealthiest private clients. In the early 1930s, surgical techniques for removing faulty glands or grafting on new ones to stimulate hormone production were controversial innovations that promised to meet a growing concern for youth consciousness and gender normativity among elite men and women. Radical glandular interventions had first become notorious after the Russian surgeon Serge Voronoff's celebrated "rejuvenation" experiments with transplanting monkey and baboon glands into humans in the late 1920s.[29] In 1941, Ray (later Rae) Bourbon, a self-described "pansy" performer who played to appreciative gay circles in urban and rural areas of the United States through the mid-1960s, was still captivated enough by the Voronoff story to release a record titled "Gland Opera." The camp lyrics revealed how some had imagined endocrinology not as a corrective measure but as a potentially subversive science. For Bourbon the relation between one's body chemistry and one's gender identity seemed far more malleable than physicians like Charles Morris could ever have anticipated:

Ain't science marvelous, ain't science grand?
It'll make worn-out libidos lib by grafting on new glands.
Now a certain worn-out bachelor, who had gone from frail to frailer,
They had no stevedore's glands in stock,
So they gave him a ladies tailor's.
But now he's camping at the beaches, making passes at the sailors!
If you've lost it, get defrosted:
All you need is new glands.[30]

   Two major developments fundamentally affected the science of endocrinology: the chemical synthesis of new types of hormone treatments, and their marketing to consumers. In the 1920s and 1930s, a loosely associated group of organic chemists working independently—such as Edward Doisy, Edward Kendall, Frederick Koch, Ernst Laqueur, and Tadeus Reichstein—solved the problem presented by the small quantities of steroid hormones occurring in nature.[31] Through rapid and successful theoretical developments in biochemistry, chemists produced hormones not by isolating them from their original source materials—ovaries, for example—but by rearranging the carbon atoms of abundant organic materials.[32] Urine, blood plasma, and even soybeans and yams could be re-organized at the molecular level to resemble original steroid hor-mone compounds.[33] These advances in organic chemistry ultimately resulted in an explosion of synthetic versions of the steroid hor-mones. Within a few years, the production of hormones through total synthesis made it possible for pharmaceutical companies such as Schering and Merck to market inexpensive versions of testos-terone, estrogen, and corticosterone (known by the late 1940s by its more familiar name, cortisone) to thousands of new patients throughout the United States. The widespread availability, and lowered cost, of these new hormone treatments transformed both reproductive and nonreproductive endocrinology. It no longer fo-cused only on managing or even curing glandular disorders per se; instead, it provided inspiration both for patients with urgent medical needs and for consumers seeking social and psychological gratification from new medical products. As Herman Bundesen, one of the organic chemists who helped isolate testosterone, declared in 1940, "If chemicals can restore the yield of worn-out soil, can we not [through hormones] hope to renew the tissues and energies of worn-out men?"[34]

New hormone treatments, emphasizing self-improvement, emerged in both professional and popular culture of the period, transforming endocrinology into medical science for the masses. A 1938 issue of the classic pulp science fiction magazine *Amazing Stories,* for example, featured a male character transformed by androgenic hormones into the "Gland Superman." An advertisement published by Schering in the June 1940 issue of the professional journal *Endocrinology* mimicked 1930s *art moderne:* the feature-less, though identifiably male figure emerges enigmatically from the vaginal folds of an enormous engineer's compass. The figure's endlessly long life, stretching out to the horizon line on a graph paper runway, is made possible by an armamentarium of hor-mones that, as the caption reads, "enable physicians to influence almost every phase of man's existence from the ovum through the span of life" (fig. 17). Both image and text gave readers a flavor for the quasi-religious fervor with which pharmaceutical companies would come to regard the utopian possibilities of hormone treatments by the end of the decade.

Newspapers, magazines, and television programs routinely used the recipients of "miracle drugs" like cortisone as fodder for topical feature stories, including before-and-after photographs of the formerly bedridden who were now walking, dancing, shopping, and ready to reenter the postwar world of productive consumption.[35] "One by one," wrote William L. Laurence in the *Ladies' Home Journal* in 1949, "we saw these [tortured] men and women—sixteen in all—transformed into smiling, happy human beings, walking jauntily, performing exercises, acting in every way like normal people."[36] After physician Philip Hench's spectacular display of arthritis sufferers who could "dance a jig" after taking cortisone at the Mayo Clinic, the popular media regularly celebrated the benefits of cortisone therapy. Its anti-inflammatory and antiallergenic properties made cortisone the miracle drug of choice for a range of illnesses, including rheumatoid arthritis, dermatitis, eye diseases such as conjunctivitis and glaucoma, bronchial asthma, hay fever, rheumatic fever, degenerative disorders, scleroderma, gastrointestinal diseases, anemia, hyperthyroidism, and metabolic conditions such as Addison's disease.[37] As one 1950 *Reader's Digest* story recounted, a woman in Hench's care who used cortisone "rolled over in bed with ease. Her arthritis vanished; within a week she went on a three-hour shopping tour in down-town Rochester."[38]

Initial outbursts of enthusiasm for hormone treatments were sometimes met with skepticism, especially by those who raised questions about the potential for the home market to degenerate into snake-oil charlatanry. A May 1950 *Consumer Reports,* for example, claimed that "any [hormone] cream which might possibly be effective is ruled out because estrogens in medically 'effective' dosages are without question unsafe for self-administration."[39] Hakon Rydin, head of Sweden's state pharmaceutical laboratory

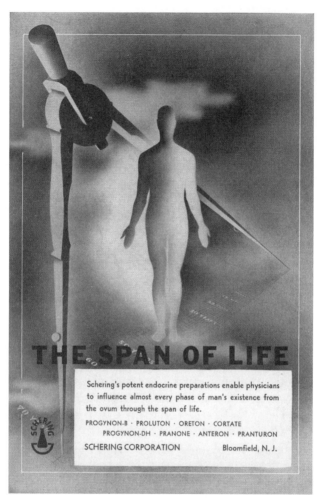

**THE SPAN OF LIFE**

Schering's potent endocrine preparations enable physicians
to influence almost every phase of man's existence from
the ovum through the span of life.

PROGYNON-B · PROLUTON · ORETON · CORTATE
PROGYNON-DH · PRANONE · ANTERON · PRANTURON

SCHERING CORPORATION                 Bloomfield, N. J.

FIGURE 17  Synthetic steroid hormones in the late 1930s appropriated the medical authority previously claimed by organotherapy products. This advertisement for Schering's new line of "endocrine preparations" promised "to influence almost every phase of man's existence from the ovum through the span of life." Originally published in the June 1940 issue of the professional journal *Endocrinology*. Reproduced with permission of Schering Corporation. All rights reserved.

in Stockholm, considered any self-applications to be dangerous, warning that hormones "particularly affect the sexual organs of women and may cause alterations or changes which can result in pathological growths and profound transformations."[40] These warnings against the potential abuses and health risks of hormone treatments did not stem the flow of over-the-counter products containing derivatives of steroid hormones. Popular period magazines such as *Charm,* "the magazine for women who work," featured numerous articles and advertisements promoting beauty products laced with estrogen. These often tapped into the anxieties of middle-class women attempting to balance their pink-collar identities with the cultural expectations of natural and enduring beauty in much the same way that advertising campaigns in earlier decades for mouthwash, deodorant, and feminine hygiene products tapped into (and perpetuated) women's deep reservoirs of bodily insecurity. One January 1954 *Charm* article declared, "After thirty-five you can fool all of the people all of the time by treating your face, throat, and hands regularly with a hormone cream or lotion. . . . There are hundreds of other 'miracles' made possible by the progress of science and chemistry."[41]

Like the cosmetic surgery techniques used on the Hiroshima Maidens, hormone treatments were also promoted in the contexts of alleviating the social and economic woes of foreign nationals. In February of the same year, *Time* related the story of surgeons in Cuba who removed the pituitary gland from a cancer patient with the mysterious name of "Señora R.," "the wife of a Havana street cleaner." The technique, adopted from Swedish surgeons, required doctors to keep the patient on a strict regimen of hormones, including cortisone, which the now-missing gland normally produced. As the article speculated, no patient would have survived such a radical move "until hormones became available from factories to replace the body's products." As a measure of the surgery's success, Señora R.— wearing "a neat linen dress and high-heeled shoes"—was invited to the Commodoro Yacht Club in Havana, where members of the Pan American Medical Association had docked during their annual

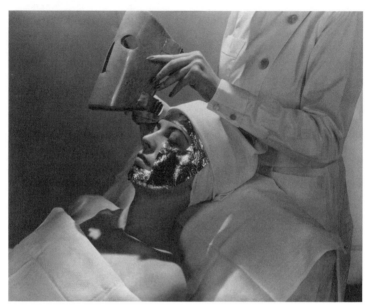

FIGURE 18 Before the arrival of synthetic steroid hormones as consumer products in the late 1930s, expensive beauty treatments such as cosmetics mogul
Helena Rubinstein's "Hormone Heat Masque," which suffused the skin with
estrogenic hormones, were aimed at elite women untouched by the financial
vagaries of the Depression. As with contemporary antiaging creams and
lotions, the efficacy of hormones applied through heat was doubtful. Photograph taken ca. 1935, © Condé Nast Archive/Corbis.

convention cruise. *Time* "did not try to forecast how long this freedom may last," a prescient prognosis for both the Señora and the
Western luxuries exhibited in that pre-Castro world of Cuban medical professionals.[42]

Despite the consumer allure imparted to these "wonder drugs,"
some endocrinologists continued to equate endocrine function and
dysfunction with social function and dysfunction. Professional and
popular discourses around hormonal imbalances before the 1940s
had reflected earlier understandings of racial primitivism. During

the economic and psychological deprivations of the 1930s, however, when the science of personality adjustment attained an authoritative stature, the equation of glandular health with psychological and social health became more nuanced.[43] With the influence of New Deal liberalism, the lure of consumerism as a democratizing force emphasized the benefits of purchasing power over the disadvantages of biology. Attaining a position in which one could buy and use new hormone products enabled one to avoid the inevitable consequences of anatomy as destiny. For many, this neutralized endocrinology's reliance on racial difference to explain physical traits or social behavior. The eugenic taint of earlier endocrinology tracts—which tried to distinguish those with faulty, inferior glands from those with productive, superior ones—seemed on the verge of disappearing. The influence of psychiatry had shifted authority away from objective explanations of glandular dysfunction and toward inclusive and subjective explanations of psychological behavior.[44]

Yet throughout the 1940s and 1950s, the equation of primitivism and pathology with the glands of certain individuals remained steadfast. Many physicians, sustained by their prewar educations and biases, continued to see hormone treatments as vehicles for the elimination of antisocial tendencies, sexual abnormalities, and unseemly physical traits. Many diagnosed with serious endocrine dysfunctions during this period were castigated as antisocial or even potentially criminal. In 1945, for example, William Wolf, a criminologist in New York City, coined the term "endocrinopath" to describe an individual for whom "faulty endocrine function [under certain conditions] may result in emotional disturbances [that] may lead to asocial, antisocial, or criminal acts."[45] Wolf perceived glandular aberrations manifest—or recognized as such— in their bodies as a kind of social recidivism.

Such ideas were occasionally challenged by endocrinologists looking to dissociate hormone therapy from the neoeugenic taint of earlier practitioners. Ralph Dorfman, an associate director at the Worcester Foundation for Experimental Biology and a research professor at Boston University School of Medicine, wrote in 1956,

"Feeble-mindedness, epilepsy, and insanity are *not* caused by . . . hormone deficiency. Such claims in the older literature were undoubtedly based on reports of persons suffering from a complex constitutional disorder to which the [glandular] defect was secondary."[46] Persistent remnants of the "older" prewar literature, however, coexisted with the new: writing in 1948, for example, New York physician Herman H. Rubin observed that "the index of the internal secretions of an individual may in the near future constitute a measure by which to fit him or her into a suitable niche in our social and ethnological system."[47] Such comments resemble the professional concerns with social and psychological readjustment that we saw among postwar prosthetists and plastic surgeons in earlier chapters. They also seem to resemble the pragmatic logic of high school teachers and vocational guidance counselors, valued touchstones given the American preoccupation with juvenile delinquency and wayward youth in the late 1940s and early 1950s.[48]

American scientists were not alone in sustaining the prewar belief that endocrinology was, at heart, a science endowed with the power of social reform. A 1951 CIBA [Pharmaceuticals'] Foundation colloquium on endocrinology, published under the title *Hormones, Psychology, and Behaviour,* affirmed this idea. Many British physicians and scientists argued that recent clinical experiments with synthetic cortisone ameliorated glandular deficiencies linked to mental health problems. As one endocrinologist commented, "The language used to describe the mental state in Addison's disease, in schizophrenia, and in patients suffering from adrenal tumours, seems to me to be precisely the same."[49] By contrast, in 1954 the French sociologist Jacques Ellul published his influential book *The Technological Society,* which conveyed the author's increasing revulsion at the seemingly totalitarian impulses that underpinned modern "surgical and medical intervention[s]." Of the five "interventions" that Ellul described, three of them originated from endocrinology's clinical repertoire: "Suppression of glandular secretions, as, for example, castration or sterilization to control antisocial and overaggressive reactions . . . injection or grafting of hormones, as, for example, in attempts to increase bodily energy, virility, femininity, or the maternal instinct . . . prolonged synthetic medication to modify metabolism."[50] The general tone of Ellul's observations about the dehumanizing effects of modern science and technology dovetailed with contemporary revelations of Nazi medical experimentation and critiques of mass conformity emerging from postwar sociological circles. Yet Ellul's ominous words of warning—"suppression . . . modify . . . control"—were ringing words of endorsement for physicians who recommended hormone therapy to their patients for "suppressing" hirsutism in women, "modifying" glandular disorders in adolescent boys, and "controlling" the pathological behaviors of criminals, sexual predators, and commonplace perverts.

The marketing of endocrinology, captured rhetorically in the belief that hormones could conquer the physical problems of defective Americans, trumped whatever eugenic or totalitarian warnings about modern culture Ellul's book raised. Endocrinologists had created a consumer demand for hormones that reflected deeply embedded social anxieties about controlling and alleviating perceived glandular dysfunction. The racial language that had been naturalized in organotherapy and, later, hormone therapy in the early decades of the twentieth century had been transmuted into the democratic and seemingly race-neutral language of universal improvement through medical science, even if the undercurrents of racial science and fears of bodily difference remained largely intact.[51] In the United States and other modern nations, hormone treatments were more than techniques of social control, as Ellul had indicated; they had become technologies used for matching one's physical body to one's idea of self. The postwar era had ushered in a new generation of hormone consumers who did not differentiate solutions to chronic illness from utopian visions of what the body might look and feel like under the right conditions. In an uncertain world poised on the brink of potential global destruction, the prudent use of hormones to promote not only good health but also physical maturity and youthful vitality provided a sense of personal

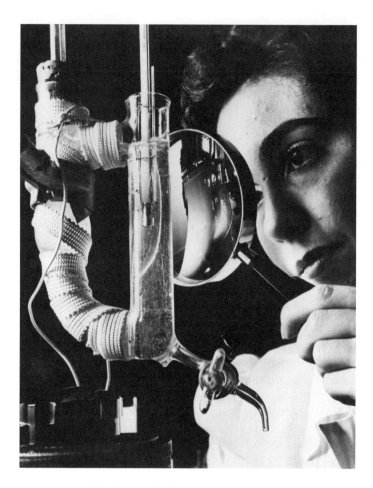

FIGURE 19 Images like this one, of a female technician making synthetic hormones at a United States–owned pharmaceutical production plant in Puerto Rico, were manipulated by the mass media to promote the benefits of both scientific advances and Cold War economic liberalism. The original caption reads, "The Commonwealth [of Puerto Rico], granted a large measure of political and economic freedom by the United States, is seen as an outstanding example of how standards of living can be raised. It offers sharp contrast with mere promises made by Soviet Russia to other countries, always with the threat of Communist enslavement attached." Photograph taken April 29, 1956, © Bettmann/Corbis.

meaning and historical revision on an intimate scale. The American body, which had been traumatized by the Depression and wartime deprivation, was suddenly free to reinvent itself and to choose its new curves and stripes the way one might pick out a new car in a showroom or a suit of clothes in a department store bulging with consumer goods. For women and men both, the use of steroid hormones became linked to a new, desirable way of living, a way to forget the disease, dysfunction, and distortion of the previous twenty years.

## SINGING THE GLAND OPERA WITH GLADYS BENTLEY

In 1952, just months before Gladys Bentley published her memoirs in *Ebony,* the eminent British mathematician and pioneer of machine intelligence Alan Turing was arrested on charges of indecency. Turing, who had worked as a cryptographer during World War II and had cracked the "enigma cipher" used by the Nazis, blithely mentioned a homosexual relationship with a local man in Manchester, England, to a police officer. The court found Turing guilty and ordered him to undergo what was then called "orgotherapy," a regimen of estrogen treatments that physicians said would "neutralize his libido" and inhibit his sexual desire for other men. Two years later, in 1954, Turing committed suicide by eating a cyanide-dipped apple; the orgotherapy had, among other things, induced gynecomastia, which had enlarged his breasts.[52]

One could read Turing's suicide as a dramatic moment in the history of endocrinology, and Cold War culture more generally. Commenting ironically on the logic of the court and of medical science, Turing chose deliberately to appropriate the symbol of the apple from both biblical and classical texts to express the death of self-knowledge rather than its traditional acquisition. Psychologists and sexual scientists, moved by what they perceived to be the glandular basis of behavior, maintained that orgotherapy—despite its embarrassing and tragic side effects—was a successful program that contained the patient's tendency toward sexual transgression. Their claim was not, as Turing had tried to express, illogical to the scientific milieu of the era. The concept of estrogen as a neutralizing force built on the prewar social control model of organotherapy. In the 1920s, it had been relatively easy to identify men who typically succumbed to gender inversion, since they supposedly did not have enough androgenic hormone (or had too much estrogenic hormone) in their bodies in the same way that women with too much or too little of the appropriate hormones, like Gladys Bentley, took on the characteristics of the opposite sex. For such individuals, a life of unnatural practices was obviously just around the corner. Turing, however, was not easily identified as a biological victim of gender inversion: to all outward appearances and biochemical assays, he would have had all of the physical and glandular characteristics of a normal male. It was therefore necessary to use hormone treatments on Turing in an entirely different way: rather than give him testosterone treatments to rejuvenate his masculinity, doctors used estrogen to neutralize the allegedly testosterone-driven basis of Turing's desire to have sex with other men. In the era of "chemical castration"—a new use of steroid hormones on convicted sex offenders, rapists, and homosexuals—the legacies of organotherapy now gave the use of steroid hormones the imprimatur of endocrinological authority.

What were the long-term effects of these kinds of applications of hormones to individuals without the telltale signs of glandular disorders? Turing's gynecomastia may have caused the patient incalculable anguish, but for physicians and scientists it was material proof of the hormonal basis of gender differentiation: estrogen had effectively produced physical characteristics clearly marked as "female." If hormones like estrogen could be shown effective in correcting primitive sexual urges, this was a sign that under the right conditions gender was not biologically fixed but entirely malleable. So, was Turing's organotherapy another version of Charles Morris's call to obliterate certain phenotypic characteristics associated with racial difference? Or was it something else altogether? Was it a version of Ray Bourbon's claim that glandular science could make presumably straight bachelors go "camping at the beaches, making passes at the sailors"? The potential radicalism of Morris's and Bourbon's understandings of glandular therapy seemed to coexist in awkward harmony with the social control model of hormone therapy propounded by Turing's physicians. Here was a production of Bourbon's "gland opera," but with Turing cast as Madame Butterfly.

Estrogen, used to punish Alan Turing for transgressing the bounds of sexual decency, was for Gladys Bentley the ticket to acquiring gender normativity and social respectability. For her, estrogen therapy was not a punitive measure but a social amenity commensurate with a newly claimed domestic stature. Photographs accompanying her "I Am a Woman Again" article in *Ebony* portrayed the new, improved version of Bentley dressing before her boudoir mirror, tasting the dinner she is cooking for her husband, newspaper columnist J. T. Gibson, and turning down the sheets of the conjugal bed (fig. 20). One caption read "Miss Bentley enjoys the domestic role that she shunned for years. She lives in modest, tastefully-appointed home directly in [the] rear of the home she purchased for her mother." Through estrogen treatments, Bentley claimed, she had been cured of not only the stigma of homosexuality but the stigma of independence. Bentley's performance of her domestic duties suggested that she had also been "cured" of her identification as a working woman, especially as one who had previously supported herself in the questionable role of cabaret entertainer. Perhaps this economic fact, more than her being a lesbian, was the root cause of her shunning the domestic role for so many decades. These photographs made visible Bentley's journey from depressed invert to bubbly hausfrau and suggested her new role as a model of middle-class black femininity.

Bentley's narrative of transformation was not unique among *Ebony*'s articles in the 1950s. The magazine published a number of stories that exposed gender difference, for example, either as an opportunity for personal triumph, as in Bentley's case, or more commonly as a lurid example of criminal transgression or obscure curiosity. In October 1951, for instance, *Ebony* printed an article

FIGURE 20 Gladys Bentley repudiates her lesbian sexuality and economic independence by showing her mastery over heterosexual domestic duties such as cooking dinner, changing bed linens, and modeling pearls at her home in Los Angeles, ca. 1952. Published in Bentley, "I Am a Woman Again," *Ebony* 7 (August 1952): 92–98.

about Georgia Black, a resident of Sanford, Florida, whom a local doctor discovered to have a "man's body."[53] "The doctor says he didn't see how I coulda married," Black told the magazine a few months before her death, "but I don't pay no 'tention to that doctor. My husbands and me had a peaceful, lovely life." Black's story and subsequent death were publicized approximately one year before the more famous case of Christine Jorgensen hit the front pages in December 1952. Interviews with and photographs of the citizens of Sanford illustrate a community that was allegedly indifferent to whether Black was a "real" woman. In November 1954 the magazine published a feature story on Annie Lee Grant of Kosciusko, Mississippi, who lived fifteen years under the identity of James McHarris, described as a "hard-working laborer" who was a "mighty tough man with the ladies."[54] The Christine Jorgensen phenomenon, which we will explore more fully in chapter 4, had already peaked—and to a certain extent fizzled out— by the time Grant's story appeared. But as with the story of Georgia Black, *Ebony* focused on community reaction in these small southern towns, and especially on what the magazine's editors probably believed were unvarnished vernacular responses to perceived imposters. Questions of propriety and respectability were what ultimately separated the stories of Georgia Black and Annie Lee Grant. Black's secret was discovered only after medical inspection by her doctor and, later, when the news was revealed publicly after her death. Grant by contrast chose a far more performative method of revealing her secret to members of the Kosciusko community. As McHarris, Grant went to court after being arrested for "driving with improper lights" and protesting a conventional search of his person. The defendant explained to Judge T. V. Rone (who also served, apparently without a conflict of interest, as the town's mayor) that he could prove that he was really a woman. According to *Ebony,* McHarris "walked to a closet, discarded shirt, pants, and male underwear. The police crowded in closer, strained their necks and jockeyed for position. When Jim walked out almost completely nude, what they saw made their mouths pop open. . . . [McHarris] was no man at all, but a fully-developed, big-breasted woman."

Bentley never tried to "pass" for a man during her appearances in New York City or Hollywood. Indeed, the success of her cabaret act rested on the delight her audiences experienced at seeing Bentley in full butch daddy regalia. But the same physical traits and social behaviors through which Bentley had expressed her (former) lesbian identity—from wearing men's clothing, to indulging in food and spirits, to performing as brazenly and provocatively as she could—were now scrutinized by the middle-class black community that Bentley so desperately wanted to be part of, the one that she hoped would lend her respectability and public legitimacy. For this reason the critical stance Bentley took toward the early stage of her own life and career as an open lesbian performer corroborated *Ebony*'s general disapproval of anyone or anything that undermined the magazine's claims to a bourgeois sensibility. Clearly, *Ebony*'s focus on gendered difference, and Bentley's overcoming of it, had a pronounced meaning in a black publication whose goal was to redefine representations of the black public sphere, no matter how compressed or circumscribed that sphere was in the early 1950s.

At the heart of Bentley's *Ebony* essay was her description of her medical interaction with her gynecologist. As she recounted in plain, confessional prose, her physician had told her, "'Your sex organs are infantile. They haven't progressed past the stage of those of a fourteen-year-old child.'" According to this observation, Bentley's labia and clitoris were small, probably the result of hypofunctional ovaries. During the 1940s, many gynecologists and general practitioners had been trained to diagnose a pronounced hypofunctioning gland as a perfect example of a condition that could be corrected through hormone therapy. Because Bentley's ovaries were thought to function incorrectly, they could be understood to produce too little estrogen, enabling an imprecise amount of androgenic hormones (such as testosterone) to dominate her glandular network and lead to distorted sexual characteristics. Such comments implied that endocrine dysfunction might also explain her lowered self-esteem and poor body image.

As absurd as his diagnoses might have appeared, Bentley's physician was not treating his patient in a vacuum. Women acknowledged throughout the nineteenth and twentieth centuries as cross-dressers, killer dykes, cradle-robbing pederasts, and "sapphic slashers" were often a species readily identified by their criminal biology.[55] Fears of the "masculinizing" effects of glandular imbalances drove gynecological choices for many midcentury physicians, most of whom were equally influenced by the social anxieties that stemmed from the contemporary fear of strong women who emasculated men, the condition that author Philip Wylie called "Momism" in his 1942 book *Generation of Vipers*. Beginning in the late 1920s, physicians in the United States and Europe frequently used endocrine therapy to treat women who self-identified as homosexual. Since many saw female homosexuality as a condition that was biologically based, glandular dysfunction was assumed to be the cause of attraction to the same sex. While Alan Turing endured his organotherapy in Britain, at least until he could take it no longer, many lesbians or nonnormative women endured both hormone therapy and surgical treatment. A doctor, for example, might trace a lesbian's "masculine" patterns of facial and body hair to a hyperactive adrenal gland and believe that removing the offending gland and administering a regimen of estrogen treatment would make the hirsutism disappear. Treating the patient with estrogen, so the logic went, would also reverse her inverted gender characteristics and thus eliminate her homosexual tendencies. In the first half of the twentieth century, surgical and hormonal interventions for homosexual women and men may have numbered in the thousands.

But what, exactly, was meant by Bentley's doctor's diagnosis of "infantile" genitals? Are the genitals of a fourteen-year-old girl in fact significantly different from those of an adult woman? Do the labia and clitoris grow to Olympic proportions after the age of fifteen? Surely any young woman with a handy compact mirror could see through such patent distortions of gynecological information.

Yet under the painful influence of the oppressive expectations that dominated biological and psychological discussions of gender in the 1950s, physicians like Bentley's could exploit such causal connections between putatively small genitalia and sexual orientation. They could use specious claims about "infantile" genitals to push through a hormonal agenda predicated on normalizing her body. Indeed, Bentley's doctor probably assumed that her depressed estrogen supply not only had caused her allegedly dysfunctional genitalia but ultimately caused her homosexuality and unhappiness. If her heroic gynecologist could straighten out Bentley's hormonal system, so the logic went, then her genitalia would mature and she would be put solidly on the path toward heterosexuality in mind as well as in body. Assuming that the balance of a woman's personality and an authentic gender identity were not only co-dependent but inextricably linked, maturing Bentley's sex organs was thought to be the ultimate cure for her domestic woes as well as for her spiritual ones.

In her defense of the estrogen treatments she pursued, Bentley identified her medical transformation as an attempt to reckon with her unhealthy past. "Throughout the world," she declared, "there are thousands of us furtive humans who have created for ourselves a fantasy as old as civilization itself: a fantasy which enables us, if only temporarily, to turn our back on the hard realism of life." It is worth paying close attention to the language in such passages. Bentley's use of "hard realism" would have been consonant with the ideas circulating in certain psychotherapeutic circles during the 1940s. Modern psychological discourse maintained that homosexuality was an arrested stage of development in human sexual functioning that, as Alan Turing's organotherapy supposedly demonstrated, could be neutralized if not overcome through a regimen of hormones. Yet the delicacy with which Bentley revealed the story of her life and labia may not have been the only reason she chose to speak so euphemistically about herself and her body. Her story of heterosexual triumph, and her commitment to the medical erasure of an earlier version of her body, would have been quite satisfying to *Ebony*'s target audience. The phrase "the hard realism of life," a statement of putative maturity, also reflected the postwar era's increasing emphasis on sobriety and realistic behavior, a time when individuals were expected to find personal meaning through civic duty and obligation to the social order.

In her narrative, Bentley described her lesbian life before hormone treatments as one filled with "a brooding self-condemnation, a sense of not being as good as the next person, a feel[ing] of inadequacy and impotence." This "inadequacy," beyond its facile assumption that one could not be a "real" woman and a lesbian at the same time, would have resonated poignantly for Bentley's reading audience. Nothing could have been more antidemocratic in the culture of the early 1950s than "not being as good as the next person." Writing in 1954, for instance, physician Warren Orr described untreated hormonal disturbances among children as potential catalysts for antisocial behavior: "A shy boy or girl who feels inferior [owing to glandular disorders] may be able to find sufficient means of expression to keep him happy. But today, in a world which is drawing closer together, the adult who doesn't like to associate with other people finds difficulty in making a living, and difficulty in integrating with the rest of society in every way."[56] As we have seen in the stories of veteran amputees and the Hiroshima Maidens, the compulsion to be "as good as the next person" was not merely an exploitation of social authority aimed at enforcing physical normativity. The postwar political moment was also one in which Americans had absorbed the potential, rhetorical or otherwise, for medical science to make their private bodies match their public selves. Americans like Gladys Bentley saw hormones, like prosthetic devices or cosmetic surgery techniques, as tools of self-actualization, even if hormone treatments merely traded the top-heavy model of organotherapy that demanded collective commitment to the social order for a more flexible, individualized model of hormone therapy that created a wider but no less demanding set of options for expressing one's commitment to the social order.

Bentley's narrative of self-fulfillment may have been inspiring in other ways as well. *Ebony*'s target audience of black middle-class consumers may have seen in her revelations a barometer of the changing conditions of African American political progress. Since World War I, African Americans had expected the economic and social momentum of black consumerism to be the engine of great political change. Although the Depression interrupted this momentum for many African Americans, by the early 1940s an increasingly conservative movement emerged again within middle-class African American circles, owing significantly to legislative successes such as Franklin D. Roosevelt's Fair Employment Act of 1941. In the decades before the civil rights movement of the mid-1950s, however, African American political leaders and social critics promulgated competing visions for gaining further political recognition.[57] Followers of Elijah Muhammad and the Nation of Islam movement defined citizenship and community as a universal world order of postdiasporic individuals of African descent. This vision of black community, which attracted the attention of young activists like Malcolm X, contrasted with definitions of citizenship and community promulgated by assimilated middle-class blacks during the same period.

The cultural ascendance of a highly visible black middle class during the 1940s convinced many African Americans that their arrival would be accompanied, at least in theory, by many of the amenities taken for granted by white Americans that were previously denied them.[58] With many black workers enjoying well-paid civil service and, during wartime production, industrial jobs, their new economic freedom gave them the illusion that enjoying the material amenities of a prosperous culture was tantamount to legal and social enfranchisement. In the early 1940s black-owned companies (as well as the "Negro" divisions of white companies) recognized this enormous marketing potential and targeted a new wave of black middle-class consumers armed with disposable income.[59] With this new purchasing power, economic observers and organizations like the NAACP predicted, middle-class African

Americans would finally be able assert their proper economic leadership in society and thus transform their social stature. According to a 1956 issue of *Fortune* magazine, in the near future black porters "will live better than the white trainman. [The porter is] shining expensive shoes all day and serving expensive whiskey. What he works with, he wants."[60] In 1960, Kenneth Clark predicted that "as the Negro increases his political power in northern communities he will influence the status of Negroes in the southern states and facilitate the general progress toward full social, political, and economic equality."[61]

After 1945, new magazines from the Chicago-based Johnson publishing dynasty became essential to this vision of comfort and security. In magazines like *Ebony* and *Jet*, periodicals that themselves self-consciously replicated the journalistic conventions and photographic slickness of mass-market publications like *Look* and *Life*, contemporary black life appeared as the most visible embodiment of antiracist democratic principles at work. Diverging from the political and community focus of black news and entertainment staples like the *Chicago Defender*, the *Negro Digest*, or the *Crisis*, this new crop of black periodicals aimed at a national market used recognizable African American celebrities to endorse beer, cars, and hair-care products. Such advertisements depended on the deeply entrenched notion that American blacks had always been, and would continue to be, active, discriminating consumers. By 1952, when Bentley's article first appeared, *Ebony* had firmly established itself as the premier magazine proclaiming a new posture for middle-class African American identity built firmly on the foundation of both black consumerism and cultural assimilation.

Yet we know that African Americans' access to the world of conspicuous consumption during the 1940s and 1950s did not erase the legacies of Jim Crow, either in the South or in the North. Despite new products and services aimed at an upwardly mobile black constituency, many African Americans experienced social progress not through consumerism but through an increased commitment to social justice after the economically lucrative period of wartime production opened their eyes to other professional and social opportunities. Many took seriously the conclusions of *An American Dilemma* (1942), Gunnar Myrdal's important study of race relations in the United States, and as a result, were divided between the seductions of a rapidly changing economic and social climate for middle-class blacks and the unavoidable legacies of institutionalized racism. Even after the paradigm-shattering triumph of the Supreme Court's 1954 decision in *Brown v. Board of Education,* the legal and social realities of "separate but equal" still dominated the United States in the middle of the decade, as evinced by the violent responses to the Montgomery bus boycotts in 1955–56 and the battles that emerged with the desegregation of Central High School in Little Rock, Arkansas, in 1957. This remains true whether the discrimination occurs in overt illegal restrictions or in covert practices such as neighborhood racial covenants or the redlining strategies deployed by banks and insurance companies.

Furthermore, the liberal economic climate that had made much black civil rights activism possible in the 1940s took a painfully ironic turn when consumerism was used against those who had made effective strides in the cause of economic and social justice. As Cedric Robinson has argued, many middle-class blacks were persuaded to distance themselves from the more radical commitments to increased civil and economic protections espoused by working-class black political activists.[62] The NAACP encouraged many African Americans during this period to fight for constitutional amendments rather than take direct action in the workplace through union-led boycotts or picket line activity. Anti-Communism infected such arguments, turning black radicals into personae non grata. Zora Neale Hurston, the famous writer and anthropologist who was Bentley's contemporary during the Harlem Renaissance, was among those who dismissed labor's appeals to a black working-class consciousness. In a 1951 essay published in the *American Legion* titled "Why the Negro Won't Buy Communism," Hurston argued that the Negro was the "ultimate capitalist,"

too busy enjoying liquor, cars, and cigarettes to be seduced by
Communism or the American Left's fantasies of a pan-African
world political movement.[63] In many ways Hurston's article was an
extreme form of the integrationist trend among African Americans
during the period, which in the early 1950s dovetailed with the
mainstream fears imparted by the McCarthyite demonization of
Leftists, labor agitators, intellectuals, and those targeted as the usual
suspects by anti-Communist rhetoric. Labor activists like A. Philip
Randolph and organizations like the Congress for Racial Equality,
founded in 1942, struggled to make white politicians recognize the
basic needs of the African American poor and working class.
Meanwhile, the NAACP and other middle-class black organizations aligned themselves with often reactionary political choices
well into the 1950s in order to distance themselves from unions or
other public markers of radicalism.

By the second half of the 1950s, the struggles of grassroots
civil rights activists in southern states like Alabama, Arkansas,
Mississippi, and North Carolina had begun to make the consumer-
based strategies of social progress advocated during the 1940s
seem like the ultimate in Uncle Tom sycophantism.[64] Writing
in 1957, E. Franklin Frazier called consumerism a form of self-
destructive assimilation, declaring that "Negroes who adopt the
standards of the white world create among the black bourgeoisie a
feeling of insecurity and often become the object of both the envy
and hatred of this class."[65] The tension that had been simmering
between political factions representing competing definitions of
black identity and community would boil over only a few years
later when the goals of middle-aged blacks yearning for social
respectability would be challenged by the expansive vision of young
black radicals. In 1965, an editorial in the *Liberator* called *Ebony*
an "imitation of both *Life* and *Playboy*," a stinging comment that
not only compared *Ebony* to two mainstream white lifestyle publications but also invoked the self-hating racial politics of Douglas
Sirk's 1957 film *Imitation of Life*.[66] By the end of the 1960s, the legislative triumph of the 1964 Civil Rights Act shared cultural

significance with, and was arguably even eclipsed by, the assassination of Malcolm X in April 1965 and that of Martin Luther King Jr. three years later in April 1968. Throughout the 1960s and 1970s, what many perceived as retrograde black conservatism endured regular criticism by radical factions of domestic and international black power activists and advocates for black pan-nationalist movements.

Bentley's *Ebony* article, not unlike Hurston's pronouncements against black radicalism in *American Legion,* could be seen as a poignant moment in the history of black American media. Such magazines, aimed nationally at a middle-class African American audience, made visible the complexities of class politics by showing black American culture at its most reactionary. Bentley and *Ebony,* it could be argued, were equally complicit in following a model established by early twentieth-century ethnic Americans who actively sought ways to assimilate into the mainstream by making overtures to a normative white identity. True, Bentley's primary claim, and the one she believed might relaunch her career, was that estrogen had allegedly enabled her to reclaim the dormant femininity that had made her a "woman" again. But hormones had also enabled Bentley to erase her past as both a lesbian and an independent woman. This claim could be interpreted as a coup for the social norms in postwar culture that conspired to force all women to challenge their bodies in order to assert an authentic femininity. To a large degree, Bentley was not unlike tens of thousands of women who had imbibed the ideal of the superfeminine that Betty Friedan would dissect a decade later in her 1962 bestseller *The Feminine Mystique.*[67] The "problem that has no name" espoused by Friedan's white middle-class interviewees, however, may have been called by a different name by nonwhite women; indeed, "it" may not have been a problem at all for these women of color or poor women. As Bentley's autobiographical sketch demonstrates, the feminine mystique may have provided access to a class stature and cultural legitimacy otherwise denied to most African American women. Nothing could have been more inimical to the formation of black bourgeois identity of the late 1940s than the idea of "not being as good as the next person."

This is why, for someone like Gladys Bentley, forging a gender-friendly body in the pre–civil rights era of the early 1950s was one of the only conduits to a truly acceptable social identity. We cannot assume, then, that the ennui of bourgeois domesticity as depicted by Friedan and others in the 1950s was a universal complaint. Bentley was lured by hormone therapy's potential because it provided instant access to a black middle-class domestic milieu that had previously shunned her. Clearly, the momentum of the civil rights movement was triggered by a world far removed from the one she lived in, a world held captive by the feminine mystique that crystallized around African American culture of the early 1950s. Perhaps assimilation through medical technology could prove equivalent to any legislative act, if not even more important.

## GLADYS ISN'T GRATIS ANY MORE

"I Am a Woman Again" did not put Gladys Bentley back in the driver's seat, as perhaps she had expected. The article's revelations did not return her to the same level of public notoriety she had enjoyed during the Harlem Renaissance, though its publication did cause some immediate ripples. Her blissful, idyllic marriage to a newspaper columnist named J. T. Gibson was apparently apocryphal: despite the photographic concoctions that appeared in *Ebony*, Gibson denied that he and Bentley had ever wed. In 1953, Bentley did marry a cook named Charles Roberts, but the two eventually divorced. In the late 1950s Bentley made an appearance on Groucho Marx's hit television show *You Bet Your Life* alongside an adolescent Candace Bergen. In her final years, having already joined the Temple of Love in Christ, Inc., as a choir member, Bentley decided to place her talents in the hands of an authority even higher than Groucho. She was studying to become an ordained minister when she died during a flu epidemic in Los Angeles in January 1960.

Although little else is known about the final years of Bentley's life, her understanding of estrogen treatments as a status symbol remains a prominent feature of hormone discourse in the United States nearly a half century after her untimely demise. In 1965, for example, Robert Wilson's best-selling *Feminine Forever* was acclaimed as *the* guidebook for menopausal women.[68] Wilson—a wealthy New York City gynecologist who established his own foundation in Brooklyn—offered his services to women who wanted to understand and, more important, to control the effects of menopause. Wilson was adamant that menopause, far from being a natural part of the biological cycle of women's physical maturation, was an unnatural and debilitating disease that could be cured through pharmaceutical intervention. Wilson publicly advocated hormone replacement therapy to correct menopause's "unnatural" state. According to Wilson, the "deprivation" of estrogen made postmenopausal women no longer "whole," but only "part woman."[69] A middle-aged woman could begin a regimen of synthetic hormones and maintain an almost preternatural, if not utopian, physiological state of authentic womanhood. In 1963 he endorsed the use of estrogen "from puberty to the grave."[70]

Wilson's choice of title for his book was deliberate. By appealing directly to the anxieties of his middle-class readers, Wilson consciously set out to repudiate the criticism of the feminine ideal that Betty Friedan had so famously articulated in *The Feminine Mystique*. Femininity, Wilson believed, was not a mysterious force oppressing women but one that could liberate them from the despair of aging. Wilson's book played on the most intimate fears of an entire generation of women in the United States who had been brainwashed by the feminine mystique and taught to fight at all costs for the elusive commodity of their own dormant or temporarily obscured femininity. Wilson's arguments in *Feminine Forever* convincingly portrayed hormone therapy as a manifest prescription for happiness, even if it also sounded ominous, like a prison sentence from which one might never be paroled.

In a brief but illuminating passage toward the end of *Feminine Forever,* Wilson attempted to conjure the image of the type of woman who was likely never to seek the help of a medical professional to deal with menopause. The passage is worth quoting at length, especially for its hyperbolic prose:

For the lower-middle-class woman, the range of available options [for dealing with menopause] is sharply curtailed. She has sense enough to know that, in her restrictive environment, a love affair in the casual suburban style is out of the question. She rarely has the inclination—let alone the time—to occupy herself with new interests such as volunteer hospital work, community service, amateur theater groups, and other activities that might help her retain a positive frame of mind. So she gradually sinks into a state of almost bovine passivity.

Such women generally flock together in small groups of three or four. Not that they have anything to share but their boredom and trivial gossip. Clustering together in monotonous gregariousness, they hide themselves from the rest of the world. They go together to the same hairdresser to have their hair tinted purple. As though they were schoolgirls again, they dress alike and buy the same little hats. They hobble slowly to the delicatessen shop to buy day after day the same cold roast beef and potato salad, for they have long ago resigned from the more challenging responsibilities of their kitchens. . . .

*This picture is by no means overdrawn.* Strolling through any drab neighborhood on a sunny afternoon, you can see such women sitting on the stoops of their houses, oblivious to everything—a total loss to themselves and their families.[71]

For Wilson, class status was what made estrogen therapy biologically comprehensible and socially meaningful. The references to the "sad lot" of poor menopausal women—with their purple-tinted hair, miniature hats, and delicatessen treats—were desperate rhetorical invocations of a culture of not only "bovine passivity" but also utter conformity and deprivation. These predictable images of women with dyed hair sitting on stoops, reminiscent of the working-class culture of early twentieth-century urban immigrants, must have deeply upset the social arriviste in Wilson. Regular access to estrogen treatments, he implied, helped to keep one's social status intact. To underscore this perspective, Wilson recommended the use of estradiol, the hormone derivative distilled from pregnant mares' urine, which he called the "Cadillac of hormones." For gynecologists like Wilson, estradiol users were likely those consumers who could eschew the base trappings of "little hats" and "cold roast beef" for something far more glamorous: an image of consumer sophistication in which a woman riding in the Cadillac of hormones could show off her body as the most necessary accoutrement of robust femininity. Such women needed to maintain a securely female identity as wives and mothers who had moved into the postreproductive phase of their adult lives. Though pursuing volunteer work and dabbling in amateur theater were not necessarily anathema to the consciousness-raising efforts that emboldened a growing feminist movement in the mid-1960s, the guilt implied by Wilson's charge that these woman had abandoned the "challenging responsibilities of the kitchen" reminds us how alluring creative cooking must have been to American audiences after Julia Child's *The French Chef* debuted in 1961. Apparently only women of the better sort had the leisure time to learn new things like French cooking, take the right drugs, and maintain their bodies in the best and most civilized spirit of medical modernity.

Gladys Bentley's journey to become "a woman again" exemplified the same mystique surrounding hormone therapy propounded by Robert Wilson and the women who basked in the glow of his paternalistic advice. By describing her newly heterosexual body as a replacement for her formerly aberrant one, Bentley laid claim to an imagined community of heterosexual, middle-class (and less explicitly, white) women whom Bentley believed to have the same normal physical features that she did. How could she think it was otherwise? Medicine had made it all come true. As her genitals were brought to their full flowering, her physical primitivism—what doctors imagined to be the cause of her homosexuality—began to disappear. Just as some of the other nonnormative individuals we have encountered in this book imagined the new possibilities provided by medical procedures, Bentley believed that she had turned herself from a passive, prosaic victim of anatomical destiny into an active, hypernormative citizen who was unequivocally "as good as the next person." The maturation of her physical body, from allegedly infantile to adult genitals, directly paralleled her shift away from the infantile same-sex eroticism of her wayward youth to the adult phase of her feminine and happily heterosexual identity. Here was a form of medical intervention that provided Bentley with access to the best of all possible worlds. Estradiol, like the fine luxury products that enticed African Americans in the pages of *Ebony,* was the Cadillac that allowed her to drive worry-free to her final destination.

Bentley's hormone-driven biography occupies an awkward place in mid-twentieth-century African American history. During the late 1920s, Bentley personified for many the cultural vanguard of the Harlem Renaissance in both physical identity and professional occupation, and she symbolized that era's celebrated attitude toward creative gender roles and sexual nonconformity. Within two decades, she came to denounce her private bodily identity as well as her personal sexual history. Yet in the few historical works that recount her life and career, Bentley is regarded as a radical lesbian who chose to live her life daringly ahead of her time. Writing a close analysis of the fluid nature of Bentley's shifting identities, Carmen Mitchell concludes that "it is extraordinary to realize what Bentley had accomplished decades before the civil rights, women's, and gay and lesbian movements."[72] According to Eric Garber and James Wilson, during the Harlem Renaissance Bentley was one member of a larger community of openly queer performers of color, creating and creolizing ethnic and sexual identities as a visible part of a public transatlantic black culture.[73]

Visibility and accomplishment may indeed characterize the first phase of her life and the significance of her early career, but by the

1950s Bentley was hardly a radical figure. Indeed, even during the late 1930s when she moved to Los Angeles, she had already started making a self-conscious—some would say opportunistic—break from her familiar past. By the late 1940s Bentley had begun actively denouncing her former lesbianism by pursuing estrogen treatments and, later, by joining a Christian ministry. At the time of her death in 1960, she was on her way to becoming an ordained minister, indicating how far her project of assimilation had taken on a spiritual dimension in addition to physical and cultural ones (fig. 21). In remaking her own body she was able to imagine simultaneously a new identity that was heterosexual, feminine, and Christian, made possible by a body that materialized her desire to enter—though perhaps not her immediate acceptance into—a respectable socioeconomic niche recognized by the black middle-class mainstream.

Bentley's desire has been deeply undervalued in the scholarly literature. Mitchell, for instance, argues that "despite the public retraction of her nonconformity to heterosexuality, Gladys Bentley remains a potent Black lesbian icon." If toward the end of her life Bentley disdained what she perceived to be her abnormal body and sought the medical and social imprimatur of normalization, why should historians persist in reading Bentley as a "lesbian"? A similar strategy of historical revisionism was made in a 1994 polemical performance piece about Bentley's life. Joana "Juba-Ometse" Clayton declared that "homophobia, uniting with racism, sexism, and classism, destroyed Bentley's ability to live creatively and freely. Today we tell the story of Gladys Bentley, a 'notorious and successful' out-of-the-closet African and lesbian artist."[74] Clayton argues that Bentley's postcareer embrace of the closet was one of the only creative choices available to African American women during the 1950s: "The privileged definition of closet does not consider that many African-American women heal ourselves in our closets. In our closets, we create different realities, collect tools and strategies for healing the deep and painful wounds of our multiple oppressions, discover a voice and language that is our life, and unearth and affirm our authentic selves."[75] Was Bentley's identity as a lesbian the only

FIGURE 21 Gladys Bentley, lounging in her caftan, examines a scrapbook of clippings from her heyday in Harlem. Although the photograph suggests a nostalgic walk down memory lane, it also affirms the necessity for Bentley to use "before" and "after" images to underscore her claim that estrogen treatments transformed her from bulldagger to superwife. Published in Bentley, "I Am a Woman Again," *Ebony* 7 (August 1952): 92–98.

one she expressed during her lifetime? If so, why is it the only one we elect to remember? Perhaps our wishful insistence on including Bentley as part of a transhistorical continuum of African American lesbians is as naive as Bentley's wishful insistence that under hormone treatments she had become "a woman again."

More than perhaps any other facet of her post-Harlem Renaissance life and career, the social and medical aspects of Bentley's abjuration of self challenge the mythic status that we often impart to "gay men and women who enriched the world." They also draw her as a much more complex figure who embodied profound contradictions and rough-hewn imperfections and even reactionary politics. For this last reason alone, Bentley's biography demands that we see her as something other than an ahistorical spokesdyke whose later stance may be "forgiven" but which does not alter the radicalism of her earlier life. As Martin Duberman has shown in his poignant memoir *Cures,* the very real experiences of denial and disavowal, despite their self-effacing and often self-hating psychological dimensions, are as much a part of a collective lesbian and gay past as the expression of nonnormative sexualities and identities in those figures that we routinely celebrate.[76] In other words, do we want so much to claim her as a sister that we are willing to disregard and even distort how Bentley understood her own life? Surely as important as canonizing her as a role model for African American lesbians or for African Americans in general is bestowing on Bentley the dignity of biographical complexity.

## FOUR

**Christine Jorgensen and the Cold War Closet**

I'm strictly a female female
And my future I hope will be
In the home of a brave and free male
Who'll enjoy being a guy having a girl like me.

"I ENJOY BEING A GIRL," FROM FLOWER DRUM SONG (1958)

ONE OF THE MOST wrenching moments of Tony Kushner's Pulitzer Prize–winning drama *Angels in America* (1993) occurs during a confrontation between lawyer Roy Cohn and the ghost of Ethel Rosenberg. Forty years earlier, in 1953, the espionage trial of Ethel and her husband, Julius, had helped catapult Cohn to professional infamy. In Kushner's play, Cohn lives in New York City during the mid-1980s, and has been diagnosed with AIDS. In a moment of transhistorical hallucination, Rosenberg appears before Cohn in his hospital bed and proclaims to her former prosecutor that "the shit's really hit the fan." Feeling both vengeance and pity, Rosenberg watches as the dying Cohn confronts his own closeted homosexuality—the specter of which, Kushner insinuates, was part of the reason Cohn pursued and vilified the Rosenbergs thirty years earlier. Cohn's exposure of Rosenberg's secret life as an alleged Communist spy permitted him to displace his own secret homosexual life so that, in his manipulation of the trial, he could transfer his own sense of guilt from himself to the defendants. The execution of Ethel and Julius Rosenberg in 1953 not only achieved the public humiliation and degradation of American Communists but helped to eradicate any associations Cohn may have had with inappropriate personal conduct, whether in his Jewish immigrant heritage or in his private sexual proclivities.

In Kushner's revenge fantasy, the relationship between Ethel and Roy is cemented through this act of revealing, and testifying on behalf of, each other's closeted alliances and subversive activities.[1] Moreover, the loose, surreal framework of *Angels in America* provided Kushner with an opportunity to show how the domestic, heterosexual, nationalistic rhetoric that crystallized around discussions of family values and individual rights during the 1980s was rooted in the immediate postwar period. Many studies of postwar American culture have attempted to show similar continuities between the 1950s and the 1980s, albeit with fewer creative liberties or dramatic flourishes than Kushner's play entails.[2] Historians such as Elaine Tyler May, Stephen Whitfield, and Stephanie Coontz have tried to demonstrate how mass media, government agencies, and religious propaganda manipulated ideas about family, nation, and "American" character to maintain control over domestic political and social behavior. But as Kushner's play suggests, the postwar trope of Americanism ultimately achieved success through what critics Peter Stallybrass and Allon White have called "displaced abjection."[3] That is, in order to secure abstract concepts such as national pride or American character, individuals or institutions had to prove that certain ideas or people were antithetical to dominant conceptions of domestic health, public safety, or national security. To demonstrate publicly how another person was abject enabled one to escape further scrutiny.

The culture of the 1950s was one of displaced abjection in which individuals and institutions regularly turned complex political issues into allegories of damnation or redemption. People could exonerate themselves for their errant ways by either publicly exposing their own personal secrets, or by exposing the secrets of their neighbors. Postwar culture framed these disavowals or confessions as narratives of conversion, ascendance, and political maturity. Some of them included highbrow tomes like *The God That Failed* (1949), which expressed the disillusionment of famous American and European intellectuals, or popular confessional autobiographies such as Whittaker Chambers's *Witness* (1952), Elizabeth Bentley's *Out of Bondage* (1950), Louis Budenz's *This Is My Story* (1951), and films such as *I Was a Communist for the FBI* (1952) and the more (in)famous *On the Waterfront* (1954).[4] Such cultural phenomena— confessionals, conversion narratives, and the multiple closets established by hidden political or sexual identities—seem particularly critical to understanding the Cold War period. Indeed, it is precisely in these circumstances that Kushner's play forces Roy Cohn to confess his true identity—not merely to the world, or to Ethel Rosenberg, but to himself. Kushner's portraits of Ethel Rosenberg and Roy Cohn illuminate the multiple closets people were routinely forced into (or were routinely evicted from) during the 1950s.

As we have seen throughout this book, medical procedures and technologies enabled individuals to emerge victoriously from the closets of shame and pathology into which they were typically forced, and provided new narrative possibilities heretofore unanticipated by the vast majority of Americans. For veteran amputees, or victims of the atomic bombing of Hiroshima, or hormone consumers like Gladys Bentley, medical procedures were not only tools of modernity but represented physical confirmation of one's normative status. The culture of rehabilitation and the novelty imputed to so-called medical miracles encouraged many Americans to transform the material substance of their bodies in order to physically articulate their private identities. This chapter looks at the early case history of Christine Jorgensen (1926–89), the first internationally known transsexual personality of the twentieth century and perhaps the most famous medical miracle of the postwar era. Admittedly, the dual effects of Jorgensen's surgical transformation and her rise to stardom hardly seem consonant with the historical moment that nourished McCarthyism and permitted the Rosenbergs' execution. Elements of Jorgensen's biography, however, reveal the ways the popular media exploited her surgical and hormonal transformation in order to link her to nationalistic values and a modern American identity. For instance, what current professionals in the field of sex reassignment surgery consider to be the definitive (some would say defining) operation for transsexuals—vaginoplasty for male-to-females and phalloplasty for female-to-males—was beyond the scope of those medical experts in Copenhagen, Denmark, in whom Jorgensen had put her faith. The best that contemporary physicians could offer in the early 1950s was electrolysis, high doses of estrogen, and amputation of the penis and testicles.

In the earliest media spectacles that accompanied her return from Copenhagen, Jorgensen assumed her new position as a full-fledged American woman. Like Gladys Bentley, whose story she somewhat mirrored, Jorgensen was now a woman whose femininity could be quantified by her estrogen levels. Jorgensen was able to maintain her celebrated place in the public eye for almost six months, during which time she was known internationally as "the most talked-about girl in the world." But when the media called on endocrinologists and surgeons to define, in layperson's terms, exactly what steps they had taken to transform Jorgensen from one gender to another, they instead announced the bitter truth about Jorgensen's inauthentic anatomy. By May 1953, newspapers around the country outed her as an "altered male." Her supporters were disappointed to discover that without a vagina, a menstrual cycle, or productive ovaries—the biological requirements of all authentic women—Jorgensen was not actually a *real* woman. Within a few months, her social significance had shifted from glamour girl and medical miracle to scientific oddity, psychological subject, and butt of countless jokes.[5]

According to a radio interview that she gave in 1968 to promote her newly published autobiography, Jorgensen did not become an anatomically correct transsexual—that is, did not have a surgically constructed vagina—until 1954, almost two years after her first appearance in the media.[6] By the time she took that last step in her transformation, however, Jorgensen's public identity and reputation had already dramatically shifted. The story of Christine Jorgensen demonstrates why the various media and medical communities welcomed and celebrated her, and why they lashed out against her within six months of her initial appearance. While medical and psychiatric discourses dominated the Jorgensen case from the outset—culminating, perhaps, in the release of Ed Wood Jr.'s unintentional masterpiece *Glen or Glenda?* (1953)—the mainstream media of the early 1950s seized on an alternative version of the Christine Jorgensen story rather than what has been recounted by historians of transsexualism.[7] Between December 1952 and April 1953, the American media refracted the image of Christine Jorgensen through a variety of cultural conventions such as fashion photography, behind-the-scenes reportage, and reprinting personal letters that Jorgensen had sent to her parents and a pilot stationed in Britain who was known briefly as her boyfriend. These provocative references had the unprecedented effect of normalizing Jorgensen rather than alienating her and thus secured her reputation as a sterling example of a real American woman. Christine Jorgensen's early success rested almost entirely on her ability to avoid the question of genital ambiguity by using patriotic rhetoric and projecting a super-feminine identity. But immediately following the revelations about her genitals that precipitated her "fall from grace," the popular media expunged from Jorgensen's biography any positive, romantic, or nationalistic attributes it had acquired just months earlier. Within six months of her initial appearance, the media attacked Jorgensen as pathological: a perfect symbol of the Cold War closet that someone like Roy Cohn, had he not had his hands full with the Rosenberg case, might eagerly have sought out in order to distance himself from his own private sexuality and maintain his reputation.

## I LOVE A GIRL IN UNIFORM

On December 1, 1952, the *New York Daily News* ran an exclusive headline across its front page: "EX-GI BECOMES BLONDE BEAUTY." Beneath the seventy-two-point capitals, usually reserved for events like MacArthur's perambulations around North Korea, was the shadowy profile of what seemed to be an attractive young woman who looked something like Marilyn Monroe. Facing to the right, with her nose crinkled and her eyes opened slightly, she seemed frozen like a mannequin—or, perhaps more fittingly, like an intro-verted celebrity caught off guard by invasive paparazzi. Beneath the grainy photograph was the caption: "George Jorgensen, Jr., son of a Bronx carpenter, served in the Army for two years and was given an honorable discharge in 1946. Now George is no more. After six operations, Jorgensen's sex has been changed and today she is a striking woman, working as a photographer in Denmark. Parents were informed of the big change in a letter Christine (that's her new name) sent to them recently."[8] Inside the front page, read-ers were treated to "before" and "after" photographs of George and Christine, including one narrow vertical shot of Jorgensen as a leggy bombshell, similar in style and pose to the pinups of Betty Grable or Rita Hayworth that George's army buddies (or George himself, perhaps) may have displayed inside locker doors or on bar-racks walls.[9] The *Daily News* printed the complete text of the letter Christine wrote to her parents, George Sr. and Florence Jorgensen of 2849 Dudley Avenue, the Bronx. In it Christine described the pain and secrecy involved in her decision to leave for Denmark and undergo two years' worth of psychiatric consultations, operations and hormone injections.

The *Daily News* first presented Jorgensen's story in a form that resembled familiar feature articles of local and national interest that were common to the media of the late 1940s and early 1950s. The *Daily News* prided itself on being the first newspaper to break the news: indeed, the story of how Jorgensen's story was captured became a corollary to the earliest accounts of her celebrated trans-formation. In one version, which was retold in syndicated ver-sions of Christine's story, *News* reporter Ben White heard about Jorgensen from a friend working at Rigs Hospital in Copenhagen, where Christine had been recuperating for several months following her surgery. Within a few days of White's initial interview and cover story, the location of Jorgensen's hospital room became public knowledge and the subsequent site of an international media circus. When major weeklies such as *Time, Life,* and *Newsweek* seized on the Jorgensen story, they did not fail to reiterate White's professional account of how he got his news, as if to suggest that the resourceful journalist's ability to obtain and disseminate the details of Jorgensen's story was as triumphant, mythical, and extraordinary as the surgery itself.[10]

But Jorgensen was, of course, no mere feature article in a newspaper tabloid—and the *News* repeatedly identified her as a former GI who had served honorably in World War II (figs. 22 and 23). This may have been because the Korean War was already in full swing, so that the residual effects of the "soldier's story"—especially the feature on the soldier returning home after many years abroad—had never really disappeared from the cultural imagination. But it may also have been because in many ways Jorgensen exuded all the insecurities of the conventional (and heterosexual) soldier's tale. From the very outset, the newspaper continued to reiterate the Christine story as a celebrity news item firmly ensconced in the tradition of military reportage, for which there were countless newspaper precedents during the period. The *New York Times* followed the *News*'s lead with a dismissive, satiric presentation of Jorgensen that was echoed in its headline, "Bronx 'Boy' Is Now a Girl: Danish Treatments Change Sex of Former Army Clerk."[11] When *Newsweek* temporarily turned from the Jorgensen case to discuss the war in Korea, an article noted that "not until the end of the week, when the travels of *another* soldier, Dwight D. Eisenhower, broke into the news did the public peek at Christine's private ordeal start dropping from the front pages."[12] When she returned from Copenhagen in February 1953, however, a *New York Times* headline announced, "Miss Jorgensen Returns from Copenhagen: Ex-GI Back 'Happy to Be Home,'" which made explicit the connection between Jorgensen's arrival in the United States and the soldier's return from war.[13] *Newsweek* announced her arrival at New York International Airport in an article called "Homecoming." According to the article, Christine was in a plush suite at the Carlyle

FIGURE 22 Portrait of the shy, reserved Private George W. Jorgensen Jr. during his brief stint as an army clerk stationed at Fort Dix, New Jersey (and not, as some believed, as a soldier on his tour of duty). During the first few days of the Jorgensen phenomenon, this photograph of Jorgensen the GI was published alongside a posed studio image that Jorgensen sent to her parents after becoming Christine. Photograph taken ca. 1945, © Bettmann/ Corbis.

FIGURE 23 First portrait of Christine Jorgensen, looking not unlike Grace Kelley, taken in late spring 1952, which Jorgensen mailed to her parents. When the New York *Daily News* broke the Jorgensen story on December 1, the family allowed wire services around the world to reprint the portrait, usually alongside the image of Private George Jorgensen as a GI. Photograph taken ca. May 1952 in Copenhagen, Denmark, © Bettmann/ Corbis.

Hotel, busily writing her memoirs for William Randolph Hearst's *American Weekly;* she intended her life story to provide spiritual and emotional guidance for those suffering in what she called "the no-man's land of sex," which may rank as one of the most provocative civilian appropriations of military jargon.[14]

Such military invocations were much more than updated versions of standard war stories like *The Red Badge of Courage* or *All Quiet on the Western Front.* Within the immediate context of American journalism during the early 1950s, Jorgensen's military identity not only exploited the success of World War II and Korean War propaganda but evoked the social reform journalism and reportage of the 1930s, when advances in photographic technology were combined with the popularizing of the social document. The soldier's story—his family background, his military exploits, his letters to family and friends—imitated self-consciously the iconographic images of the common man that WPA artists and writers a generation earlier had used to endorse New Deal programs and policies. This is precisely what Walker Evans had attempted to capture in his "Labor Anonymous" photos in *Fortune* discussed in chapter 1. But whereas the conventions of social realism, which reached its aesthetic maturity in the cultural work of the Popular Front movement, provoked a deliberate confrontation with the Depression's widespread suffering and constituted an implicit mandate for change, the wartime appropriation of such common images became a way to conceal and ultimately displace the more unsettling, and less altruistic, economic and political imperatives that motivated the war. Journalists during the mid-1940s such as John Hersey—whose narrative portraits of the Reverend Kiyoshi Tanimoto and the Hiroshima Maidens we explored in chapter 2— became famous for their military descriptions of Douglas MacArthur's troops, even if they were made entirely from the safety of the Time-Life Building in midtown Manhattan. Hersey wrote tenderly about the brave red-blooded American boys conscripted from farm fields, the Dust Bowl, city streets, and college quadrangles. Such portraits were meant to assuage American consumers' eagerness to affix national, familiar, and sentimental qualities to the abstract war statistics that confronted them daily.[15] By elevating the common man to heroic stature, the media were able to achieve ideological assent from the citizenry and could successfully trade the unpleasant images of death and violence for a wholesome, democratic, and ultimately mythologized American masculine identity.[16] Hersey's ability to convey large national stories through the extraordinary portraits of ordinary men, such as Tanimoto, found its apotheosis in his best-selling book *Hiroshima* (1946).[17]

To what degree, if at all, did these journalistic conventions change to accommodate a soldier who had been allegedly transformed into the opposite gender? Major periodicals tended to represent Jorgensen within the familiar strategies of wartime reportage—not to mention the hyperbolic language of tabloid journalism—in order to legitimate her putative realness. Yet photographs and feature articles blurred the distinctions between Jorgensen's dual identities as ex-GI and aspiring starlet. These were highly negotiable, if not collapsed outright. According to one *Daily News* article, "The Girl Who Used to Be a Boy Isn't Quite Ready for Dates," Christine was "a former GI who became a beautiful blonde with silken hair," a tendentious statement that allowed the reporter to endow Christine with erotic qualities ("silken hair") that George never could have possessed (or never could have openly acknowledged) when he was a soldier. Jorgensen's wistful, camp response—"I'm womanly enough to be glad that it is such nice blonde hair"—suggested that she knew only too well what might happen if a soldier made an explicit statement about another man's hair.[18] None of these emphatic comments about her female authenticity seemed to conflict awkwardly with her military identity; indeed, even Christine's parents framed the discussion of their (new) daughter's transformation in terms of military service. In a *Daily News* piece, "Folks Proud of GI Who Became Blonde Beauty," father George declared, "[She] deserves an award higher than the Congressional Medal of Honor. She volunteered to undergo this guinea pig treatment for herself and to help others." Florence Jorgensen expressed delight and frustration similar to those of many army mothers when she explained, "You send a person over [to Europe] and you have a completely different person coming back." When a reporter asked if Jorgensen had enjoyed his service in the army, Florence replied, "Who likes the Army? She was very brave. And she is a beautiful girl, believe me."[19]

If Jorgensen's public representation seemed to waver conspicuously between her former military male identity and her new civilian female one, it was not simply because she could be inserted into the established schema of wartime journalism. Building on the existing conventions of social realism within newspaper reportage, postwar military culture encouraged the news media to quantify and reproduce every intimate moment, every private heartbreak, and every recognizable human experience for mass consumption. In this way all cultural rituals—births, graduations, wedding celebrations, and deathbed scenes—took on a self-consciously performative aspect that softened the more corrosive aspects of military life.[20] As we discussed in chapter 1, successful postwar films such as *The Best Years of Our Lives* (1946), *The Men* (1950), and *The Man in the Gray Flannel Suit* (1954) traced the journeys of male war veterans back to civilian life in order to examine the traumatic psychological, emotional, and economic effects of the war. The war had invested popular culture with a fertile and highly profitable commodity, the human interest story, distilled from the wounded masculine psyche.[21] The media's emphasis on Jorgensen's previous military identity seemed to commingle strangely with her postwar gender identity and thus connected her not only to the genre of wartime reportage but to images of innocence and vulnerability that such journalism hoped to instill in its readers. In a bizarre twist on the standard military hospital scene, *Time*'s initial Jorgensen story, "The Great Transformation," described her "lying in a hospital bed, her long yellow hair curling on a pillow. . . . Christine widened her grey-blue eyes and lifted her hands in a surprised frightened gesture," which made her sound like a cross between a wounded fawn and a soldier recuperating after a bloody battle.[22] The fact that Jorgensen had never seen the theater of battle—George joined the army in late 1945 after the war had already ended, and never served his country as anything more brawny than a clerk typist and photographer at Fort Dix, New Jersey—was deliberately ignored to perpetuate the idea of the beautiful blonde as an ex-GI.

If soldiers were supposed to be stoic heroes impervious to pain on the battlefield, then they were supposed to succumb to human frailty while they were hospitalized, a rhetorical move that helped to make their formerly indestructible bodies more pathetic and thus render the enemy more reprehensible. But unlike her fellow soldiers' bodies, Jorgensen's body was wounded voluntarily, and with complications for which there were neither shiny medals nor elevations in military rank. In fact, her surgical transformation aggravated the image of wounded soldiers' bodies by blurring the male-coded wounds of the military hospital with the female-coded wounds of transsexual surgery. Given popular culture's predilection for images of insecure war veterans and amputees who had to adjust to civilian life, Jorgensen's surgical transformation may have seemed like the logical outcome of military service: it aligned her with the ways traumatized veterans were sometimes feminized, however temporarily, by their physical or mental inactivity. It was as if, by her conversion from agile manhood to fragile womanhood, Jorgensen stood symbolically for the vulnerable American male body besieged by a foreign power.[23] Jorgensen's reputation as a man who had become a woman was secured, not denied, because of these military embellishments on her identity. They were strategies developed to ensure that patriotic Americans would understand her exclusively as an object of heterosexual male desire. Given how far the news media embraced her as a woman, Jorgensen's military identity seemed to coexist peacefully with her feminine one.

Several days after her initial appearance, the *Daily News* featured an article that identified Jorgensen's boyfriend as Air Force Staff Sergeant Bill Calhoun, who hailed from the town of Everman, Texas (a place whose very name might have made Christine feel restless). According to the article, which was reprinted in numerous though often abbreviated versions, Calhoun met Jorgensen while on a weekend pass from a U.S. Air Force base in the provocatively named city of Bentwater, England. "I was on leave in Copenhagen this Spring [of 1952] with nothing much to do," Calhoun explained. "I saw this good looking blonde in a park. She looked like an American, and I decided to ask her." After she took him on a brief tour through the city, Calhoun had to leave, but the two agreed to exchange letters. In September, Calhoun returned to Copenhagen on a six-day pass to spend time with Christine "on the continent"; he remarked later, "I can honestly say that it was the best time of my life." Calhoun claimed it was not until that December, when Jorgensen's medical transformation was announced publicly, that he discovered his girlfriend's special *je ne sais quoi*. According to Calhoun, a fellow serviceman noticed that a picture of "the sergeant's blonde pinup girl" resembled a woman featured in *Stars and Stripes,* the U.S. military's newspaper. Calhoun admitted that finding out the truth about Christine was like going on "a trip to the moon," but he defended his girlfriend's honor as well as his own: "When I met her she was a girl and, as far as I'm concerned, she's a girl now. She's got a personality that's hard to beat, the best looks, best clothes, best features, and best body of any girl I ever met. . . . I consider it a very intimate friendship." The *Daily News* explained that "[Calhoun's] feelings for Christine have not changed but . . . he had 'taken a ribbing from boys on the base'—good naturedly."[24]

What did it mean that Calhoun recognized Jorgensen as an American? What, after all, did an American woman look like in 1952, and by which traits or characteristics would a serviceman recognize one? And what did Calhoun mean when he described his relationship with Christine as "a very intimate friendship"? In recounting the fairy-tale romance of Bill and Christine, several important and suggestive themes emerge, both in terms of how the news media framed and packaged their relationship and in terms of what information was emphasized, or alternately repressed, by such framing and packaging. For immediate consumption, the story was framed as a military romance, in the purest sense of the phrase: a tale of the handsome young soldier who, on leave, discovered the girl of his dreams—the American girl, one might argue, on whose behalf Calhoun had vowed to defend his country in the first place. Their story was so saturated with both the romantic rituals of courtship and the conventions of military journalism that there was nothing about their relationship that could be coded as different or illicit. Indeed, the news was so utterly banal that the mockery of Bill's friends was presented as nothing more than the gentle derision that any heterosexual male might expect from his peers. Yet what remains so intriguing about this episode is that this conflation of Jorgensen's multiple identities seems to have provoked little or no discomfort in the military itself, as evidenced by the prominent article in *Stars and Stripes*. Perhaps this is because the news media's focus on her as a medically engineered woman subsumed all other aspects of her biography. An article from early December 1952, titled "'I Could Have Gone for the He-She Girl,' Says Reporter," offered another perspective on Jorgensen's military romance. In it, *Daily News* writer Paul Ifverson admitted to his readers that "Chris is now a girl I could have fallen in love with had I met her under different circumstances." Even though doctors were still trying to "help Christine adjust her still masculine mentality and to become truly feminine," Ifverson had no qualms about commenting on the "beautiful, emotional, feminine hands" of "the chic, obviously American girl."[25]

The emphatic attention to Jorgensen's American characteristics in both Calhoun's and Ifverson's accounts must be regarded as more than simply nationalistic pride. With historical hindsight, we know Jorgensen was not at the time an anatomically correct female with a surgically constructed vagina. This may or may not have been known to Calhoun and Ifverson. But it was the constant effort to emphasize Jorgensen's explicitly feminine appearance and her externally projected gender identity that simultaneously elevated the overt heterosexual conventions of her public behavior and diminished the covert homosexual implications of her private sexuality.

For Ifverson there was nothing incompatible in his description of Jorgensen's "blue eyes sparkling and her blonde hair in pretty curls around her broad shoulders." And for that matter it comes as no surprise when Ifverson's article closes dramatically with the statement, "Today, Chris looked up, her mouth as luscious as Joan Crawford's, and said, 'I'm happy.'" In both cases, it was the attention Ifverson paid to Jorgensen's femininity that legitimated his infatuation and defused the homoerotic tensions of his description. And it was the same attention Bill Calhoun paid to "the best looks, best personality, best features, and best body" of Jorgensen that sanctioned a publicly celebrated romance that in different circumstances (as an open same-sex couple) would surely have branded Calhoun a homosexual and forced him to leave the Air Force via court-martial or dishonorable discharge. Bill's and Christine's status as a couple was made safe not only through the familiar conventions of military reportage and heterosexual romance, but through photographs, hyperbolic narratives, and personal testimonies that revealed the terms by which men during the early 1950s understood the attributes of American femininity. Just as the media's emphasis on her status as a former GI normalized her new life, her romance with Bill Calhoun normalized her new identity in the face of systemic homophobia fomented by military, journalistic, and family institutions.[26]

In these ways, Jorgensen's routine reiteration of her natural femininity and the obvious qualities of her American persona helped to mitigate any associations she, or even Bill, might have had with subversive behavior or dangerous sexuality. Such rhetorical moves served to reinforce each other, thereby making it entirely possible for both reporters and readers to naturalize Jorgensen's claims to authenticity and displace the social or sexual anxieties that typically would have attended such revelations. This is also why, during these early moments of Jorgensen's life, her desire to be seen as categorically female ("I'm womanly enough to be glad that it is such nice blonde hair") could effectively diminish what contemporary physicians and psychiatrists might have otherwise dismissed as the behavior of someone with a deviant personality or pathological glandular disorder.[27] Although Jorgensen was not anatomically a woman (this was not known publicly), her identity could be affirmed culturally as the material apotheosis of a modern military-industrial nation still reeling from the patriotic fervor of its geopolitical adventures abroad. Jorgensen embodied essentially the story of the solider who in the end defies convention, follows his own heart, and remains happily-ever-after not *with,* but *as,* the beautiful blonde. The appellation first used by the *Daily News* to announce Christine Jorgensen to the world—"Ex-GI Becomes Blonde Beauty"—satisfied the binary terms on which American postwar culture understood gender, and helped to explain what those terms actually meant. The ubiquitous, recurring tropes of Americanism throughout her early case history tempered confusion about her gender status, while her femininity was exploited as part of the inviolable bulwark of nationalistic propaganda that could be used to justify why governments waged wars and put men's lives on the line in the first place.

## THE PLACE OF SKULLS, OR THE NO-MAN'S-LAND OF SEX

Jorgensen's military reputation and domesticated personality carried potent rhetorical strength. Clearly, the media's attention to her natural female character traits gave audiences a familiar conceptual framework for the physical and even perhaps the philosophical dilemmas posed by her new identity. But it also served to clear up the confusion voiced by some of the more disconcerted members of the press, who were unable to imagine Jorgensen's transformation within the terms established by socially prescribed gender roles. During her first interview from her Copenhagen hospital room, for example, *Time* reported that Christine was forced to field questions such as, "Do you sleep in a nightgown or pajamas?" "Do you still have to shave?" and "Are your interests male or female? I mean, are you interested in, say, needlework, rather than a ball game?"[28] One reporter, in a slightly more hostile tone, observed that Jorgensen "lit a cigarette like a girl, husked 'Hello' and tossed off a Bloody Mary like a guy, then opened her fur coat. Jane Russell has nothing to worry about."[29]

From the very beginning, Jorgensen's external features were the most vigorously contested aspect of her personality, needing constant attention and affirmation. Her clothes and mannerisms—her personal habits or effects that could be enumerated, through which she could articulate her femininity—were at least as important as what she said or which boyfriend she was currently dating. Rather than passively allowing her image to be manipulated by news agencies or journalistic conventions, however, Jorgensen herself played an extremely important part in producing and disseminating her own identity. Like a good politician, she knew how to mobilize personal integrity and public virtue to manage her image. As a media star, Jorgensen herself was amazingly good at structuring the way she dressed and what she said in public. After her return from Copenhagen, the *New York Times* noted, "Wearing a loose fitting nutria coat and carrying a mink cape over one arm, the blonde woman declared: 'I'm happy to be home. What American woman wouldn't be?'"[30] Like her comments about her hair, Jorgensen's poised gestures, expensive and tasteful ensemble, and quick wit—all of which seem endowed with a self-consciously camp flourish—were structured as a kind of physical rhetoric that allowed her to fit comfortably within the limits of the heterosexual imagination. Only the fiercest drag queen might venture to dispute Jorgensen's authority as a woman in such passages, since she obviously knew exactly how to present herself, both physically and socially, in order to pass according to the cultural tenets of American womanhood.[31] For these reasons, most accounts of Jorgensen's public appearances during this period did not fail to mention, and consequently reify, her innumerable female accoutrements, which were repeatedly couched in the familiar, glamorous language of fashion journalism. The *Daily News* reported that Jorgensen was "dressed in a sophisticated tailored black suit. . . . Christine used pearls as the only jewelry to relieve the severe black of her costume. A pearl cluster adorned the side of her black hat and another cluster her high-collared blouse. Pearl earclips added the final, brightening touch. . . . [She was] manifestly pleased at the attention bestowed on her feminine charm."[32]

If the public seemed to scrutinize Jorgensen unceasingly, it is because she self-consciously confused or collapsed those social gestures and mannerisms that, in the early 1950s, were thought to be the outward signs of masculinity and femininity. Comments such as "I am very happy to be a woman" and "I'm just a natural girl" were inherently strategies of self-promotion, but Christine also used them to challenge and parody the assumptions that people brought, often cynically, to her new life.[33] Such comments not only legitimated her claim to an American female identity but refuted the homosexual innuendo involved in such a claim. Jorgensen's self-promotion, not unlike Gladys Bentley's, was predicated almost entirely on exploiting the performative, or theatrical, aspects of what constituted a female gender identity.[34] Her clothes, gestures, and physical presence became openly dramatized events that were buttressed by the media's perpetual retelling or reenactment of the myths and secrets that surrounded her life story. Moreover, Jorgensen's newly constructed persona functioned as a public disavowal of her former male identity, of her former life as a soldier, and of whatever physical or psychological male attributes she still felt burdened with. Whether intended or not, Jorgensen's self-generated female virtues, and her self-styled vampish behavior, distanced her not only from the dangerous sexual implications of her surgery but also from her unglamorous, unsexy former life as the son of a Bronx carpenter.

Clothing and mannerisms, however, were only part of Jorgensen's strategy to authenticate herself as a legitimate woman. To be exonerated from possible associations with antisocial behavior, which Christine was in perpetual danger of exposure to, required ceremony and ritual, and in this regard Jorgensen was no different from any of her Cold War contemporaries. While she may have performed a coherent gender identity through her external appearance, it was on the question of Christine's soul that the jury was still out. The letter she wrote to her parents in the summer of 1952 serves as a highly accessible inroad on the Jorgensen phenomenon (fig. 24). As a cultural artifact in its own right, it also speaks to many of the questions of authenticity raised by Jorgensen's own public displays and announcements.[35]

At first glance, the letter bears an unfaltering resemblance to what is now called, in popular parlance, a coming-out letter: a claim, defense, or partial explanation for her struggle with, and triumph over, her gender identity. "Right from the beginning," Jorgensen announced, "I realized that I was working toward the release of myself from a life I knew would always be foreign to me. Just how does a child tell its parents such a story as this?" Yet given the delicacy, poignancy, and emotional investment one would normally expect from a such a life-altering document, its narrative content seems anything but private or domestic. Nothing in Jorgensen's letter strikes one as particularly cryptic or inaccessible in the way intimate family correspondence often is; that is, no editorial annotations are necessary to clarify her meaning. Indeed, Christine's words bear a remarkable similarity to those of Gladys Bentley, whose writing was also intended for public consumption. Like Bentley, Jorgensen tried to find the most eloquent and soul-searching method of explaining her decision to seek medical help and undergo estrogen treatments:

Sometimes a child is born and to all outward appearances seems to be of a certain sex. During childhood, nothing is noticed; but at the time of puberty, where the sex hormones come into action, the chemistry of the body seems to take an opposite turn and chemically the child is not of the supposed sex, but rather of the opposite sex. . . . I was one of those people. . . . It was not an easy fact to face but only for the happiness it brought me I should not have had the strength to go through these two years. . . . I am still the same old Brud, but, my dears, nature made a mistake which I have had corrected and now I am your daughter.

Jorgensen's prose—deliberately honest, familiar, and reassuring—was more than simply calculated to assuage the confusion and anxieties presumably produced by her physical appearance. The letter's goal was to seize the voice of reason and the language of confession: its stylistic conventions, readerly expectations, and utterly predictable language would be familiar to any audience, including Jorgensen's parents. Like Christine herself, the body of the text seems carefully and self-consciously constructed from the inside out, with a public audience and its bewildered reception firmly in mind. Jorgensen's letter invoked this generic language and tone precisely because she herself expected—and rightly so—that this was what her readers, parents and tabloids alike would want to hear in a description of a postoperative recipient of sex reassignment. One anticipates the buildup to the revelation, the protracted explanations of circumstance ("I was one of those people") mixed with wispy camp flourishes ("my dears"). Anything more unfamiliar or cryptic might have placed Christine's case beyond the reach, both intellectually and morally, of her parents' affection, not to mention the discriminating palate of mass culture.

In these and many other passages, Christine demonstrated her obvious compulsion to explain herself and choose a singular life from the enigmatic haze of her formerly ambiguous gender identity. Jorgensen's words combined the implicit desire for immediate control with the explicit desire to generalize about, and therefore avoid, external pressures and problems, so that her decision to change her gender became a positive choice that brought with it the ever elusive commodity of personal happiness. "Life is a strange affair and seems to be stranger as we experience more of it," Jorgensen meditated. [We] strive through science to answer the great question of 'Why'—Why did it happen, where did something go wrong and, last but not least, what can we do to prevent it and cure it if it has already happened?" By assuming the rhetorical "we," Christine pleaded for compassion and universality ("We strive through science to answer the great question of 'Why?'") while also envisioning her own anxiety as part of a larger shared cultural anxieties ("Why did it happen? Where did something go wrong? . . . what can we do to prevent it and cure it if it has already happened?"). Jorgensen's prose in these passages took on an almost spiritual dimension: representing her surgery as a type of religious conversion, Christine described her struggle as a triumph of spirit over flesh wherein she chose to alter, through the miracle of modern medicine, the poor hand she had been dealt in life. Whatever other qualities, transparent or otherwise, that Jorgensen's letter possessed, it was without doubt a work of confession, equal parts declaration, explanation, and revelation.

Jorgensen was only one of many public personalities during the early 1950s whose celebrity status and popularity were clinched by the success of such personal expositions about life and career. True, the rhetoric she used in her letter was quite specific, a public translation of her anxieties about the mysteries of gender that made her story more generically familiar, or more accessible or highly prized, to the culture at large. But the letter's confession of innocence that anchored her claims to authenticity also seemed to mirror the rhetoric of other confessional tracts popularized during the postwar period. These were especially popular after 1950, when the onset of domestic anti-Communist propaganda catalyzed the rise to power of Senator Joseph McCarthy and reinforced the efforts of the House Committee on Un-American Activities (otherwise known HUAC) in the first few years of the decade.[36]

One of the most famous confessionals of this type was Whittaker Chambers's epic work *Witness* (1952), which became a Book-of-the-Month Club selection not long after Chambers read sections of it on a national radio broadcast in July 1952, the very month that Jorgensen's parents received the first news of their new daughter.[37] Chambers's embrace of anti-Communist hysteria serves as an interesting departure point for a discussion of Jorgensen. *Witness* enacted publicly the cultural contradictions of the early 1950s, especially as embodied by closet dwellers like Roy Cohn. In exposing and vilifying Alger Hiss, Chambers was attempting to disguise any guilty associations he himself may have had with the Communist

Party. Writing *Witness,* which helped to endear him to the American public, provided him with an ideal (although an apparently common) opportunity: like Cohn with his manipulation of the Rosenberg trial, Chambers could bring Alger Hiss to public obloquy and at the same time manipulate the facts of his personal history. Chambers's book humanized his own identity as an otherwise inaccessible and intimidating public figure who, like many HUAC participants and informers, required a public image sweetened by virtuous recantings and Christian allegories to naturalize and protect acts of domestic terrorism.

*Witness*—especially its prologue, "Foreword in the Form of a Letter to My Children"—used and abused a host of sentimental devices that were as accessible and effective for Chambers as they were for Christine Jorgensen. In the "Foreword" to *Witness,* for instance, Chambers explained to his children his decision to rescue himself from his deluded former life as a Communist. Chambers insisted that "one day [American Communists] have to face the facts. They are appalled at what they have abetted. They spend the rest of their days trying to explain, usually without great success, the dark clue to their complicity." Although such ruminations sound like Gladys Bentley's apologia for her sexual past, for Chambers the moment of political uncertainty was a moment of freedom from the soul's inner torment and the brain's inner sickness: "The Communist who suffers this singular experience then says to himself: 'What is happening to me? I must be sick.' . . . It is recognized frankly as a sickness. There are ways of treating it—if it is confessed." In one deft motion, Chambers's narrative conflated the terms of popular psychology and religious conversion so that his desire for spiritual change and moral rehabilitation became the ultimate expression of his Americanism.

It is not simply that Chambers saw Communism as an illness that could be cured. More precisely, he suggested that Communism could be cured only by enacting or articulating certain patriotic forms that would allow an individual to express the ideological soul of his nation. For Chambers, a true American soul expressed the uniform, religious desire for what he called political freedom: "Freedom is the need of the soul, and nothing else. It is in striving toward God that the soul strives after a condition of freedom. . . . External freedom is only an aspect of interior freedom." This is not so dissimilar from how Jorgensen described her desire to become a woman, which she saw as nothing more than an "aspect of [her] interior freedom." As Jorgensen herself claimed, "I realized that I was working toward the release of myself from a life I always knew would be foreign to me." Jorgensen's emphasis on the "foreign" served the same function as Chambers's emphasis on "sickness" did: reiterating such terms not only permitted the two writers to expose the dangerous, even insidious, forces they had saved themselves from but allowed them to completely evade and displace other questions about the exact nature of their personal histories. Chambers fashioned *Witness* as a highbrow political jeremiad that would win over those who doubted his integrity or the sincerity of his intentions. This explains why and how Jorgensen's letters could, and did, follow the same rhetorical pattern as Chambers's book. Both authors knew how to manipulate publicly sanctioned ideas of oppression and freedom so that their personal experiences, however different from one another, made complete sense within the political milieu of the Cold War.

At a February 1953 press conference, Jorgensen announced that she intended to use her fame to endorse medical interventions for those individuals who suffered in what she called the no-man's-land of sex, It was because she felt, as Chambers did, that she had the authority to offer spiritual and psychological guidance to those in need. The covert, subtle triumph of Jorgensen's narrative of conversion and escape from the no-man's-land was achieved in much the same way that the overt, exaggerated emphases on her former military identity and her real feminine appearance established her as a reputable American woman. Chambers concluded his "Foreword" with a similar authority: although written for his children, it was intended to persuade and sustain those who had chosen to follow his footsteps to righteousness. "I am leading you, not through cool pine woods, but up and up a narrow defile between bare and steep rocks from which in shadow things uncoil and slither away. It will be dark. . . . I will have brought you to Golgotha—the place of skulls. This is the meaning of the journey." Chambers appropriated the image of a vast, dangerous wasteland to describe the journey facing deluded Communists who seek conversion to democratic purity. It was the ideal Christian allegorical space. "The place of skulls," as a physical and spiritual terrain, served exactly the same purpose for Chambers as the no-man's-land of sex did for Jorgensen. Both analogies were powerful symbolic spaces that individuals who desired conversion and change would have to traverse to reach their final destination.

*Witness,* as an affirmation of change, conviction, and spiritual ascendance, paralleled the way that Jorgensen, trapped by her biologically male body, fashioned a new identity consonant with what she contended were her many female virtues. Just as Jorgensen used the confessional to defend herself from her detractors, Chambers seized on the cultural disposition toward public proclamations of innocence and experience to produce an easily digestible (though intellectually spurious) anti-Communist tract. For both parties the physical and intellectual act of confession not only articulated the essentialized tenets underpinning Jorgensen's avowed femininity and Chambers's avowed political maturity but made visible the role that the confession played in the deployment of Americanism during the Cold War. But whereas Chambers's hyperbolic journey resulted in a published work, Jorgensen's resulted in a new gender identity. Her surgical and hormonal transformation did not simply emulate the act of confession. It *was* the act of confession. It was her attempt to soulfully render the commitment she had made, from the moment she understood what she wanted to become, to putting her private body and her public identity into permanent alignment. Her surgery—like the letters she sent home, or like the perpetual performance of her femininity—was the material proof of Jorgensen's redemption from her former life as a man.

## GOOD-BYE NEW YORK, HELLO LAS VEGAS

On April 20, 1953, only four months after the *Daily News* first broke the story of Jorgensen's transformation, *Time* ran a lengthy article titled "The Case of Christine":

For a while, having achieved notoriety, she was Manhattan's No. 1 glamour girl. A blonde with a fair leg and a fetching smile, she seemed to be everywhere that was anywhere, with everybody who was anybody. Columnist Leonard Lyons introduced her to a gaggle of celebrities. Broadway star Yul Brynner and she grinned at each other over a couple of highballs at El Morocco. She appeared in Madison Square Garden at a charity rally sponsored by Walter Winchell, on half a dozen television programs, and was photographed in a soft *tailleur* for the Easter Parade. . . .

Last week came the revelation that Christine Jorgensen was no girl at all, only an altered male.[38]

Within several days of *Time*'s announcement, the media descended on the Jorgensen case and exposed her secret to a disenchanted, and visibly offended, American popular audience. Her secret—that she had not undergone genital surgery that converted her from one gender to another—made her physical and rhetorical performances seem more than patently unreal. It exposed her as nothing more than an unmitigated sham (fig. 25). But had Jorgensen really betrayed the public's trust and confidence? Had she blatantly lied or misled people? Or was she merely caught in the ideological net of Cold War culture, which both framed and consumed her according to its own political commitments and cultural ideals?

After April 1953, references to her former military life and professions of her female authenticity began to vanish from the popular media, replaced by the sober pronouncements of medical science. A May 1953 *Newsweek* confirmed that "latest medical testimony seems to indicate that the now celebrated Christine Jorgensen is not a hermaphrodite, not a pseudohermaphrodite, and not a female. The former George Jorgensen is a castrated male."[39] The article's

FIGURE 25 Surrounded by fabulous gowns, Jorgensen defends her womanhood
at a press conference in Hollywood, California, following her April 1953 outing
as an "altered male." "Danish doctors," the original caption reads, "were quoted
as saying Christine is not a female, but an emasculated male. She would neither
confirm nor deny it." Jorgensen stated somewhat enigmatically, "I don't have to.
There are boundaries to a human being's rights, and good taste." Photograph
taken May 7, 1953, © Bettmann/Corbis.

continuum of biologically coded gender identities, and its pragmatic reiteration of Jorgensen's given male name, not only shows that Jorgensen's transformation was under serious scrutiny but demonstrates how control over the word "testimony" had shifted ultimately from Jorgensen to the medical profession. Jorgensen's personal narrative had initially inspired American readers with the kind of warm, family comfort that seemed anathema to the more formal scientific world of surgery or psychiatry. But as an exposed, illegitimate woman—and perhaps, more powerfully, an illegitimate *man*—Christine had betrayed more than just the trust and goodwill of the American public. Later references to Jorgensen labeled her a "fugitive" who had been "emasculated" to "suit his inclinations," and descriptions of Jorgensen were based, as *Time* related, on "more pity than facts."[40]

When Jorgensen had been identified as a real woman, it would have been unthinkable for media pundits to put her under any kind of scrutiny. Considering the decorum of 1950s public culture, which dictated what was proper or improper to discuss in the public sphere, to openly question Jorgensen's gender authenticity would have been a social transgression far too indelicate for a lady of Jorgensen's glamorous stature to endure. But when medical experts intervened to demystify the tenets of Jorgensen's alleged womanhood for popular audiences, they exposed her as an "altered male"—and, later, a "morbid" transvestite. With the authoritative voice of medical science tempering her popularity, many members of the public found Jorgensen to be nothing more than a female impersonator whose distorted mind and body were confirmed as a reassuring subject for the Manichaean microscope focused on psychological and sexual deviance. In *Angels in America,* Roy Cohn materializes as the self-hating Jewish *feygele* for whom redemption comes at the hands of his manufactured mortal enemy, Ethel Rosenberg. In that one moment when Ethel confronts Roy, the duplicity and ideological terror of an entire age are made manifest in Rosenberg's act of "outing" Cohn, his secret life, and his physical and mental deterioration. Outing Jorgensen, as it were, served the same impulses for Cold War culture as praising her female authority and feminine wiles had done six months earlier.

After May 1953, the ambiguous qualities imputed to Jorgensen's gender identity inspired numerous examples of public animosity. A summer 1954 broadcast of the *Jack Benny Show,* for instance, featured a sketch in which Benny and Bob Hope, dressed as jungle explorers, capture a tiger that, when turned over, was revealed to be a leopard.[41] The Hope-Benny routine was on one level a standard vaudeville sketch about the great white hunter out to capture wild beasts and subdue untamed natives.[42] Far from being merely nostalgic for vaudevillian simplicity, however, the satire demonstrated that the familiar mythology surrounding Jorgensen's early reputation had been replaced by a cultural mythology even more familiar to American audiences (if not more insidious). Hope, taking full advantage of the immediacy provided by early live television, examined the animal's hybrid body and remarked to an especially anxious Benny that the tiger "must have gone to a veterinarian in Denmark. . . . He had his paw on his hip when I shot him. . . . Look, his claws have been manicured."

The simple reference to "a veterinarian in Denmark" as the slapstick vignette's punch line could have easily sustained the scene. Yet Hope's reiteration of "he" and "him" throughout the sketch registered the public's reaction to Jorgensen's alleged failure at persuading audiences that she was a surgically and socially constructed woman. Hope's improvised line about manicured claws also revealed the logical progression of intolerance subsequent to her eviction from the closet of gender authenticity. In her fall from medical miracle to gender invert, Jorgensen was seen as nothing more than a limp-wristed queer who indulged in activities culturally identified as female and therefore effeminate. That the longevity and popularity of both Benny's and Hope's careers rested on their willingness to perform in drag seems, in this context, nothing more than an ironic insight. The conflation of Jorgensen's reputation with the imagined attributes of early 1950s homosexual identity—posturing, vain, dramatic—was the only possible conclusion for the Jorgensen case in the popular imagination. Not only did such sketches transform her into the butt of jokes about gay behavior (she was certainly not the first, nor would she be the last), but they implicitly demoted her to the level of a transvestite, which denied her any of the privileges of womanhood—however socially circumscribed in the early 1950s—to which she so conspicuously aspired.

Although the benevolent treatment of Jorgensen in the popular media seemed to have disappeared, what did not disappear as a consequence of her public exposure was her status as a public spectacle who was forced to tread the fine line between museum exhibit and sideshow act. In 1953 a prominent Las Vegas casino offered Jorgensen a contract to perform in a supper club-cabaret at salary of $12,000 a week. Building on this success, she also toured the United States, Hawaii, South America, the Philippines, Cuba, and parts of Western Europe throughout the 1950s and 1960s. Early on, Jorgensen's act consisted mainly of talking about her transformation, changing in and out of designer gowns while standing behind a screen, and narrating a photographic slide show of her two years in Copenhagen. She also engaged in what the late Quentin Crisp remembered as "jaunty little dance numbers, although she couldn't sing or dance to save her life."[43] On some level, however, she was destined to remain a gender refugee, trapped forever in a cultural no-man's-land between risqué entertainment and high kitsch. In the late 1950s her nightclub act culminated in Jorgensen's parading around the stage dressed in a Wonder Woman costume and knee-high boots while holding lighted sparklers. Although one is tempted to read her performance as Wonder Woman—the all-American comic book heroine who helped the Allied Forces during World War II—as a reference to her former military career, when she identified as male, the performance also demonstrates that after 1953 Jorgensen could earn her salary only by playing exaggerated cartoon roles that mocked

FIGURE 26 Christine Jorgensen does her version of the "Red Shoes" ballet during a performance at Café Society in Greenwich Village, New York City. While her managers believed that dance and comedy sketches at sophisticated venues like Café Society helped to expand Jorgensen's range as an entertainer, such vignettes also helped to crystallize Jorgensen's reputation as a camp icon. Photograph taken April 28, 1956, © Bettmann/Corbis.

her attempts to legitimate herself as an authentic woman deeply committed to her national character.[44]

For much of the decade, and through the mid-1960s, Jorgensen's managers commissioned writers and composers to produce for her what was known in the entertainment business at the time as "special material." They encouraged her to expand her repertoire to include customized versions of popular songs as well as burlesque parodies of *Madame Butterfly* and the Ballet Russe (fig. 26). She also tried her hand at comedy, telling witty jokes designed to show off her ability to sustain rapport with her band and members of the audience. Jorgensen had only slightly greater success with this new material, which she passively accepted as her fate. Apparently her good friend and show biz legend Jimmy Durante had explained this to her bluntly. As she told an interviewer in 1957: "When I first started in the business I told a few jokes, very nice jokes, but I didn't get any response from the audience. And I remember one evening [Durante] looked at me and he said, 'You know, Christine, you could tell the funniest joke ever written on stage in the first fifteen minutes of your act and you won't get a laugh. *They're too busy looking at you.*'"[45]

The Golden Slipper Show

IN DECEMBER 1956, a rising young fashion illustrator named Andy Warhol premiered the first major exhibition of his own work in an art gallery. Warhol's "Golden Slipper Show, or Shoes Show in America," which debuted at the Bodley Gallery on Fifty-seventh Street in Manhattan, was notable for its novel approach to the art of celebrity portraiture. Warhol had conceived of approximately forty celebrities not by rendering them in pen-and-ink drawings or watercolors but by personifying them as exquisitely stylish shoes covered with gold leaf and trimmed with lace from chocolate boxes sold in expensive Fifth Avenue candy emporiums. Warhol, even then a canny arbiter of sophisticated tastes, included a sizable number of personalities who would become gay cult icons if they were not already so by the time he memorialized them: Truman Capote, James Dean, Zsa Zsa Gabor, Judy Garland, Kate Smith, Diana Vreeland, and Mae West. "Where else in the fifties," costume historian Richard Martin observed, "could have existed the fey, gold-leafed fetish objects Warhol made, suggestive of [Joseph Cornell's] keepsakes while partaking of the racket in celebrity relics?"[1]

In early January 1957, *Life* magazine allotted two full pages—printed on lusciously glossy stock for the weekly's mass readership—to many spectacular examples of Warhol's podiatric art.[2] Even the straightest arrow had to marvel at the texture and imagination of Warhol's shoes, let alone the glory and grandeur of the gold leaf, a material more suited to ancient Buddhist temples or medieval illuminated manuscripts than to middlebrow weeklies. But what, exactly, was Warhol trying to say about these celebrities by way of their shoes? What did it mean, for example, that the full-figured Mae West was depicted as a delicate pump resting on a spindly heel? Or that Elvis Presley was characterized as a gold-encrusted pirate boot? These were images that had nothing to do with the images that the celebrities, their agents, or the Hollywood system cultivated in the popular media. So was the shoe merely a reference to a surreptitious fetish that the celebrity kept from public view? Or did it represent some fundamental truth about each celebrity's identity after they had been exposed to the cold light of day?

One celebrity portrait that was *not* included in the *Life* spread was that of Christine (née George) Jorgensen, the Bronx-bred former GI who achieved international status as the first American man to become a woman. *Life*'s omission of Jorgensen from the roster of famous footwear was certainly not a result of her lack of fame. Jorgensen was as well known as any of the public figures she kept company with at the Bodley Gallery, especially since she had been known for years as "the most talked-about girl in the world." Perhaps it was the way Warhol had chosen to represent Jorgensen that decided *Life*'s omission. She was the sole celebrity Warhol had depicted as two separate shoes. The two shoes seemed innocent enough, gingerly touching at the heels like the feet of a adolescent girl trying to cultivate an image of graceful femininity. Yet one of the shoes wore a cameo brooch, while the other—pointing across the canvas in an opposing direction—sported a bulbous gold leaf butterfly looking suspiciously like a penis and testicles. The visual confection seemed to imagine Jorgensen as a fusion of gendered characteristics rather a differentiation of gender roles, which Jorgensen and her supporters insisted was at the core of her transformation. As art critic Trevor Fairbrother has argued, "The shoes are mismatched and seem to be different sizes, suggesting Jorgensen's various dualities."[3]

One could argue that the sensibility that permeated Warhol's portraits depended, among other things, on the cultural syntax of camp, the privileged vocabulary of ironic play defined by Susan

Sontag in her influential 1964 essay "Notes on Camp," in which the critic famously observed that camp was the "answer to the problem [of] how to be a dandy in an age of mass culture."[4] The shoe portrait of Jorgensen as a pair of glittery pumps seemed to emphasize one other aspect of Warhol's dandyism: in camp, there is nothing "natural" about the body. Instead, what is deemed natural is only a false front that makes visible the inherent disconnect between the body we show in public and the one we hold in private. The disjunction between how one identifies one's body and how one performs one's body in public—an instantly recognizable strategy of survival for those who experience the world through some form of nonnormative subjectivity—is essential to the language of camp, the winking parody and ironic double entendre of which Warhol's shoe portraits are perfect examples.

Warhol's approach was not new, and certainly not new among those who identified as members of the avant-garde. In a media-saturated culture, representations of celebrities that depend on the constant dissemination of their bodies will always overpower (or possibly be at odds with) what a given individual does or says, making their physical bodies equivalent to their professional reputation, if not more important. In the 1930s, for instance, German artists such as John Heartfield and Hannah Höch applied this notion to their photomontages of Adolf Hitler and other members of the Third Reich. But whereas their photomontage portraits conveyed the increasing horror of German citizens who opposed the Nazis, Warhol's portraits were also commentaries on the idea of celebrity itself. In the 1930s political propagandists like Heartfield and Höch manipulated public images to define an overtly political consciousness rather than an exclusively aesthetic one. In the postwar era, however, camp's manipulations of the codes of popular culture served an entirely different constituency. As Andrew Ross has argued, in the 1950s camp's power resided in its reverence for outdated cultural forms or genres that no longer possessed immediate ideological power but instead exposed the artifice of whatever power they had heretofore contained. Warhol's famous 1960s portraits of

Jackie Kennedy, Marilyn Monroe, and Elizabeth Taylor were, according to Ross, "trashy tributes to the demise of the star system, while the images themselves were created by means of the mass production techniques endemic to the making of that star system."[5] But even in his earlier works, Warhol reduced the representation of his celebrities to symbols that simultaneously conveyed the power of celebrity and the elasticity of its authority by overlapping the complex cultural meanings of celebrity with the aesthetic codes of camp. Rather than turning Elvis into a logical metonym of his own life—a guitar, for instance, or a pomaded coiffure—Warhol recognized the delicious transgression that resided in turning one of the world's most famous entertainers into a pirate boot, a theatrical accoutrement that was as far as possible from Elvis's own popular image.

Jorgensen, too, seemed initially to understand the language of camp. Like Warhol, she knew how to subvert the codes of fame and celebrity, all the while embracing their mythic power. During her first few days in the spotlight, for instance, she was often quoted as saying, "I'm just a natural girl," which in the early 1950s might as well have meant that she was a lifelong devotee of Ivory soap.[6] But while Jorgensen claimed that her private body and public identity were no longer in direct conflict, the telltale traces of that conflict emerged in the jokes and double entendres through which the general public perceived her sex reassignment surgery. For all her claims to the "natural," Jorgensen's transformation did nothing but highlight the transparency of the natural body, since medical science now offered a method of aligning one's body with what one believed it truly was. Unknown even to her, the juxtaposition of Jorgensen's achievement of fame and glamour and her commitment to her reputation as a "natural girl"—an outmoded way of understanding femininity in the age of medical transformation—was essential to her reputation as a camp icon.

Warhol's gold-leaf fantasia intended to distill meaning from the relation between Jorgensen's public image and her private body, perhaps because he saw some of Jorgensen's dualities in himself. The Czechoslovakian American Warhola chose the more easily digestible Warhol for himself in much the same way that the Danish American Jorgensen chose her new name in honor of Dr. Christian Hamburger, the Copenhagen endocrinologist who offered her the opportunity to undergo sex reassignment. Their shared middle-class roots, and the obsessions and limitations of their youths in the 1930s and their coming of age in the 1940s, not only had affected their formative years but also had shaped the content of their professional lives in profound ways. Both the Bronx-bred Jorgensen and Warhol, Pittsburgh's most awkward son, aspired to a kind of international celebrity style that would enable them to pursue their respective interests. Warhol's fascination with expensive women's shoes was a coherent expression of the glamorous lifestyle he idealized in his artwork in much the same way that Jorgensen's sartorial affectations—wearing designer gowns, mink coats, and dazzling jewelry—were coherent expressions of her femininity when she was understood as a biological woman.

Both Warhol and Jorgensen also used the latest medical procedures to reconcile the physical and psychological tensions that seemed to exist between their private and public selves and that they believed inhibited them from leading normal lives. In 1957, shortly after the Bodley Gallery show, Warhol underwent elective surgery to reshape his nose; soon afterward he began his lifelong practice of wearing artificial hair. Like the thousands of others who sought out rhinoplasty in the 1950s, Warhol believed this medical intervention would solve his social and psychological problems, as the popular magazines and medical journals of the era concurred. By undergoing a nose job, Warhol wanted to replace his most ethnically identifiable body part with something more compatible with the often WASP Manhattan tastemakers who helped pay his rent and with whom he would always maintain a relationship no matter how fabulous he became. Even though Warhol was not entirely happy with the results of his plastic surgery, the theme would continue to surface in his work: from his famous early parody of advertising *Before and After, 4* (1962) (fig. 27) to the cryptic pencil sketch *Cosmetic Surgery* (1985–86), completed only a year before

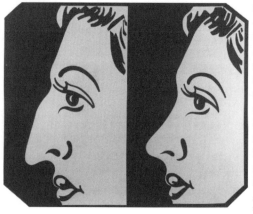

FIGURE 27 *Before and After*, 4 (1962), one of the most famous of Andy Warhol's early silk-screening experiments with newspaper clippings—in this case, an advertisement promising miraculous results from plastic surgery. Reprinted with permission of the Whitney Museum of American Art and the Andy Warhol Foundation for the Visual Arts/ARS, New York, © 2004.

his death in 1987. Rhinoplasty, tummy tucks, facelifts, and other cosmetic enhancements remained cultural shorthand for the vain celebrity culture he idealized.

Warhol and Jorgensen shared a more pronounced connection to medical procedures after Valerie Solanas attempted to assassinate Warhol in 1968. Following the shooting, Warhol's multiple surgical scars become a touchstone for photographer Richard Avedon and painter Alice Neel, both of whom memorialized Warhol's disfigured torso as part of the visual excess of the 1960s counterculture. One could even argue that Chris Burden's infamous 1971 performance piece, in which the artist shot himself in the arm with a gun, was an outgrowth of the macabre embodiment of celebrity spectacle and physical violence that Warhol's shooting provoked.

Jorgensen had a less tumultuous experience reconciling her perception of her public body with her private identity. Indeed, as far as she was concerned, the camp traces imputed to her appearances were the result of the public's miscomprehension. For her there was no dissonance to speak of. She ignored popular distortions of her private identity and instead presented herself as an entertainer, photographer, and writer who was more domestic than exotic, more middlebrow than avant-garde (fig. 28). Her sensibilities were tied much more to the restrained, bourgeois pretensions of her Danish American family than to the jet-set circles she frequently traveled in. In March 1959, for instance, Jorgensen and her then fiancé, Howard Knox, applied for a marriage license at city hall in downtown Manhattan (fig. 29). In what became a much-touted news feature in national and local papers, the New York City Bureau of Licenses refused to grant the couple their wish because Knox did not have the appropriate papers to prove he had been divorced from his first wife. While they waited for the papers to be delivered from Knox's hometown of Chicago, Jorgensen and Knox decided to call off the wedding, preferring to remain just good friends.[7]

BEFORE          AFTER          TODAY

FIGURE 28 This publicity triptych chronicles Jorgensen's evolution from prewar photography student in New York (1943) to postwar blonde beauty in Copenhagen (1952) to established celebrity icon in Los Angeles (ca. 1975). The sexual liberation movements of the 1960s and 1970s encouraged Jorgensen to temper her glamour queen image, but by the time of her fiftieth birthday in 1976, she had achieved grande dame status in the transsexual subculture. Triptych ca. 1975, © Bettmann/Corbis.

FIGURE 29 Christine Jorgensen, in fur wrap and sunglasses, poses with her sharkskin-suited fiancé, Howard J. Knox, at La Guardia Airport in New York City. In the moment preceding the mainstream civil rights era, the name of the airline painted on the tail of the plane offers a provocative comment on the status of the couple standing beneath it. Photograph taken March 31, 1956, © Bettmann/Corbis.

Jorgensen never wanted to push the cultural envelope beyond her belief that, under the right conditions, people should follow certain medical procedures—from plastic surgery and hormone treatments to depilatory waxing—to make themselves feel more whole. She wanted everyone to see that, while George had lived the early part of his life in a gendered limbo, Christine had ulti-mately shifted to the other side with great success. Having already arrived, she was no longer in the process of becoming. By the 1960s, Jorgensen's insistence on a smooth and continuous alignment between her private body and her public identity—her belief that the world saw her as an old-fashioned girl and glamorous celebrity—only served to heighten her camp stature. For those emboldened by the civil rights and women's and gay liberation movements of the era, her static claims to femininity made her less interesting. While many of her supporters during the 1950s evolved into untrust-worthy thirtysomethings, a younger generation had emerged that was more attracted to cultural dissonance than to cultural coherence.

By contrast, the secret language of camp that Warhol had ex-ploited in the late 1950s had become, by the mid-1960s, the basis for pop art's demythologizing of the iconic in American culture.[8] In his "Screen Tests," which lovingly mocked the golden age of the Hollywood studio system, and his fascination with American prod-ucts like Brillo pads and Campbell's soup, Warhol celebrated the unnatural as a site of aesthetic inspiration. Meanwhile, what Susan Sontag had regarded as camp's affected dandyism had been absorbed into a new international language of style that revolved around a heightened sense of play and artifice—from Mary Quant's miniskirts and André Courrèges's white ankle-length boots to Verner Panton's injection-molded plastic chairs and the flag designed by Emilio Pucci that was carried by the Apollo 15 astro-nauts to the moon in 1971. Like Jorgensen, Warhol increasingly disidentified with the role foisted upon him at birth; unlike Jorgensen, however, he became a fluid, ambiguous figure unfazed by normative expectations of gender, sexuality, or even the new homo-sexual masculinity that emerged in the postwar era.[9] Because of this, a specialized constituency of artists, performers, scene-makers, fashionistas, and queers of all stripes and inclinations embraced him. As long as Warhol maintained his status as a cultural outsider (though he remained a devout and lifelong Catholic) who sought

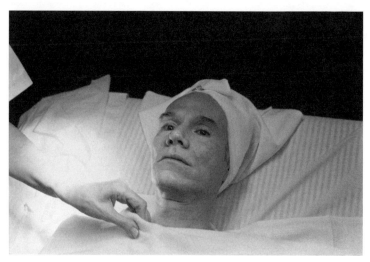

FIGURE 30 Andy Warhol having a facial in the early 1980s. Although this image was probably intended to document his fabulous New York social life, the sterile cotton sheets and austere head wrap, along with the surgical light and the tight grip of the technician's hand beneath the client's vulnerable gaze, suggest that the lure of cosmetic procedures had always been part of Warhol's gestalt. Photograph ca. 1981, © Robert Levin/Corbis.

out and championed the unnatural in almost every aspect of his life, the distinction he drew between his private body and his public reputation remained tangible. Artifice, the direct opposite of Jorgensen's claims to the natural, was the new coin of the realm.

In the end, Jorgensen never would have fallen in with the Factory crowd that gathered around Warhol. She may have embodied the 1950s camp sensibility Warhol thrived on, and she may even have inspired the likes of Candy Darling, Warhol's pre-op ingenue, but she would have never claimed Darling as one of her own progeny. Like her eponymous shoes at the Bodley Gallery show, Jorgensen only wanted to be fabulous but sensible, like Jackie Kennedy, rather than fabulous but reckless, like Marilyn Monroe.

ACKNOWLEDGMENTS

THIS BOOK BEGAN as a mere slip of a thing, an essay written for a seminar in graduate school. It later mutated into an article, then a dissertation, and *per ardua ad hoc* what you now hold in your hands. Along the way I have accumulated a list of more than a few people and institutions to whom I owe a great deal of gratitude for their unswerving support of this project as it has evolved over the course of a decade.

My dissertation advisers in American Studies at New York University, Andrew Ross and Daniel Walkowitz, supported this project from the very beginning and through their example taught me the value of doing politically engaged scholarship. Lizabeth Cohen, Robin D. G. Kelley, Barbara Kirshenblatt-Gimblett, and George Yúdice offered helpful suggestions and important insights during gestation. I also had the privilege of working with the late Dorothy Nelkin, from whom I learned how to be fearless about doing science. The Graduate School of Arts and Sciences at NYU encouraged my initial forays into the strange world of medical technology through a Dean's Summer Research Fellowship and annual travel grants. During the writing of the dissertation, I received helpful research grants from the American Institute for the History of Pharmacy and the Chemical Heritage Foundation as well as a Mellon Fellowship from the American Philosophical Society. The last phase of writing took place while I was a Smithsonian Predoctoral Fellow at the National Museum of American History.

During the initial editing and revising of this book, I served as a historian-in-residence in the History of Medicine Division of the National Library of Medicine. The NLM provided me with a clean and well-lighted cubicle to call home and offered the support and encouragement of colleagues including James Cassedy, Elizabeth Fee, Walter Hickel, Christie Moffatt, Greg Pike, and Paul Theerman. I received additional financial support through residential fellowships from the New York State Archives and the Wood Institute of the College of Physicians of Philadelphia. In 2000, I was deeply honored to receive the inaugural Jack D. Pressman-Burroughs Wellcome Career Development Award in Twentieth Century Science or Medicine. Faculty development awards from Albright College and Bard College have enabled me to reproduce many of the beautiful images that grace these pages.

Research was conducted under the guidance and insight of many excellent archivists, curators, historians, and librarians. They include Jennifer Belt of the Whitney Museum of American Art; Jill Bloomer of the Henry Dreyfuss Memorial Library and Study Center at the Cooper-Hewitt Museum; James Folts and Richard Andress of the New York State Archives; Roy Goodman of the American Philosophical Society Library; Patricia Gossel, Katherine Ott, and Fath Davis Ruffins of the National Museum of American History; Amy Hau of the Isamu Noguchi Foundation; David Hett, formerly of the Peace Resource Center, Wilmington College; the helpful and attentive staff at the Massachusetts Institute of Technology's Institute Archives, especially for their multimedia assistance with the Norbert Wiener Papers; David Hans Plotkin at Corbis Images; John Powell at the Newberry Library; Michael Rhode of the Otis Historical Archives, Armed Forces Institute of Pathology; Leo B. Slater, formerly of the Chemical Heritage Foundation; Mary Ternes, formerly of the Washingtoniana Division, Martin Luther King Jr. Memorial Library; and the fabulous Gretchen Worden of the Mütter Museum at the College of Physicians of Philadelphia. My research assistant, Mark Santangelo, continuously impressed me with his resourcefulness, and his capacity for excavating hidden gems remains matchless. Chapter 2 is dedicated to the late Dr. Bernard E. Simon (1912–99), the last surviving member of the Hiroshima Maidens' surgical team, with whom I spent several unforgettable afternoons in deep conversation about the politics of medicine in the mid-twentieth century.

At the University of Chicago Press, Doug Mitchell, my editorial champion and gastronomic hero, has been an ally since our first tea together on a blustery autumn day in Montreal; thank you, Doug, for your patience and faith as well as your unremitting loyalty. John Howard and Bill Brown provided much-needed comments on early drafts, and their luminous insights helped to give this book its wings. Alice Bennett and Carol Saller, my manuscript editors, performed miracles with a delicate touch. Joan Davies, Renate Gokl, Mark Heineke, and Tim McGovern worked tirelessly to make this book the best it could be.

These acknowledgments would be incomplete without some shout-outs to those whose support, inspiration, and friendship have sustained me during the completion of this book. Great thanks are in order to Ron Amstutz, Matt Acheson, Dave Bullwinkle, Steven Capsuto, Brian Conley, Robyn Dutra, Dan Froot, David Gissen, Deana Headley, Rebecca Herzig, John Howard, Dan Hurlin, Jeffrey Kastner, Nina Katchadourian, Rebekah Kowal, Regina Kunzel, Jesse Lerner, Michael Lerner, David Levithan, Robert McRuer, Tanya Melich, Sina Najafi, Steve Rippon, Frances Richard, Andrew Ross, Alice Joan Saab, Rachel Schreiber, Lynn and Roger Selznick, Noel Silverman, Marc Stein, Robin Veder, Alan Wald, Greg Williams, and Danny Walkowitz.

Katherine Ott, at whose feet I worship, has been my guru and friend from the moment she first entered my life, and it is because of her continuous influence that I see the world with the eyes and conscience of a historian and an activist. Amanda Bailey, my rock and redeemer, has been a partner in crime since our initiations into the evil cabal that was graduate school, and she remains a singular source of intellectual and emotional sustenance. Carol Carpenter is simply the most treasured girlfriend any gay man could ever have, and besides being the funniest *mamacita* on this or any other planet is also the most generous reader any writer could ever ask for. To my mother, Renee Serlin, thank you for all the love and support you have given over the years to your sad-eyed boy. And saving the best for last, I give thanks daily for Brian Selznick, my irreplaceable partner and sweet pea, the person who gave this book its title and so much more than mere words could ever convey. You amaze me.

**INTRODUCTION**

1. For more about this concept see Rosemarie Garland Thomson's ground-breaking *Extraordinary Bodies: Figuring Physical Disability in American Culture and Literature* (New York: Columbia University Press, 1997).

2. Deirdre N. McCloskey, *Crossing: A Memoir* (Chicago: University of Chicago Press, 1999), xv–xvi. Interestingly, McCloskey waited until the mid-1990s before she made the decision to put her private body and public self into alignment through sex reassignment surgery.

3. Nancy Tomes, "Merchants of Health: Medicine and Consumer Culture in the United States, 1900–40," *Journal of American History* 88, no. 2 (September 2001): 519–47.

4. For more about the social and political promotion of consumerism in the postwar era see Lizabeth Cohen, *A Consumer's Republic: The Politics of Consumption in Postwar America* (New York: Alfred A. Knopf, 2003).

5. Henry La Cossit, "Can Humans Be Rebuilt? A Progress Report," *Collier's*, June 3, 1950, 70.

6. "Spare Parts for Humans," *Ebony* 8, no. 6 (April 1953): 16.

7. Paul Starr, *The Social Transformation of American Medicine* (New York: Basic Books, 1982), 336.

8. Stanley Hiller, *Exporting Our Standard of Living* (San Francisco: John Howell, 1945), 30.

9. John Edgar Hoover, "Let's Keep America Healthy," *Journal of the American Medical Association* 144, no. 13 (November 25, 1950): 1094–95.

10. For an interesting examination of the Physicians' Forum, see Monte Poen, *Harry S. Truman versus the Medical Lobby: The Genesis of Medicare* (Columbia: University of Missouri Press, 1979), and Sheri David, *With Dignity: The Search for Medicare and Medicaid* (Westport, CT: Greenwood Press, 1985).

11. Richard Wright, unknown article in *Free World* (possibly September 1946), quoted in George D. Cannon to Ernst Boas, November 7, 1946, from

the Physicians' Forum folder, ser. 1, Ernst P. Boas Papers, in the collection of the American Philosophical Society.

12. Committee of Fifteen mass mailing to physicians, dated May 16, 1949, from the Physicians' Forum folder, ser. 1, Ernst P. Boas Papers, in the collection of the American Philosophical Society.

13. See The Wagner-Murray-Dingell bill, introduced as S. 1161 in 1943, circulated in Congress for several years before the Physicians' Forum lobbied for it at the end of the decade.

14. Mass letter from Ernst Boas to members of the Physicians' Forum, ca. 1953, from the Physicians' Forum folder, ser. 1, Ernst P. Boas Papers, in the collection of the American Philosophical Society. See also Henry A. Turner, "New Power at the Polls: The Doctors," in *Politics in the United States: Readings in Political Parties and Pressure Groups* (New York: McGraw-Hill, 1955), 180–85.

15. Robert Hunter, Ross Anthony, and Nicole Lurie, "Make World Health the New Marshall Plan," *RAND Review* 26, no. 2 (Summer 2002): 20–22.

16. See W. E. B. Du Bois, *The Souls of Black Folk* (1903; New York: Bantam, 1995), 3.

17. See Allan M. Brandt, *No Magic Bullet: A Social History of Venereal Disease in the United States since 1880* (New York: Oxford University Press, 1987); Katherine Ott, *Fevered Lives: Tuberculosis in American Culture since 1870* (Cambridge: Harvard University Press, 1996); and Suzanne Poirier, *Chicago's War on Syphilis, 1937–1940: The Times, the Trib, and The Clap Doctor* (Urbana: University of Illinois Press, 1995).

18. K. Walter Hickel, "War, Region, and Social Welfare: Federal Aid to Servicemen's Dependents in the South, 1917–1921," *Journal of American History* 87, no. 4 (March 2001): 1362–96.

19. Devon Francis, "How We're Healing the Scars of Battle," *Popular Science,* June 1945, 90; emphasis added.

20. See Glenn Gritzer and Arnold Arluke, *The Making of Rehabilitation: A Political Economy of Medical Specialization, 1890–1980* (Berkeley: University of California Press, 1985).

21. See Simon A. Cole, *Suspect Identities: A History of Fingerprinting and Criminal Identification* (Cambridge: Harvard University Press, 2001); and Allen Sekula, "The Body and the Archive," *October* 39 (Winter 1986): 3–64.

22. See Alan M. Kraut, *Silent Travelers: Germs, Genes, and the "Immigrant Menace"* (New York: Basic Books, 1994).

23. For more about the eugenics movement in the United States see Troy Duster, *Backdoor to Eugenics* (New York: Routledge, 1990); Mark Haller, *Eugenics: Hereditarian Attitudes in American Thought* (New Brunswick, NJ: Rutgers University Press, 1984); and Martin Pernick, *The Black Stork:*

*Eugenics and the Death of "Defective" Babies in American Medicine and Motion Pictures since 1915* (New York: Oxford University Press, 1996).

24. See Gail Bederman, *Manliness and Civilization: A Cultural History of Race and Gender in the United States, 1890–1917* (Chicago: University of Chicago Press, 1995), and John D'Emilio and Estelle Freedman, *Intimate Matters: A History of Sexuality in America,* 2nd ed. (Chicago: University of Chicago Press, 1998).

25. See Lynne Curry's "'Lesser Sacrifices': Law and Medicine in *Buck v. Bell*" (unpublished essay, author's collection).

26. Charles B. Davenport and Albert G. Love, *Defects Found in Drafted Men: Statistical Information* (Washington, DC: Government Printing Office, 1920), and Charles B. Davenport and Albert G. Love, *Army Anthropology: The Medical Department of the United States Army in the World War* (Washington, DC: Government Printing Office, 1921).

27. See William Sheldon's two influential books, the prewar *Varieties of Human Physique: An Introduction to Constitutional Psychology* (New York: Harper and Brothers, 1940), and the postwar *Atlas of Men: A Guide for Somatotyping the Adult Male at All Ages* (New York: Harper and Brothers, 1954). For a contemporary example of the resilience of somatotyping in the social sciences, see J. E. Lindsay Carter and Barbara Honeyman Heath, *Somatotyping: Development and Applications* (New York: Cambridge University Press, 1990).

28. Sigmund Freud, *Civilization and Its Discontents* (1930), in *The Freud Reader,* ed. Peter Gay (New York: W. W. Norton, 1989).

29. See Sander Gilman, *Making the Body Beautiful: A Cultural History of Aesthetic Surgery* (Princeton, NJ: Princeton University Press, 1999); Thomson, *Extraordinary Bodies;* Elizabeth Haiken, *Venus Envy: A History of Cosmetic Surgery* (Baltimore: Johns Hopkins University Press, 1997); Valerie Hartouni, *Cultural Conceptions: On Reproductive Technologies and the Remaking of Life* (Minneapolis: University of Minnesota Press, 1997); and Donald Lowe, *The Body in Late-Capitalist USA* (Durham, NC: Duke University Press, 1995).

30. See Gail Bederman, *Manliness and Civilization: A Cultural History of Gender and Race in the United States, 1880–1917* (Chicago: University of Chicago Press, 1995); John Howard, *Men Like That: A Southern Queer History* (Chicago: University of Chicago Press, 1999); Kathy Peiss, *Hope in a Jar: The Making of America's Beauty Culture* (New York: Metropolitan Books, 1998); Siobhan B. Somerville, *Queering the Color Line: Race and the Invention of Homosexuality in American Culture* (Durham, NC: Duke University Press, 2000); and Robyn Wiegman, *American Anatomies: Theorizing Race and Gender* (Durham, NC: Duke University Press, 1995).

31. See Paul Boyer, *By the Bomb's Early Light: American Thought and Culture at the Dawn of the Atomic Age* (Chapel Hill: University of North Carolina Press, 1994); Mary Dudziak, *Cold War Civil Rights: Race and the Image of American Democracy* (Princeton: Princeton University Press, 2000); Elaine Tyler May, *Homeward Bound: American Families in the Cold War Era* (New York: Basic Books, 1988); Alan Nadel, *Containment Culture: American Narrative, Postmodernism, and the Atomic Age* (Durham, NC: Duke University Press, 1995); and Stephen Whitfield, *The Culture of the Cold War* (Baltimore: Johns Hopkins University Press, 1991). Some of the major themes charted by this historiography include the shift from a wartime to a civilian economy and the consolidation of the military-industrial complex; geopolitical containment as foreign policy, mirrored in civil defense as domestic policy; heightened and paranoiac patriotism resulting from anti-Communist hysteria and fear of a nuclear attack; the legislative and social accomplishments of the mainstream civil rights movement; the social, scientific, and legal restrictions placed on gender and sexual expression; the rise of religious and economic conservatism and the birth of the New Right; and the tension between forged consensus and the birth of the New Left leading to a counterconsensus in the early 1960s.

32. For important examples of this scholarship, see Kathryn Pauly Morgan, "Women and the Knife: Cosmetic Surgery and the Colonization of Women's Bodies," *Hypatia* 6, no. 3 (Fall 1991): 25–53; Susan Bordo, *Unbearable Weight: Feminism, Western Culture, and the Body* (Berkeley: University of California Press, 1993); Kathleen Davis, *Reshaping the Female Body: The Dilemma of Cosmetic Surgery* (New York: Routledge, 1994); and Eugenia Kaw, "Medicalization of Racial Features: Asian American Women and Cosmetic Surgery," *Medical Anthropology Quarterly* 7, no. 1 (March 1993): 74–89.

**CHAPTER ONE**

1. See Walker Evans, "Labor Anonymous," *Fortune* 34, no. 5 (November 1946): 152–53.

2. James Agee and Walker Evans, *Let Us Now Praise Famous Men* (1939; New York: Houghton Mifflin, 1988).

3. See Terry Smith, *Making the Modern: Industry, Art, and Design in America* (Chicago: University of Chicago Press, 1994). See also *Fortune: The Art of Covering Business*, ed. Daniel Okrent (Layton, UT: Gibbs Smith, 1999).

4. Evans, "Labor Anonymous," 153. In James R. Mellow's biography *Walker Evans* (New York: Basic Books, 1999), 485–504, the author posits that Evans did indeed write the text that accompanied this *Fortune* photo-essay.

5. For more about the transition of large American cities from industrial to service economies, see Robert Fitch, *The Assassination of New York* (New York: Verso, 1994).

6. Susan Hartmann, "Prescriptions for Penelope: Literature on Women's Obligations to Returning World War Two Veterans," *Women's Studies* 5 (1978): 224.

7. For historical studies of amputation and prosthetics in a nineteenth-century United States context, see O'Connor, "Fractions of Men," and Lisa Herschbach, "Prosthetic Reconstructions: Making the Industry, Re-making the Body, Modelling the Nation," *History Workshop Journal* 44 (Autumn 1997): 22–57. On prosthetics and amputation with reference to British society after World War I, see Seth Koven, "Remembering and Dismemberment: Crippled Children, Wounded Soldiers, and the Great War in Great Britain," *American Historical Review* 99, no. 4 (October 1994): 1167–1202, and Bourke, *Dismembering the Male.* For French and German responses to soldiers after World War I, see Roxanne Panchasi, "Reconstruction: Prosthetics and the Rehabilitation of the Male Body in World War I France," *Differences: A Journal of Feminist Cultural Studies* 7, no. 3 (1995): 109–40; Anson Rabinbach, *The Human Motor: Energy, Fatigue, and the Origins of Modernity* (Berkeley: University of California Press, 1990); and Heather Perry, "Re-arming the Disabled Veteran: Artificially Rebuilding State and Society in World War One Germany," in *Artificial Parts, Practical Lives: Modern Histories of Prosthetics,* ed. Katherine Ott, David Serlin, and Stephen Mihm (New York: New York University Press, 2002), 60–95.

8. See Celia Lury, *Prosthetic Culture: Photography, Memory, and Identity* (New York: Routledge, 1998), and Gabriel Brahm Jr. and Mark Driscoll, eds., *Prosthetic Territories: Politics and Hypertechnologies* (Boulder, CO: Westview Press, 1996).

9. Kathleen Woodward, "From Virtual Cyborgs to Biological Time Bombs: Technocriticism and the Material Body," in *Culture on the Brink: Ideologies of Technology,* ed. Gretchen Bender and Timothy Druckery (Seattle: Bay Press, 1994), 50.

10. See Glenn Gritzer and Arnold Arluke, *The Making of Rehabilitation: A Political Economy of Medical Specialization, 1890–1980* (Berkeley: University of California Press, 1985), and Jafi Alyssa Lipson, "Celluloid Therapy: Rehabilitating Veteran Amputees and American Society through Film in the 1940s" (unpublished senior thesis, Harvard University, 1995), author's collection.

11. More than half a century after the film's release, *The Enchanted Cottage* is still seen as a cautionary tale about narcissism, which reduces the content of the film to its most ahistorical form. According to one online movie review service, the film is about "two people [who] are thrown together and find love in their mutual unhappiness. Sensitive, touching romantic drama."

12. See Arthur Wing Pinero, *The Enchanted Cottage: A Fable in Three Acts* (Boston: Baker, 1925).

13. For contemporary examples of this literature, see United States Veterans Administration, *Manual of Advisement and Guidance* (Washington, DC: Government Printing Office, 1945), and James Bedford, *The Veteran and His Future Job: A Guide-Book for the Veteran* (Los Angeles: Society for Occupational Research, 1946).

14. David Gerber, "Anger and Affability: The Rise and Representation of a Repertory of Self-Presentation Skills in a World War II Disabled Veteran," *Journal of Social History* 27 (Fall 1993): 6. For more about the film, see Gerber, "Heroes and Misfits: The Troubled Social Reintegration of Disabled Veterans in *The Best Years of Our Lives*," *American Quarterly* 46, no. 4 (December 1994): 545–74.

15. See George Roeder Jr., *The Censored War: American Visual Experience during World War Two* (New Haven: Yale University Press, 1993).

16. "50,000 Mark Passed in Drive to Aid Army Multiple Amputee," *Washington Evening Star*, August 30, 1945.

17. See photograph of Wilson and Myerson, *Washington Times-Herald*, January 31, 1946. See also material on Wilson in Bess Furman's *Progress in Prosthetics* (Washington, DC: National Science Foundation, 1962).

18. Arthur Edison, "Iwo Jima Vet First to Get Amputee Car," *New York Times-Herald,* September 5, 1946.

19. *Goodwill,* Washington, DC edition, 7, no. 2 (Fall 1945): 1; capitals in original.

20. Newspaper clippings from the *Washington Evening Star,* probably 1945 or 1946. From the scrapbooks of the Donald Canham Collection, Otis Historical Archives, Armed Forces Institute of Pathology, Walter Reed Army Medical Center.

21. See Tom Engelhardt, *The End of Victory Culture: Cold War America and the Disillusioning of a Generation* (New York: Basic Books, 1995).

22. See Matthew Naythons, *The Face of Mercy: A Photographic History of Medicine at War* (New York: Random House, 1993).

23. *Congressional Record,* 1951, 5579, quoted in David M. Oshinsky, *A Conspiracy So Immense: The World of Joe McCarthy* (New York: Free Press, 1983), 196.

24. See Alan Trachtenberg, *Reading American Photographs: Images as History from Matthew Brady to Walker Evans* (New York: Noonday, 1989). See also Michael Rhode, *Index to Photographs of Surgical Cases and Specimens and Surgical Photographs,* 3rd ed. (Washington, DC: Otis Historical Archives, Armed Forces Institute of Pathology, Walter Reed Army Medical Center, 1996).

25. Kathy Newman, "Wounds and Wounding in the American Civil War: A Visual History," *Yale Journal of Criticism* 6, no. 2 (1993): 63–86.

26. For examples of scholarship in this area, see Leslie Fiedler, *Freaks: Myths and Images of the Secret Self* (New York: Simon and Schuster, 1978); Robert Bogdan, *Freak Show: Presenting Human Oddities for Amusement and Profit* (Chicago: University of Chicago Press, 1987); Rosemarie Garland Thomson, ed., *Freakery: Cultural Spectacles of the Extraordinary Body* (New York: New York University Press, 1996); and Rosamond Purcell, *Special Cases: Natural Anomalies and Historical Monsters* (San Francisco: Chronicle Books, 1997).

27. Detlev W. Bronk, foreword to *Human Limbs and Their Substitutes* (1954; New York: Hafner, 1968), iv.

28. Wilfred Lynch, *Implants: Reconstructing the Human Body* (New York: Van Nostrand Reinhold, 1982), 1.

29. For more about the uses of new products developed in tandem with postwar materials science, see *Proceedings of the International Symposium on the Application of Automatic Control in Prosthetic Design* (Belgrade, Yugoslavia, 1962).

30. Cornelia Ball, "New Artificial Limbs to Be Power-Driven," *Washington Daily News*, August 27, 1945.

31. All material on Milton Wirtz and the Naval Graduate Dental Center is from the collection of the Division of Science, Medicine, and Society, National Museum of American History, Smithsonian Institution, Washington, DC.

32. Miles Anderson and Raymond Sollars, *Manual of Above-Knee Prosthesis for Physicians and Therapists* (Los Angeles: University of California School of Medicine Program, 1957), 40.

33. Army psychologists who feared that one bad apple could spoil the whole bunch taunted recruits with effeminate mannerisms and "code words" perceived to be the performative gestures and underground lingo of a vast homosexual conspiracy. The military also administered urine tests to determine whether soldiers' bodies had appropriate levels of testosterone and rejected those with too much estrogen. See "Homosexuals in Uniform," *Newsweek,* June 9, 1947, reprinted in Larry Gross and James Woods, eds., *The Lesbian and Gay Reader in Media, Society, and Politics* (New York: Columbia University Press, 1999), 78.

34. Allan Bérubé, *Coming Out Under Fire: The History of Gay Men and Women in World War Two* (New York: Free Press, 1990).

35. New York University College of Engineering Research Division, *The Function and Psychological Suitability of an Experimental Hydraulic Prosthesis for Above-the-Knee Amputees,* National Research Council Report 115.15 (New York: NYU/Advisory Committee on Artificial Limbs, 1953), 48; emphasis added.

36. Donald Kerr and Signe Brunnstrom, *Training of the Lower Extremity Amputee* (Springfield, IL: C. C. Thomas, 1956), vii, 3–4.

37. Quoted in Steven Hall, "Amputees Find Employers Want Only Supermen," *Washington Daily News,* October 2, 1947.

38. Louise Maxwell Baker, *Out on a Limb* (New York: McGraw-Hill, 1946), 37.

39. See, for example, Serge Guibault, *How New York Stole the Idea of Modern Art* (Chicago: University of Chicago Press, 1983), or Robert Haddow's discussion of the circulation of American objects during the Cold War in *Pavilions of Plenty: Exhibiting American Culture Abroad in the 1950s* (Washington, DC: Smithsonian Institution Press, 1997).

40. For an interesting discussion of pinup girls as domestic politics, see Robert B. Westbrook, "'I Want a Girl, Just Like the Girl, That Married Harry James': American Women and the Problem of Political Obligation in World War Two," *American Quarterly* 42 (December 1990): 587–614.

41. See Barbara Ehrenreich, *The Hearts of Men: American Dreams and the Flight from Commitment* (Garden City, NY: Anchor Books, 1983). See also Angel Kwolek-Folland, "Gender, Self, and Work in the Life Insurance Industry, 1880–1930," in *Work Engendered: Toward a New History of American Labor,* ed. Ava Baron (Ithaca, NY: Cornell University Press, 1991). For historical background on the image of the white-collar corporate organization man, see C. Wright Mills, *White Collar* (New York: Oxford University Press, 1951), and William H. Whyte, *The Organization Man* (New York: Simon and Schuster, 1954).

42. See Ellen Herman, *The Romance of American Psychology: Political Culture in the Age of Experts* (Berkeley: University of California Press, 1994), and David Riesman, Nathan Glazer, and Reuel Denney, *The Lonely Crowd: A Study of the Changing American Character* (1950; Garden City, NY: Doubleday, 1953).

43. Anderson and Sollars, *Manual of Above-Knee Prosthesis for Physicians and Therapists,* 20.

44. New York University College of Engineering Research Division, *Function and Psychological Suitability of an Experimental Hydraulic Prosthesis for Above-the-Knee Amputees,* 21–22.

45. See Elspeth Brown, "The Prosthetics of Management: Motion Study, Photography, and the Industrialized Body in World War I America," in *Artificial Parts, Practical Lives: Modern Histories of Prosthetics,* ed. Katherine Ott, David Serlin, and Stephen Mihm (New York: New York University Press, 2002), 179–219. See also Rabinbach, *Human Motor,* esp. 280–88, and Michael Adas, *Machines as the Measure of Men: Science, Technology, and Ideologies of Western Dominance* (Ithaca, NY: Cornell University Press, 1989).

46. Ralph Parkman, *The Cybernetic Society* (New York: Pergamon Press, 1972), 215.

47. Norbert Wiener, "The Second Industrial Revolution and the New Concept of the Machine" (manuscript dated September 13, 1949), from folder 619, Norbert Wiener Papers, Institute Archives, Massachusetts Institute of Technology.

48. For further exploration see Peter Galison's important essay "The Ontology of the Enemy: Norbert Wiener and the Cybernetic Vision," *Critical Inquiry* 21 (Autumn 1994): 228–66.

49. Sandra Tanenbaum, *Engineering Disability: Public Policy and Compensatory Technology* (Philadelphia: Temple University Press, 1986), 34. For further elaboration on Weiner's impact on the development of cybernetics, see Steve Heims, *Constructing a Social Science for Postwar America: The Cybernetics Group, 1946–1953* (Cambridge: MIT Press, 1993); Evelyn Fox Keller, *Refiguring Life: Metaphors of Twentieth-Century Biology* (New York: Columbia University Press, 1995), esp. 81–118; and Lily E. Kay, "Cybernetics, Information, Life: The Emergence of Scriptural Representations of Heredity," *Configurations* 5, no. 1 (Winter 1997): 23–91.

50. For further information about the history of the Soviet arm, see A. Y. Kobrinski, "Utilization of Biocurrents for Control Purposes," Report of the USSR Academy of Science, Department of Technical Sciences, Energetics, and Automation 3 (1959), folder 812, Norbert Wiener Papers, Institute Archives, Massachusetts Institute of Technology.

51. Parkman, *Cybernetic Society,* 254.

52. See Amy Sue Bix, *Inventing Ourselves Out of Jobs? The Debate about Technology and Work in the Twentieth Century* (Baltimore: Johns Hopkins University Press, 2000).

53. Henry Dreyfuss, *Designing for People* (New York: Simon and Schuster, 1955), 160.

54. All information about Dreyfuss Associates is taken from chronologies in Dreyfuss's "Brown Books" microfiche, Henry Dreyfuss Papers, Henry Dreyfuss Memorial Study Center, Cooper-Hewitt National Museum of Design, New York City.

55. See Stephen Mihm, "'A Limb Which Shall Be Presentable in Polite Society': Prosthetic Technologies in the Nineteenth Century," in *Artificial Parts, Practical Lives: Modern Histories of Prosthetics,* ed. Katherine Ott, David Serlin, and Stephen Mihm (New York: New York University Press, 2002), 220–35.

56. A. A. Marks annual merchandise catalog (New York, 1908), 226. From the collection of Katherine Ott.

57. Dreyfuss, *Designing for People,* 29.

58. For more about disruptions of gender normativity (and their conse-
quences) in the late 1940s and early 1950s, see, for example, Richard Corber,
*In the Name of National Security: Hitchcock, Homophobia, and the Political
Construction of Gender in Postwar America* (Durham, NC: Duke University
Press, 1993), and Alan Nadel, *Containment Culture: American Narratives,
Postmodernism, and the Atomic Age* (Durham, NC: Duke University Press,
1995), esp. 117–54.

59. See "Playboy's Penthouse Apartment" (1956), reprinted in Joel Sanders,
ed., *Stud: Architectures of Masculinity* (New York: Princeton Architectural
Press, 1995), 54–65.

## CHAPTER TWO

1. For a comprehensive overview of Noguchi's activities in the 1950s,
see Diane Apostlos-Cappadoria and Bruce Altshuler, *Isamu Noguchi: Essays
and Conversations* (New York: Isamu Noguchi Foundation/Harry N.
Abrams, 1994), and *Isamu Noguchi 1931–50–51–52 Japan* (Tokyo: Bijutsu
Shuppan-Sha, 1953).

2. Sachio Otani, "A Memory of Isamu Noguchi," in *Isamu Noguchi and
Louis Kahn: Play Mountain* (Tokyo: Watari Museum of Contemporary
Art/Isamu Noguchi Foundation, 1996), 140.

3. Isamu Noguchi, *Isamu Noguchi: A Sculptor's World* (New York: Harper
and Row, 1968), 163.

4. Noguchi actually designed two sculptures for the Peace Memorial Park,
though neither of them was fully realized. According to Noguchi's autobiographical survey of his own work, the first design Noguchi submitted was a
"Bell Tower for Hiroshima," a seventy-foot tower "from which symbolic
fragments—sun, moon, helmets, bells, and 'bones'—[were] suspended, as
though collected randomly after an atomic explosion" (Noguchi, *Isamu
Noguchi,* 164).

5. For a fuller discussion, see Bert Winther, "The Rejection of Noguchi's
Hiroshima Cenotaph," *Art Journal* 53, no. 4 (Winter 1994): 23–27.

6. Noguchi, quoted in "Isamu Noguchi," *Arts and Architecture* 67, no. 11
(November 1950): 24. For many years afterward, Noguchi sought a public
space for his sculpture—including sites in Washington, DC, and near the
United Nations building in New York City—but his memorial cenotaph never
was erected.

7. A full account of Tanimoto's involvement with the "Keloid Girls," the
name that preceded the more famous "Hiroshima Maidens," can be found in
many sources, the most prominent of which is John Hersey's *Hiroshima* (1946;
New York: Vintage, 1989).

8. Yoshio Hiraga, "The Double Eyelid Operation and Augmentation Rhinoplasty in the Oriental Patient," *Clinics in Plastic Surgery* 7, no. 4 (October 1980): 553.

9. Lisa Yoneyama, *Hiroshima Traces* (Berkeley: University of California Press, 1999). See also Michael J. Hogan, ed., *Hiroshima in History and Memory* (New York: Cambridge University Press, 1996), and Kyo Maclear, *Beclouded Visions: Hiroshima-Nagasaki and the Art of Witness* (Buffalo: State University of New York Press, 1999).

10. For examples of this rhetoric in books aimed at the lay public in the 1930s, see Jacques W. Maliniac, *Sculpture in the Living: Rebuilding the Face and Form by Plastic Surgery* (New York: Pierson, 1934), and Maxwell Maltz, *New Faces, New Futures: Rebuilding Character with Plastic Surgery* (New York: Smith, 1936).

11. Some recent scholarship on postwar Japanese society has argued that the image of a conflict-free, diligent, and satisfied Japanese society (what Herman W. Smith has called "the myth of Japanese homogeneity") was partly a rhetorical myth concocted by Cold War politicians and policymakers in the United States. The myth argues that First World superpowers were eager to transform Japan from a disjointed, awkward, humiliated nation into a model of emotional and political equilibrium that postwar cultures (and economies) around the globe could emulate. While this "myth" may have had all the appearances of truth, the stories of Noguchi's sculpture and the Hiroshima Maidens vividly reflect how citizens of Hiroshima questioned Japan's putatively homogeneous culture during the period of massive urban reconstruction immediately following the war. See Herman W. Smith, *The Myth of Japanese Homogeneity* (Commack, NY: Nova Science, 1995). See also William K. Tabb, *The Postwar Japanese System* (New York: Oxford University Press, 1995).

12. Carl Mosk, *Making Health Work: Human Growth in Modern Japan* (Berkeley: University of California Press, 1996), 88.

13. Masao Watanabe, *The Japanese and Western Science*, trans. Otto Theodor Benfey (Philadelphia: University of Pennsylvania Press, 1990), 1.

14. See Watanabe, *Japanese and Western Science*, and Hideo Yoshikawa and Joanne Kauffman, *Science Has No National Boundaries: Harry C. Kelly and the Reconstruction of Science and Technology in Postwar Japan* (Cambridge: MIT Press, 1994).

15. Sachio Otani, "Memory of Isamu Noguchi," 140. Noguchi's design for the cenotaph was based on *haniwa,* a traditional, minimalist, and deeply symbolic Japanese form that deliberately linked those killed by the bomb with their premodern, preatomic ancestors. As Noguchi wrote in 1950, "When all the possibilities of modern technology are lost, one returns more to basic

things, to basic materials, to basic thoughts. One starts all over again, and I think it good." See "Isamu Noguchi," *Arts and Architecture* 67, no. 11 (November 1950): 24–27.

16. Quoted in James R. Bartholomew, *The Formation of Science in Japan: Building a Research Tradition* (New Haven: Yale University Press, 1989), 279. See also Hideo Sato, "The Politics of Technology Importation in Japan: The Case of Atomic Power Reactors," paper presented at the Conference on Technological Innovation and Diffusion in Japan, Kona, Hawaii, February 7–11, 1978.

17. See, for example, Michael Yavenditti, "The Hiroshima Maidens and American Benevolence in the 1950s," *Mid-America* 2 (1983): 21–39; Lawrence Wittner, "Menace of the Maidens," *Proceedings of the Conference of the International Peace Research Association,* Malta, November 2, 1994, 1–9; and Martha Gaie, "Healing the Hiroshima Maidens: A Historic Lesson in International Cooperation," *Journal of the American Medical Association* 276, no. 5 (August 7, 1996): 1546–48.

Robert Jay Lifton's monumental and award-winning study *Death in Life: Survivors of Hiroshima* (1967) examined the psychological trauma of bomb survivors, including many of the women who were members of the original Maidens group, and was groundbreaking in its understanding of postatomic trauma.

In *The Hiroshima Maidens* and *Faces of Hiroshima* (both 1985), journalists Rodney Barker and Anne Chisholm, respectively, enumerate the phases of the Maidens' journey, including their emotional and social development during their sojourn in the United States. Barker's book reminds us of the deep personal commitment by so many of those involved, either directly or peripherally, in the Maidens project, rendered all the more realistically since Barker's family hosted several of the Maidens during their surgeries.

Historian M. Susan Lindee's *Suffering Made Real: American Science and the Survivors at Hiroshima* (1994) briefly discusses the Maidens project against the contemporary backdrop of the Atomic Bomb Casualty Commission, a U.S.-sponsored research unit established in Hiroshima for the sole purpose of collecting and recording information about the *hibakusha,* the survivors of the atomic bombing. Lindee describes how Japanese and American critics of the Hiroshima Maidens project interpreted their surgeries as symbolic acts of spiritual atonement and psychic repair for the United States' accumulated guilt.

18. Edmund Wilson, "Prologue," in *Patriotic Gore* (New York: Oxford University Press, 1962), xxx.

19. Rodney Barker, *The Hiroshima Maidens* (New York: Penguin, 1985). See also Martha Gaie, "Healing the Hiroshima Maidens: A Historic Lesson in International Cooperation," *Journal of the American Medical Association* 276, no. 5 (August 7, 1996): 351–53.

20. Earlier, Tanimoto had appealed for help to prominent public figures including Eleanor Roosevelt. But the famous former first lady chose not to get involved in so complex an issue, especially since it raised serious foreign policy concerns and questions about American imperialism despite its obvious humanitarian dimension. See Hersey, *Hiroshima*.

21. See Selma Robinson, "A Maiden from Hiroshima," *Redbook* (December 1956): 42–44, 78–84.

22. Before arriving in the United States with the Maidens, Norman Cousins and Kiyoshi Tanimoto made members of the American press sign agreements that they would refrain from harassing the shy and vulnerable young Japanese women. Within days of their arrival, most photographers (especially in New York) had already broken their agreements many times over, much to Cousins's and Tanimoto's outrage.

23. Photograph probably April 1955, author's collection, a gift from the late Dr. Bernard Simon.

24. See the photographs in Gloria and Peter Kalischer, "Love Helped to Heal 'the Devil's Claw Marks,'" *Collier's,* October 26, 1956, 48–49.

25. For more about mass culture and visual propaganda in the postwar period, see Marianne Fulton, *Eyes of Time: Photojournalism in America* (Boston: Little, Brown, 1988); Wendy Kozol, *"Life's" America* (Philadelphia: Temple University Press, 1994); and Eric Sandeen, *Picturing an Exhibition: "The Family of Man" and 1950s America* (Albuquerque: University of New Mexico Press, 1995).

26. See, for example, "When the Atom Bomb Struck—Uncensored," *Life,* September 29, 1952, 19–25. See also Susan D. Moeller, "Pictures of the Enemy: Fifty Years of Images of Japan in the American Press, 1941–1992," *Journal of American Culture* 19, no. 1 (Spring 1996): 29–42, and George Roeder Jr., *The Censored War: American Visual Experience during World War Two* (New Haven: Yale University Press, 1993).

27. Internal memo, June 2, 1955, from RG 59, Department of State Files, 1955–59, box 4186, file 811.558/1–755, National Archives.

28. For more about the seductive power of postwar French photography as a tool of political and aesthetic propaganda, see Peter Hamilton, "Representing the Social: France and Frenchness in Post-war Humanist Photography," in *Representation: Cultural Representations and Signifying Practices,* ed. Stuart Hall (Thousand Oaks, CA: Sage/Open University Press, 1997), 75–150. See also Kristin Ross, *Fast Cars, Clean Bodies: Colonization and French Culture* (Cambridge: MIT Press, 1995).

29. Associated Press photographs and captions, from the files of the *Washington Evening Star,* Washingtoniana collection, Martin Luther King Jr. Memorial Library, Washington, DC.

30. Cousins, quoted in Sheila Johnson, *The Japanese through American Eyes* (Palo Alto: Stanford University Press, 1988), 50.

31. See Watanabe, *The Japanese and Western Science*. See also Hideo Yoshikawa and Joanne Kauffman, *Science Has No National Boundaries: Harry C. Kelly and the Reconstruction of Science and Technology in Postwar Japan* (Cambridge: MIT Press, 1994).

32. Sheldon Garon, *Molding Japanese Minds: The State in Everyday Life* (Princeton: Princeton University Press, 1997), 163.

33. Figures from Office of Budget, Directorate for Finance and Administration, Agency for International Development, *U.S. Overseas Loans and Grants and Assistance from International Organizations: Obligations and Loan Authorizations July 1, 1945–September 30, 1992* (Washington, DC: Government Printing Office, 1992), 128.

34. See Elizabeth Gray Vining, *Windows for the Crown Prince* (New York: Harper and Row, 1952).

35. Ruth Benedict, *The Chrysanthemum and the Sword: Patterns of Japanese Culture* (1946; Boston: Houghton Mifflin, 1989). For an interesting critique of Benedict as an interesting reflection of midcentury liberalism, see Christopher Shannon, "A World Made Safe for Differences: Ruth Benedict's *The Chrysanthemum and the Sword*," American Quarterly 47, no. 4 (December 1995): 659–80.

36. Garon, *Molding Japanese Minds*, 149–53.

37. For more on the relations between Japanese architecture and Western modernism, see Egon Tempel, *New Japanese Architecture* (New York: Praeger, 1969), and Arthur Drexler, *The Architecture of Japan* (New York: Museum of Modern Art, 1955), esp. 240–61.

38. Kenzo Tange Team, *A Plan for Tokyo, 1960: Toward a Structural Reorganization* ([Tokyo]: Shikenchikusha, 1961), 10.

39. See Drexler, *Architecture of Japan*, 255.

40. *Japan Letter* 2, no. 8 (August 1955): 15. See also "Chronology of Events Related to the Peace Memorial Park/Peace Boulevard," *Chugoku Shimbun*, January 29, 1995, translation courtesy of the Isamu Noguchi Foundation Archives.

41. Associated Press, "City of Life and Fear," *Washington Evening Star*, July 25, 1965.

42. Hersey, *Hiroshima*, 109.

43. See Norman Klein, *The History of Forgetting: Los Angeles and the Politics of Memory* (New York: Verso, 1997). See also Robert Fitch, *The Assassination of New York* (New York: Verso, 1994), and Manuel Castells, *City, Class and Power* (New York: St. Martin's Press, 1978).

44. For historical and critical accounts of the City Beautiful movement as a form of social control, see, for example, M. Christine Boyer, *Dreaming the*

*Rational City: The Myth of American City Planning* (Cambridge: MIT Press, 1983), and Elizabeth Wilson, *The Sphinx in the City: Urban Life, the Control of Disorder, and Women* (Berkeley: University of California Press, 1992).

45. *Japan Letter* 2, no. 8 (August 1955): 20, from the special issue commemorating the tenth anniversary of the atomic bombing.

46. Memo telegram, May 6, 1955, from RAG 59, Department of State Files, 1955–59 Central Decimal File, box 4186, file 811.558/1–755, National Archives.

47. "Chronology of Events Related to the Peace Memorial Park/Peace Boulevard."

48. See Serge Guibault, *How New York Stole the Idea of Modern Art* (Chicago: University of Chicago Press, 1983).

49. Johnson, *Japanese through American Eyes*, 48–49.

50. Drexler, *Architecture of Japan*, 262. For an interesting review of the relation between Japanese architects and Western design during this period, see Maitland Jones's review of "Revealing New Ground," an exhibition held at the Yale School of Architecture, February 11–March 8, 2002, in *Constructs* 5, no. 1 (Fall 2002): 13.

51. Theo Wilson, "Hiroshima Maids Here for Aid," New York *Daily News,* May 10, 1955.

52. Paul Tobenkin, "Hiroshima Girls Here, to Rest Before Surgery: Feel Friendship for U.S.," *New York Herald Tribune,* May 10, 1955.

53. Minowa, quoted in Carol Taylor, "25 A-Burned Girls Here for Surgery," *New York World-Telegram,* May 9, 1955.

54. Herbert Feis, *From Trust to Terror: The Onset of the Cold War, 1945–1950* (New York: Norton, 1970); Harry Bayard Price, *The Marshall Plan and Its Meaning* (Ithaca, NY: Cornell University Press, 1955); Theodore Harold White, *Fire in the Ashes: Europe in Mid-century* (New York: Sloane, 1953).

55. Tomin Harada, *Hiroshima Surgeon* (Newton, KS: Faith and Life Press, 1983). Harada's title also suggests the conceptual linkages between surgical and architectural reconstruction as overlapping discourses in postwar Japan.

56. Telegram of travel itinerary, May 5, 1955, in RG 59, Department of State Files, 1955–59 Central Decimal File, box 4186, file 811.558/1–755, National Archives.

57. Jane Cochran, "A-Scarred Japanese Women Reach U.S.," *Newark Star-Ledger,* May 9, 1955.

58. Memorandum of conversation, June 2, 1955, in RG 59, Department of State Files 1955–59 Central Decimal File, box 4186, file 811.558/1–755, National Archives.

59. Max Milliken and Walt Whitman Rostow, *A Proposal: Key to an Effective Foreign Policy* (New York: Harper and Row, 1957), 8. The *Proposal,*

which began as a conference at MIT in 1952, was written during 1953–54 and circulated among members of Congress for input and ideas in 1956 before publication in 1957.

60. For a compelling example of this approach see Wendell Wilkie, *One World* (New York: Simon and Schuster, 1943). For more about the "altruistic" motivations of Cold War liberals and foreign policy experts, see James Guimond, *American Photography and the American Dream* (Chapel Hill: University of North Carolina Press, 1991), and Sandeen, *Picturing an Exhibition.*

61. "25 Hiroshima Girls in N.Y. for Surgery," *Newark Evening News,* May 9, 1955, 1, 8.

62. Barker, *Hiroshima Maidens,* 64.

63. For contemporary receptions to the film *Hiroshima,* see Bosley Crowther, "Screen: Hiroshima after the Bomb," New York *Times,* May 18, 1955, 35, and Donald Richie's groundbreaking essay "'Mono No Aware': Hiroshima in Film" (1961), reprinted in *Hibakusha Cinema: Hiroshima, Nagasaki, and the Nuclear Image in Japanese Film,* ed. Mick Broderick (New York: Kegan Paul International, 1996), 20–37. For more about the film, see also Amos Vogel, "The Atom and Eve of Destruction," *Film Comment* 19, no. 1 (January–February 1983): 76–77, and Tadako Sato, *Currents in Japanese Cinema,* trans. Gregory Barrett (Tokyo: Kodansha, 1982), 197–200.

64. Office memo, May 13, 1955, from RG 59, Department of State Files, 1955–59 Central Decimal File, box 4186, file 811.558/1–755, National Archives.

65. Memorandum of conversation, June 2, 1955, from RG 59, Department of State Files, 1955–59 Central Decimal File, box 4186, file 811.558/1–755, National Archives.

66. Norman Cousins to William J. Sebald, June 20, 1955, from RG 59, Department of State Files, 1955–59 Central Decimal File, box 4186, file 811.558/1–755, National Archives.

67. Author's interview with Dr. Bernard Simon, September 6, 1996.

68. "War Surgery: The Battle of Wound Reconstruction Still Goes On," *Life,* February 11, 1946, 60–71.

69. Bernard Nosier, "Surgeons' Knife Battling A-Bomb," *New York World-Telegram and Sun,* August 22, 1955.

70. Lindee, *Suffering Made Real,* 122–28.

71. For further exploration of the history of the internment camps and their impact on Japanese Americans, see Roger Daniels, *Prisoners without Trial: Japanese Americans in World War II* (New York: Hill and Wang, 1993); Lawson Fusao Inada, ed., *Only What We Could Carry: The Japanese American Internment Experience* (Berkeley: Heyday Books, 2000); and

Tetsuden Kashima, ed., *Personal Justice Denied: Report of the Commission on Wartime Relocation and Internment of Civilians* (Seattle: University of Washington Press, 1997).

72. Cecil R. King to Thruston [*sic*] B. Morton, June 6, 1955, in RG 59, Department of State Files, 1955–59 Central Decimal File, box 4186, file 811.558/1–755, National Archives.

73. Johnson, *Japanese through American Eyes,* 109. See also Clay Lancaster, *The Japanese Influence in America* (New York: Walton H. Rawls, 1963).

74. The United States government apparently predicted the need for softening the Japanese reputation in the public imagination from very early on. According to Sheldon Harris, in 1945 American POWs who had been liberated from Japanese prison camps that were suspected of conducting biological warfare experiments were forced by the army to sign statements "stating [that they] would not tell [their] experiences or conditions, what happened to [them] in the prison camps, before any audiences or the newspapers, under threat of court martial." One of the prisoners assumed that "this was an attempt to harmonize the American public to get to like the Japanese." See Sheldon H. Harris, *Factories of Death: Japanese Biological Warfare 1932–45 and the American Cover-Up* (New York: Routledge, 1994), 120.

75. "Kiyoshi Tanimoto" episode, originally broadcast May 11, 1955, excerpts of which can be seen in the video documentary *After the Cloud Lifted,* dir. Richard M. Santoro (1996; Northbrook, IL: Film Ideas, 2001). Despite the overwhelming success of *This Is Your Life* in syndication and on home video release, the Tanimoto episode has never been (officially) released in any format by Ralph Edwards Productions. No information about this episode exists in the NBC Archives in Madison, Wisconsin.

76. For a complete description (though lacking analysis) of this television moment, see "Prologue: *This Is Your Life,*" in Barker, *Hiroshima Maidens,* 3–12.

77. Robert Lewis's speech on "This Is Your Life," excerpted in *After the Cloud Lifted;* my transcription.

78. Lewis's story was recounted by Koko Tanimoto Kando, the daughter of Kiyoshi Tanimoto, in *After the Cloud Lifted.*

79. Barker, *Hiroshima Maidens,* 9.

80. Otani, "Memory of Isamu Noguchi," 140.

81. Harada's description, retold in Anne Chisholm, *Faces of Hiroshima* (London: Jonathan Cape, 1985), 88–89.

82. Handwritten lists and charts, probably late May 1955 (possibly by Society of Friends secretary Ida Day), from the Archives of the Society of Friends New York, Haviland Historical Room, currently part of the Hiroshima

Maidens files at the Mount Sinai Hospital Archives, New York. I have made the decision to keep anonymous the identities of those named on the Friends' lists.

83. For a brilliant discussion of the distinction between "denotation" and "connotation," see D. A. Miller's essay "Anal *Rope*," in *Inside/Out: Lesbian Theories, Gay Theories,* ed. Diana Fuss (New York: Routledge, 1991).

84. Frances Macgregor's pioneering work *Facial Deformities and Plastic Surgery: A Psychosocial Study* (Springfield, IL: C. C. Thomas, 1953), was based largely on her M.A. thesis, "The Sociological Aspects of Facial Deformities" (University of Missouri, 1947). For a brief overview of the historical importance of Macgregor's work for sociologists and psychologists, see Thomas Pruzinsky, "Social and Psychological Challenges for Individuals with Facial Disfigurement," in *Special Faces: Understanding Facial Disfigurement,* ed. R. Bo chat (New York: National Foundation for Facial Disfigurement, 1994), 15–24.

85. Macgregor, *Facial Deformities and Plastic Surgery,* 78–79.

86. Macgregor, *Facial Deformities and Plastic Surgery,* 79.

87. As Macgregor writes, "Because of large-scale warfare and the mounting number of industrial mishaps and of train, plane, and automobile accidents, more people than ever before are being facially disfigured. Besides these persons disfigured by trauma are those deformed by the sequelae of such diseases as cancer and osteomyelitis and still others who are deformed from birth. . . . [T]he premium placed upon facial beauty in the United States today, its importance for jobs, marriage, and 'success' in our culture, has intensified the impact of facial deformity upon the person who is so afflicted." *Facial Deformities and Plastic Surgery,* 3–4.

88. For example, see Elizabeth Gail Haiken, *Venus Envy: A History of Cosmetic Surgery* (Baltimore: Johns Hopkins University Press, 1997).

89. Sander L. Gilman, *Creating Beauty to Cure the Soul: Race and Psychology in the Shaping of Aesthetic Surgery* (Durham, NC: Duke University Press, 1998).

90. Haiken, *Venus Envy,* and Joan Jacobs Brumberg, *The Body Project: An Intimate History of American Girls* (New York: Random House, 1997).

91. "Disfigured Jap Girls to Get Facelifting," *Newark Star–Ledger,* May 4, 1955; Taylor, "25 A-Burned Girls Here for Surgery."

92. Belle Montague, letter to the editor of *the Daily Worker,* May 23, 1955.

93. Mimeographed copy of list of surgical procedures compiled and typed about November 1956, author's collection, a gift from the late Dr. Bernard Simon.

94. Author's interview with Dr. Bernard Simon, September 6, 1996.

95. See Robert Jay Lifton and Greg Mitchell, *Hiroshima in America: Fifty Years of Denial* (New York: G. P. Putnam's Sons, 1995), esp. 245–70.

96. For more about the importance of board certification and the creation of the American Society of Plastic and Reconstructive Surgeons, see Haiken, *Venus Envy,* 25–45.

97. Pick, quoted in "Pretty Does as Pretty Is?" *Time,* October 13, 1947, 52. See also "New Faces on Life," *Newsweek,* October 13, 1947, 46. For more information about the relation between personal appearance and economic mobility after World War II, see Haiken, *Venus Envy,* 131–74.

98. Ben Pearse, "How to Get a New Face," *Saturday Evening Post,* September 16, 1950.

99. See, for example, "Face Clinic Mends Shattered Lives," *New York Times,* April 29, 1956.

100. James F. Scheer, "A New Face for Christmas," *American Mercury,* December 1958, 43–48.

101. Author's interview with Dr. Bernard Simon, September 6, 1996.

102. Arnold Brophy and Dave Rosenblatt, "25 Japanese Girls Arrive Here to Erase the Scars of Hiroshima," *New York Newsday,* May 9, 1955, 4, and Arnold Brophy and Stan Green, "U.S. Opens Eyes, Heart to Hiroshima Victims," *New York Newsday,* May 10, 1955.

103. Norman Cousins, "Interim Report on the Maidens," *Saturday Review,* October 15, 1955, 22–23.

104. Minowa, quoted in Kenneth Ishii, "Atom Blast Ruined Beauty, Sighs Girl Hiroshima Victim," *Journal-American,* April 28, 1955, and Sako, quoted in Taylor, "25 A-Burned Girls Here for Surgery."

105. Selma Robinson, "A Maiden from Hiroshima," *Redbook* (December 1956): 78.

106. Caption taken from photograph distributed by Worldwide Photos, April 29, 1955.

107. "Victims of Hiroshima," *New York World-Telegram,* May 12, 1955.

108. The Canadian artist Robert Lepage debuted his epic *Seven Streams of the River Ota* in 1996; American artist Dan Hurlin's piece, *Everyday Uses of Sight No. 9: Hiroshima Maiden,* debuted in 2004. While Lepage uses the Maidens obliquely as part of a larger meditation on postwar Japanese culture, Hurlin's piece engages directly with the Maidens' pre- and post-U.S. stories, combining both traditional Japanese puppetry and avant-garde performance techniques (including a poignant moment in which a young Hurlin, watching 1950s television, switches between *I Love Lucy* and the Maidens' appearance on *This is Your Life*).

109. Daniel James Sundahl, *Hiroshima Maidens: Imaginary Translations from the Japanese* (Lewiston, NY: Edwin Mellen Press, 1994), 5.

110. See, for example, L. R. Fernandez, "Double Eyelid Operation in the Oriental in Hawaii," *Plastic and Reconstructive Surgery* 25 (1960): 257–64, and J. Uchida, "A Surgical Procedure for Blepharoptosis Vera and for Pseudo-blepharoptosis Orientalis," *Journal of Plastic Surgery* 15 (1962): 271–76. For a very good overview of this phenomenon, see Eugenia Kaw, "Medicalization of Racial Features: Asian American and Cosmetic Surgery," *Medical Anthropology Quarterly* 7, no. 1 (March 1993): 74–89.

111. Hiraga, "The Double Eyelid Operation and Augmentation Rhino-plasty in the Oriental Patient," 544.

112. See Gabrielle Glaser, "Audi, Champagne, and Liposuction: Capitalism Arrives for Many Poles," *New York Times,* October 15, 1991, A14; Uli Schmetzer, "Cosmetic Surgery Alters Face of Post-Mao China," *Chicago Tribune,* January 24, 1989, sec. 1, 6; Nicholas Kristof, "In China, Beauty Is a Big Western Nose," *New York Times,* April 29, 1987, C4; "Koreans Seek Lifts for Careers," *Wall Street Journal,* February 23, 1993, A17; and Shirley Lord, "Images: Reshaping Moscow," *Vogue* 197, no. 4 (April 1989): 166–70.

113. Yu Min Kyung, a twenty-seven-year-old music teacher, quoted in Steve Glain, "Cosmetic Surgery Goes Hand in Hand with the New Korea," *Wall Street Journal,* November 23, 1993, A1.

#### CHAPTER THREE

1. All references are to Gladys Bentley, "I Am a Woman Again," *Ebony* 7, no. 10 (August 1952): 92–98.

2. See Carl Van Vechten, *Parties: Scenes from Contemporary New York Life* (New York: Alfred A. Knopf, 1930), and Blair Niles, *Strange Brother* (1931; New York: Avon, 1952). For further references to Bentley, see Clement Wood's study of interracial romance, *Deep River* (1934), as well as Langston Hughes's autobiography, *The Big Sea* (1951). For more about the Harlem Renaissance, see David Levering Lewis, *When Harlem Was in Vogue* (New York: Penguin, 1988).

3. See Eric Garber, "Gladys Bentley: The Bulldagger Who Sang the Blues," *Out/Look* 1, no. 1 (Spring 1988): 52–61. For more historical context about Bentley and her circle see also Eric Garber, "A Spectacle in Color: The Lesbian and Gay Subculture of Jazz Age Harlem," in *Hidden from History: Reclaiming the Gay and Lesbian Past,* ed. Martin Duberman et al. (New York: Meridien, 1990).

4. For more about this concept, see Kevin Mumford, *Interzones: Black and White Sex Districts in New York and Chicago in the Twentieth Century* (New York: Columbia University Press, 1997).

5. For more about Bentley's appearance at Mona's Club 440, see the Museum of the City of San Francisco's Web site at www.sfmuseum.org/hist10/mona.html.

6. Juliet Parker Filler, *The Female Hormones* (New York: Booktab, 1947) 5. For more about the pharmaceutical history of steroid hormones, see Harry Marks, "Cortisone, 1949: A Year in the Political Life of a Drug," *Bulletin of the History of Medicine* 66 (1992): 419–39, and G. Hetenyi Jr. and J. Karsh, "Cortisone Therapy: A Challenge to Academic Medicine in 1949–52," *Perspectives in Biology and Medicine* 40, no. 3 (Spring 1997): 426–39.

7. Herman H. Rubin, *Your Life Is in Your Glands: How Your Endocrine Glands Affect Your Mental, Physical, and Sexual Health, Your Appearance, Personality, and Behavior* (New York: Stratford House, 1948), 139–40.

8. David Roediger, *The Wages of Whiteness: Race and the Making of the American Working Class* (London: Verso, 1991); also Gail Bederman, *Manliness and Civilization: A Cultural History of Gender and Race in the United States, 1880–1917* (Chicago: University of Chicago Press, 1994), esp. chapter 4, "Not to Sex, but to Race."

9. Matthew Frye Jacobson, *Whiteness of a Different Color: European Immigrants and the Alchemy of Race* (Cambridge: Harvard University Press, 1998), 91.

10. See Londa Schiebinger, *Nature's Body* (New York: Beacon Press, 1993).

11. See Julia Ellen Rechter, "'The Glands of Destiny': A History of Popular, Medical and Scientific Views of the Sex Hormones in 1920s America" (Ph.D. diss., University of California at Berkeley, 1997).

12. Charles Evans Morris, *Modern Rejuvenation Methods* (New York: Scientific Medical Publishing, 1926), 57.

13. Kathy Peiss, *Hope in a Jar: The Making of America's Beauty Culture* (New York: Henry Holt, 1998), 208.

14. Wallace Thurman, *The Blacker the Berry . . . A Novel of Negro Life* (New York: Macaulay, 1929); Nella Larsen, *Passing* (New York: Alfred A. Knopf, 1929); George Schuyler, *Black No More: Being an Account of the Strange and Wonderful Workings of Science in the Land of the Free, A.D. 1933–1940* (New York: Macaulay, 1931).

15. See Ruth Feldstein, *Motherhood in Black and White: Race, Sex, and Liberalism in the United States, 1930–1960* (Ithaca, NY: Cornell University Press, 2000). See also Elaine Tyler May, *Homeward Bound: American Families in the Cold War Era* (New York: Basic Books, 1987).

16. For a larger discussion of Brown-Séquard, see Merriley Borrell, "Organotherapy and the Emergence of Reproductive Endocrinology," *Journal of the History of Biology* 18, no. 1 (Spring 1985): 1–30.

17. See Diana Long Hall, "Biology, Sexism and Sex Hormones in the 1920s," in *Women and Philosophy: Toward a Theory of Liberation,* ed. Carol C. Gould and Marx W. Wartofsky (New York: Putnam, 1976), and Nelly

Oudshoorn, *Beyond the Natural Body: An Archaeology of Sex Hormones* (New York: Routledge, 1994).

18. See Chandak Sengoopta, "Glandular Politics: Experimental Biology, Clinical Medicine, and Homosexual Emancipation in Fin-de-Siècle Central Europe," *Isis* 89, no. 3 (September 1998): 445–73; Stephanie H. Kenen, "Who Counts When You're Counting Homosexuals? Hormones and Homosexuality in Mid-Twentieth-Century America," in *Science and Homosexualities*, ed. Vernon A. Rosario (New York: Routledge, 1996), 197–218; and Bernice L. Hausman, *Changing Sex, Transsexualism, Technology, and the Idea of Gender* (Durham, NC: Duke University Press, 1995), esp. 21–48.

19. The title of a workshop organized by Chris Lawrence and Chandak Sengoopta and sponsored by the Wellcome Institute for the History of Medicine, London, June 13, 1997, which recognized the intellectual impact of reproductive glands on historians of the biological sciences, medical anthropologists, and historians of gender and sexuality. The conference title seems also to playfully pay homage to the late historian Lily E. Kay's influential study of mid-twentieth-century molecular biology, *The Molecular Vision of Life: Rockefeller, Caltech and the New Biology* (New York: Oxford University Press, 1992).

20. See Donna Haraway, *Primate Visions: Gender, Race, and Nature in Modern Science* (New York: Routledge, 1989), and Jennifer Terry, *An American Obsession: Science, Medicine, and Homosexuality in Modern Society* (Chicago: University of Chicago Press, 2000). For other notable examples of this scholarship, see Adele Clark, *Disciplining Reproduction: Modernity, American Life Sciences, and the "Problem of Sex"* (Berkeley: University of California Press, 1998); Anne Fausto-Sterling, *Body Building: How Biologists Construct Sexuality* (New York: Basic Books, 2000); Ruth Hubbard, *The Politics of Women's Biology* (New Brunswick, NJ: Rutgers University Press, 1992); and Marianne van den Wijngaard, *Reinventing the Sexes: The Biomedical Construction of Masculinity and Femininity* (Bloomington: Indiana University Press, 1997).

21. For an excellent discussion of how these developmental themes overlapped, see Julian Carter, "Normality, Whiteness, Authorship: Evolutionary Sexology and the Primitive Pervert," in *Science and Homosexualities*, ed. Rosario, 155–76.

22. Siobhan Somerville, *Queering the Color Line: Race and the Invention of Homosexuality in American Culture* (Durham, NC: Duke University Press, 2000), esp. chap. 1, "Scientific Racism and the Construction of the Homosexual Body," 15–38.

23. Terry, *American Obsession*, 41.

24. Frank R. Starkey, "Organotherapy in Relation to the Practice of Medicine," *Northwest Medicine* (January 1916). See also Frank R. Starkey, "The Combined Use of Thyroparathyroid, Pituitary, Ovarian, and Testicular Extracts," *New York Medical Journal* 122 (June 15, 1912).

25. L. R. Broster, Clifford Allen, H. W. C. Vines, Jocelyn Patterson, Alan W. Greenwood, G. F. Marrian, and G. C. Butler, *The Adrenal Cortex and Intersexuality* (London: Chapman and Hall, 1938), 73.

26. Theodore H. Larson, *Why We Are What We Are: The Science and Art of Endocrine Physiology and Endocrine Therapy* (Chicago: American Endocrine Bureau/W. B. Conkey, 1929), 107.

27. See Alfred Chandler, *The Visible Hand: The Managerial Revolution in American Business* (Cambridge: Harvard University Press, 1977); Olivier Zunz, *Making America Corporate, 1870–1920* (Chicago: University of Chicago Press, 1990); and Angel Kwolek-Folland, "Gender, Self, and Work in the Life Insurance Industry, 1880–1930," in *Work Engendered: Toward a New History of American Labor,* ed. Ava Baron (Ithaca, NY: Cornell University Press, 1991), 168–90.

28. George B. Alexander, *You: The Story of Your Ductless Glands* (Boston: George B. Alexander, 1929), frontispiece.

29. See Rechter, "'The Glands of Destiny.'" Also see Diana Long Hall, "Monkey Glands," author's collection.

30. Ray Bourbon, *Gland Opera* (Hollywood, CA: Imperial Records 108-A, [1941?]), transcribed by author. From the collection of Randy Riddle (www.coolcatdaddy.com).

31. For more about the chemical history of steroid hormone production before and after the invention of the techniques of total synthesis, see Edward Kendall, *Cortisone* (New York: Charles Scribner's Sons, 1971).

32. See Robert Kohler, *From Medical Chemistry to Biochemistry: The Making of a Biomedical Discipline* (New York: Cambridge University Press, 1982).

33. See Leo B. Slater, "Organic Synthesis and R. B. Woodward: A Historical Study in the Chemical Sciences" (Ph.D. diss., Princeton University, 1997). See also the article about African American chemist Percy Julian's total synthesis of testosterone using soybeans in Franklin Fosdick, "New Hope for Old Men," *Negro Digest* 9 (March 1951): 52–56.

34. Herman Bundesen, quoted in Paul de Kruif, *The Male Hormone* (Garden City, NY: Garden City Publishing, 1945), 14.

35. See Marks, "Cortisone, 1949," 419–20.

36. William L. Laurence, "Miracle Relief from Arthritis," *Ladies' Home Journal* 46 (August 1949): 51.

37. From Merck and Company, *Hydrocortisone and Cortisone* (Rahway, NJ: 1956), 53.

38. Paul de Kruif, "The Mysterious Power of Cortisone," *Reader's Digest* 57 (November 1950): 119.

39. From the May 1950 *Consumer Reports,* reprinted in "On the Lookout," *Theosophy* 39, no. 2 (December 1950): 88.

40. Rydin, as quoted in the February 17, 1950, edition of the Washington, DC, *Times Herald,* reprinted in "On the Lookout," 89.

41. Kay Torrey, "You Feel Better Because . . . ," *Charm* (January 1954), 57. From the Estelle Ellis Collection, Archives Center, National Museum of American History, Smithsonian Institution.

42. "The Case of Señora R.," *Time,* February 1, 1954, 53–54.

43. See, for example, Dale Carnegie, *How to Win Friends and Influence People* (New York: Simon and Schuster, 1936).

44. For a concise overview of some endocrinological debates in the 1930s and 1940s, see Kenen, "Who Counts When You're Counting Homosexuals?"

45. William Wolf, "The Role of the Endocrine Glands in Emotional Disturbances, Crime and Rehabilitation," *Journal of Clinical Psychopathology* 7, no. 3 (January 1946): 539.

46. Ralph Dorfman, *Androgens: Biochemistry, Physiology, and Clinical Significance* (New York: John Wiley, 1956), 319; emphasis in original.

47. Herman H. Rubin, *Your Life Is in Your Glands: How Your Endocrine Glands Affect Your Mental, Physical, and Sexual Health, Your Appearance, Personality, and Behavior* (New York: Stratford House, 1948), 120.

48. See James Gilbert, *A Cycle of Outrage* (New York: Oxford University Press, 1986).

49. Professor Zuckerman, quoted in J. S. L. Browne, "Effects of ACTH and Cortisone on Behaviour," in G. E. W. Wolstenholme, ed., *Hormones, Psychology, and Behaviour* (London: J. and A. Churchill, 1952), 208.

50. Jacques Ellul, *The Technological Society* (1954; New York: Knopf, 1964), 384–85.

51. For important contributions to the literature on consumerism and social identity in the twentieth century United States, see T. J. Jackson Lears and Richard Wightman, eds., *The Culture of Consumption: Critical Essays in American History, 1880–1980* (New York: Pantheon, 1983); Roland Marchand, *Advertising the American Dream: Making Way for Modernity* (Berkeley: University of California Press, 1986); and Joan Jacobs Brumberg, *The Body Project: An Intimate History of American Girls* (New York: Random House, 1997).

52. See Andrew Hodges, *Alan Turing: The Enigma* (Simon and Schuster, 1983).

53. "The Man Who Lived 30 Years as a Woman," *Ebony* 6, no. 12 (October 1951): 23–26.

54. "The Woman Who Lived as a Man for 15 Years," *Ebony* 10, no. 1 (November 1954): 93.

55. See Lisa Duggan, *Sapphic Slashers: Sex, Violence, and Modernity in Modern America* (Durham, NC: Duke University Press, 2001), esp. chap. 1, "The Trials of Alice Mitchell."

56. Warren Henry Orr, *Hormones, Happiness, and Health* (New York: Macmillan, 1954), 41.

57. For a more extensive discussion of black postwar politics see, for example, Manning Marable, *Race, Reform, and Rebellion: The Second Reconstruction in Black America, 1945–1990* (Jackson: University of Mississippi Press, 1991); and George Lipsitz, *Rainbow at Midnight: Labor and Culture in the 1940s* (Urbana: University of Illinois Press, 1994).

58. See Regina Austin, "'A Nation of Thieves': Consumption, Commerce, and the Black Public Sphere," in *The Black Public Sphere*, ed. Black Public Sphere Collective (Chicago: University of Chicago Press, 1995), 229–52.

59. See Robert Weems, *Desegregating the Dollar* (New York: New York University Press, 1997).

60. Emmett John Hughes, "The Negro's New Economic Life," *Fortune* 54 (September 1956): 131.

61. Kenneth Clark, "The New Negro in the North," in *The New Negro*, ed. Matthew H. Ahmann (Notre Dame, IN: Fides, 1961), 26.

62. See Cedric Robinson, *Black Movements in the United States* (New York: Routledge, 1997).

63. Zora Neale Hurston, "Why the Negro Won't Buy Communism," *American Legion* 50 (June 1951): 15.

64. Some of the legal and social triumphs of the early movement include the Montgomery bus boycotts (1955–56), the desegregation of Central High School in Little Rock, Arkansas (1957), the Freedom Rides (1957), the founding of the Southern Christian Leadership Conference (1957), and the Greensboro, North Carolina, sit-ins and the birth of the Student Non-Violent Coordinating Committee (1960–61). These set the tone for the March on Washington (1963), the Mississippi "Freedom Summer" of voter registration (1964), and the emergence of the black power movement in the aftermath of the Watts riots (1966).

65. E. Franklin Frazier, *Black Bourgeoisie: The Rise of a New Middle Class in the United States* (New York: Macmillan, 1957), 180.

66. Editorial, quoted in Abby Arthur Johnson and Ronald Maberry Johnson, *Propaganda and Aesthetics: The Literary Politics of African-American Magazines in the Twentieth Century,* 2nd ed. (Amherst: University of Massachusetts Press, 1991), 162.

67. Betty Friedan, *The Feminine Mystique* (1962; New York: Dell, 1984).

68. Robert Wilson, *Feminine Forever* (New York: M. Evans, 1965).

69. Wilson, quoted in Margaret Lock, *Encounters with Aging: Mythologies of Menopause in Japan and North America* (Berkeley: University of California Press, 1993), 326.

70. See Wilson's influential "The Fate of the Nontreated Postmenopausal: A Plea for the Maintenance of Adequate Estrogen from Puberty to the Grave," *Journal of the American Geriatrics Society* 11 (April 1963): 347–62.

71. Wilson, *Feminine Forever,* 103; emphasis added.

72. Carmen Mitchell, Creations of Fantasies/Constructions of Identities: The Oppositional Lives of Gladys Bentley," in *The Greatest Taboo: Homosexuality in Black Communities,* ed. Delroy Constantine-Simms (Boston: Alyson, 2000), 223.

73. See Garber, "Gladys Bentley," and James F. Wilson, "Bulldykes, Pansies, and Chocolate Babies: Performance, Race, and Sexuality in the Harlem Renaissance" (Ph.D. diss., City University of New York, 2000), esp. 258–346.

74. Joana "Juma-Ometse" Clayton, "Closet Ain't Nothin' but a Dark and Private Place for . . . ?" *Art Journal* 55, no. 4 (Winter 1996): 51.

75. Ibid., 53.

76. Martin Duberman: *Cures: A Gay Man's Odyssey* (New York: Plume, 1992).

**CHAPTER FOUR**

1. Tony Kushner, *Angels in America, Part One: Millennium Approaches* (New York: Theatre Communications Group, 1992), esp. 111. Later references are to this edition.

2. See Elaine Tyler May, *Homeward Bound: American Families in the Cold War Era* (New York: Basic Books, 1988); Stephen Whitfield, *The Culture of the Cold War* (Baltimore: Johns Hopkins University Press, 1991); and Stephanie Coontz, *The Way We Never Were: American Families and the Nostalgia Trap* (New York: Basic Books, 1992). For other recent historical studies of the period, see David Halberstam, *The Fifties* (New York: Villard, 1993); Dan Wakefield, *New York in the Fifties* (Boston: Houghton Mifflin/Seymour Lawrence, 1992); Alan Nadel, *Containment Culture* (Durham, NC: Duke University Press, 1996); and Wini Breines, *Young White and Miserable: Growing Up Female in the Fifties* (Boston: Beacon Press, 1992).

3. This concept, which owes its ideological undergirding to Mikhail Bakhtin, is developed by in Peter Stallybrass and Allon White, *The Politics and Poetics of Transgression* (Ithaca: Cornell University Press, 1986), 19, 53.

4. See Richard Crossman, ed., *The God That Failed* (1949; New York: Regnery Press, 1987); for the popularity of confessional literature, also see Victor Navasky, *Naming Names* (New York: Penguin, 1980), 16–19, 199–222.

5. Audio recording of 1968 radio interview with Jorgensen by well-known psychologist and radio personality Dr. Lee Steiner, published as *Male and Female* (New York: Jeffrey Norton, 1969). The word "transsexual" itself, which was coined by D. O. Cauldwell in 1949, was made popular in 1967 by Harry Benjamin, who also provided the preface for *Christine Jorgensen: A Personal Autobiography* (New York: Bantam Books, 1968). To a large extent, the controversy surrounding Jorgensen kept the surgical/medical binaries of "male" and "female" securely in place until the late 1960s, when gender dysphoria clinics such as the one at Johns Hopkins helped to create a more welcoming climate—not to mention a working vocabulary—for those wanting to undergo transsexual surgery. In this respect, both Jan Morris and Renée Richards had the surgical and cultural precedent established by Jorgensen against which they could maintain their new identities. See, for points of comparison, Morris's *Conundrum* (New York: Harcourt Brace Jovanovich, 1974) and Richards's *Second Serve: The Renée Richards Story* (New York: Stein and Day, 1983). For historical details about male to female operations as they occurred in Jorgensen's time, see Deborah Heller Feinbloom, *Transvestites and Transsexuals: Mixed Views* (New York: Delacorte Press, 1976), 25, 227, or even Janice G. Raymond's vulgar radical feminist diatribe, *The Transsexual Empire* (Boston: Beacon Press, 1979).

6. See "The Case of Christine," *Time*, April 20, 1953, 82–84. After identifying Jorgensen as not a "real woman" but actually a male transvestite, the article offers us a 1950s medical definition of transvestism: "a morbid desire to dress in the clothing of the opposite sex."

7. See Marjorie Garber, *Vested Interests: Cross-Dressing and Cultural Anxiety* (New York: Routledge, 1992); Annie Woodhouse, *Fantastic Women: Sex, Gender, and Transvestism* (New Brunswick, NJ: Rutgers University Press, 1989); Catherine Millot, *Horsexe: Essays on Transsexuality,* trans. Kenneth Hylton (Brooklyn: Autonomedia, 1990); and Kate Bornstein, *Gender Outlaw: On Men, Women, and the Rest of Us* (New York: Routledge, 1994). For another interpretation of the Jorgensen phenomenon see Joanne Meyerowitz, *How Sex Changed* (Cambridge: Harvard University Press, 2002).

8. This and following references are to "Ex-GI Becomes Blonde Beauty: Operations Transform Bronx Youth," *New York Daily News*, December 1, 1952, A1.

9. For a fascinating discussion of the use of female pinups as domestic propaganda during the war, see Robert B. Westbrook, "'I Want a Girl, Just Like the Girl That Married Harry James': American Women and the Problem of Political Obligation in World War Two," *American Quarterly* 42, no. 4 (December 1990): 587–614.

10. Ben White's travails were reprinted in "The Great Transformation," *Time,* December 15, 1952, 58; "Talk of the Town," *New Yorker,* January 24, 1953, 12; and "Christine and the News," *Newsweek,* December 15, 1952, 64–66.

11. "Bronx 'Boy' Is Now a Girl: Danish Treatments Change Sex of Former Army Clerk," *New York Times,* December 2, 1952, A18.

12. "Christine and the News"; emphasis added.

13. "Miss Jorgensen Returns from Copenhagen: Ex-GI Back 'Happy to Be Home,'" *New York Times,* February 13, 1953, A38.

14. "Homecoming," *Time,* February 23, 1953, 28. Sandra Gilbert and Susan Gubar have seized on this term for their volume of literary criticism, *No Man's Land: The Place of the Woman Writer in the Twentieth Century* (New Haven: Yale University Press, 1994). Though deliciously appropriate as a sub-verted military term, Christine's use of the phrase "no-man's-land" seems slightly inaccurate to her situation, especially for someone who had, at least to all outward appearances, chosen and arrived at a conclusive gender identity.

15. See John Morton Blum, *V Was for Victory: Politics and American Culture during World War II* (New York: Harcourt Brace Jovanovich, 1976), esp. 53–64. For more about generic conventions during the war years, see William S. Graebner, *The Age of Doubt: American Thought and Culture in the 1940s* (Boston: Twayne, 1991), 1–18, 138–40, and Warren Susman, *Culture as History: The Transformation of American Society in the Twentieth Century* (New York: Pantheon, 1984), esp. the chapter on American culture during the thirties. For WPA art, see Barbara Melosh, *Engendering Culture: Manhood and Womanhood in New Deal Public Art and Theater* (Washington, DC: Smithsonian Institution Press, 1991). For WPA photography, see Alan Trachtenberg, *Reading American Photographs: Images as History, Matthew Brady to Walker Evans* (New York: Noonday Press, 1989); and as a good introduction, see Vicki Goldberg, *The Power of Photography* (New York: Abbeville Press, 1993).

16. For an interesting treatment of political assent, see Simon Shepherd, "Gramsci-the-Goalie: Reflections in the Bath on Gays, the Labour Party, and Socialism," in *Coming on Strong: Gay Politics and Culture,* ed. Simon Shepherd and Mick Wallis (Boston: Unwin Hyman, 1989), 287–300. See also George H. Roeder Jr., *The Censored War: American Visual Experience during World War Two* (New Haven: Yale University Press, 1993).

17. See John Hersey, *Hiroshima,* rev. ed. (1946; New York: Vintage, 1985), esp. 134–52.

18. "The Girl Who Used to Be a Boy Isn't Quite Ready for Dates," New York *Daily News,* December 2, 1952, C4.

19. Theo Wilson, "Folks Proud of GI Who Became Blonde Beauty," New York *Daily News,* December 2, 1952, C4.

20. For a near contemporary analysis of this approach, see Erving Goffman, *The Presentation of Self in Everyday Life* (New York: Anchor, 1959).

21. For analyses of these films within the historical context of the period, see Graebner, *Age of Doubt,* 14, 40–42. For issues of masculinity and homoeroticism in films of late 1940s and early 1950s, see Steven Cohan, *Masked Men: Masculinity and the Movies in the Fifties* (Bloomington: Indiana University Press, 1997), and Vito Russo, *The Celluloid Closet* (New York: Harper and Row, 1987), 100–115.

22. "Great Transformation," 58.

23. Postwar masculine anxieties are discussed in Barbara Ehrenreich, *The Hearts of Men: American Dreams and the Flight from Commitment* (New York: Doubleday, 1983). The effeminacy of soldiers and its implications for gay war veterans returning to American communities are treated in Allan Bérubé, *Coming Out Under Fire: the History of Gay Men and Women in World War Two* (New York: Free Press, 1991).

24. All references in this paragraph are to "Christine's GI Beau Pops Up: Boy, Wotta Gal!" New York *Daily News,* December 5, 1952, A1. The story of the Jorgensen-Calhoun relationship was recounted throughout the media but was emphasized (and strangely edited) in *Time*'s "Great Transformation."

25. Paul Ifverson, "'I Could Have Gone for the He-She Girl,' Says Reporter," New York *Daily News,* December 3, 1952, A1.

26. While this chapter does not purport to explore homophobia per se during the early 1950s, it is important to note that Jorgensen's "fall" followed, to a great extent, this same rhetorical and political trajectory. The most crucial document of the period is the notorious, and often quoted, *Senate Report on the Employment of Homosexuals and Other Sex Perverts in Government* (Washington, DC Government Printing Office, 1950). See also William B. White, "Inquiry by Senate on Perverts Asked," *New York Times,* May 20, 1950. For background reading that examines the persecution of gay men and lesbians (and, frequently, resistance to such persecution) during the McCarthy period, see David Savran, *Cowboys, Communists, and Queers* (Chicago: University of Chicago Press, 1992); Richard Corber, *In the Name of National Security: Hitchcock, Homophobia, and the Political Construction of Gender in*

*Postwar America* (Durham, NC: Duke University Press, 1993); John D'Emilio, *Sexual Politics, Sexual Communities: The Making of a Homosexual Minority in the United States, 1940–1970* (Chicago: University of Chicago Press, 1983); Jonathan Ned Katz, *Gay American History* (New York: Meridian, 1992); Eric Gordon, *Mark the Music: The Life of Marc Blitzstein* (New York: St. Martin's Press, 1987); and Stuart Timmons, *The Trouble with Harry Hay* (Boston: Alyson Press, 1990).

27. For a typical example of a contemporary article, see Karl Bowman and Bernice Engel, "The Problem of Homosexuality," *Journal of Social Hygiene* 39 (March 1953): 2–16.

28. "Great Transformation," 58.

29. From an undated New York *Daily News* article, cited in "Homecoming," 28.

30. "Miss Jorgensen Returns from Copenhagen," A38.

31. Presentation of gender identity is a key concept in Woodhouse, *Fantastic Women,* esp. 5–21, and in Garber, *Vested Interests,* esp. 35–42.

32. "Chris in Public Bow; Aims to Grind Camera, Not Mug It," New York *Daily News,* December 12, 1952, C2.

33. Both quotations are from "Girl Who Used to Be a Boy Isn't Quite Ready for Dates."

34. For a greater discussion of the performative aspects of gender, see Judith Butler, *Gender Trouble: Feminism and the Subversion of Identity* (New York: Routledge, 1991).

35. All references to Jorgensen's letter throughout the chapter are from "Ex-GI Becomes Blonde Beauty," *New York Daily News,* December 1, 1952, A1. Almost every periodical that followed the story during the first two months of Jorgensen's initial appearance quoted from the letters, often emphasizing the "personal" rather than the descriptive medical passages. The scope of this chapter does not allow discussing Jorgensen's letter to Calhoun, reprinted in the *Daily News*'s "Christine's GI Beau Pops Up: Boy, Wotta Gal!" in which Jorgensen asks Calhoun if, on his weekend passes around England, he had "found a little *cockney*?" (italics mine).

36. Navasky, *Naming Names,* 199–222.

37. This and other references are to Whittaker Chambers, *Witness* (New York: Random House, 1952), esp. 3–22.

38. "The Case of Christine," 82.

39. "Boy or Girl," *Newsweek,* May 4, 1953, 91–92.

40. Jorgensen's reputation and medical history were partially rehabilitated the following year when a twenty-eight-year-old American, Charlotte (née Charles) McLeod, also traveled to Denmark to undergo the equivalent of a back-alley castration. See "In Christine's Footsteps," *Time,* March 8, 1954,

63–64. Two years later, Jorgensen was still a touchstone for discussions of transvestism and homosexuality in "Altered Ego," *Time*, April 18, 1955, 91.

41. According to television historian Steven Capsuto, the controversial material here from the broadcast version of this episode of *Jack Benny* (ca. June 1954) was wholly improvised. See Steven Capsuto, *Alternate Channels: Queer Images on Prime Time TV and Radio, 1930s–1990s* (New York: Ballantine, 2000), 84.

42. The vaudevillian scene may have had an awkward resonance considering military activity in Korea and the political anxieties driven by Western fear of the newly established People's Republic of China.

43. Author's telephone interview with Quentin Crisp, April 11, 1993. Crisp remembered seeing Jorgensen perform the Wonder Woman routine in London in the late 1950s.

44. Jorgensen seems to have worn a Wonder Woman outfit when she revived her stage act in the early 1980s, so it is possible that the costume remained in her repertoire throughout her career as a performer.

45. Jimmy Durante, as quoted by Jorgensen on the LP *Christine Jorgensen Reveals* (New York: J Records, [1957?]), transcribed by author.

### EPILOGUE

1. Richard Martin, "Illuminations—Warhol in the 1950s," in *The Warhol Look: Glamour, Style, Fashion*, ed. Mark Francis and Margery King (New York: Bulfinch Press/Andy Warhol Museum, 1997), 75. For an appreciation of Warhol's gay sensibility in the context of his Bodley Gallery show, see Trevor Fairbrother, "'Tomorrow's Man,'" in *"Success Is a Job in New York . . .": The Early Art and Business of Andy Warhol* (New York: New York University Grey Art Gallery, 1989), 59–74. For a broader overview of Warhol's early work see also *Andy Warhol: Drawings and Illustrations of the 1950s* (New York: Distributed Art Publishers/Goliga Books, 2000).

2. "Crazy Golden Slippers: Famous People Inspire Fanciful Footwear," *Life*, January 21, 1957, 12–13.

3. Trevor Fairbrother, "'Tomorrow's Man,'" in *"Success is a Job in New York . . . ,"* 67.

4. Susan Sontag, "Notes on Camp," in her *Against Interpretation* (New York: Farrar, Strauss, and Giroux, 1966), 288.

5. Andrew Ross's comments are part of his excellent discussion about camp in *No Respect: Intellectuals and Popular Culture* (New York: Routledge, 1989), 166.

6. "The Girl Who Used to Be a Boy Isn't Quite Ready for Dates," *New York Daily News*, December 2, 1952, C4.

7. Associated Press (New York bureau) news story, March 31, 1959.

8. Moe Meyer has argued that the post-1950s uses of camp have all but eliminated its original homosexual or queer sensibility. See Meyer's "Reclaiming the Discourse of Camp," in *The Politics and Poetics of Camp,* ed. Moe Meyer (New York: Routledge, 1994), 1–22.

9. For a discussion of the new configurations of homosexual masculinity in postwar but pre-Stonewall American culture, see Matthew Tinkcom's analysis of the films of Kenneth Anger in *Working Like a Homosexual: Camp, Capital, Cinema* (Durham, NC: Duke University Press, 2002), esp. chap. 3. See also Juan Antonio Suarez, *Bike Boys, Drag Queens, and Superstars: Avant-Garde, Mass Culture, and Gay Identities in the 1960s Underground Cinema* (Bloomington: Indiana University Press, 1996).